CEME✝ERY GA✝ES

Saints & Survivors of the Heavy-Metal Scene

RONNIE JAMES DIO LEMMY KILMISTER

BON SCOTT OZZY OSBOURNE

JOHN BONHAM NIKKI SIXX

PETER STEELE DAVE MUSTAINE

CLIFF BURTON AXL ROSE

DIMEBAG DARRELL TRENT REZNOR

PAUL GRAY SLASH

LAYNE STALEY MARILYN MANSON

DEAD (PER YNGVE OHLIN) VARG VIKERNES

JIMMY 'THE REV' SULLIVAN COREY TAYLOR

CEME✝ERY GA✝ES

Saints & Survivors of the Heavy-Metal Scene

Mick O'Shea

Plexus, London

Copyright © 2013 by Plexus Publishing Limited
Published by Plexus Publishing Limited
25 Mallinson Road
London SW11 1BW
www.plexusbooks.com

British Library Cataloguing in Publication Data

O'Shea, Mick.
Cemetery gates: saints and survivors of the heavy-
metal scene.
1. Rock musicians--Biography. 2. Heavy metal
(Music)
I. Title II. Coulman, Laura.
782.4'2166'0922-dc23

ISBN-13: 978-085965-483-8

Cover photos by Mick Hutson/Redferns/Getty
Images; Steve Brown/Photoshot/Getty Images; Larry
Busacca/Getty Images; Ann Summa/Getty Images;
Jack Lue/Michael Ochs Archives/Getty Images;
James Cumpsty/Getty Images

Cover and book design by Coco Wake-Porter
Printed in Great Britain by Bell & Bain Ltd

Acknowledgements
Professional thanks to Laura Coulman, Sandra Wake,
Laura Slater, and Tom Branton at Plexus for their
assistance in bringing the book in on schedule. Personal
thanks to Tasha 'Bodacious Babe' Cowen and Shannon
'Mini-B' Stanley for again keeping the tea flowing and
the sweet bowl filled, Lisa 'T-Bag' Bird, Paul Young
(not the singer), Rupert Tracy, Sharon Hilton Boyd and
Simon Godfrey, Zoe Meadows-Johnson, Martin and
Angela Jones, and Phil and Nicola Williams.

Kind thanks are also owed to Darcie Bowen and all
those who've shared profoundly personal memories via
Fortheloveofpetesteele BlogSpot; as well as Lauren Pringle
of the Oxford Union, who kindly arranged for Laura to
be present at Corey Taylor's motivational speech.

Putting together Cemetery Gates entailed a wide-
ranging exploration of the music media. Books that
were particularly useful included: Walker, Clinton
Highway To Hell: The Life and Times of AC/DC Legend
Bon Scott (UK Pan 2006); Wall, Mick When Giants
Walked the Earth: A Biography Of Led Zeppelin (UK Orion
2009); Osbourne, Ozzy I Am Ozzy (UK Sphere 2010);
Mötley Crüe with Neil Strauss The Dirt - Mötley Crüe:
Confessions of the World's Most Notorious Rock Band (US
Regan 2002); Sixx, Nikki The Heroin Diaries: A Year In
The Life Of A Shattered Rock Star (US Pocket Books 2008);
Sixx, Nikki This is Gonna Hurt (US William Morrow
2011); Kilmister, Lemmy White Line Fever: Lemmy – The
Autobiography (US Pocket Books 2003); McIver, Joel To
Live Is To Die: The Life and Death of Metallica's Cliff Burton
(UK Jawbone 2009); Stenning, Paul Guns N' Roses:
The Band that Time Forgot (UK Chrome Dreams 2004);
Slash with Anthony Bozza Slash: The Autobiography (UK
Harper 2008); Wall, Mick W. Axl Rose: The Unauthorized
Biography (UK Pan 2008); Wall, Mick Guns N' Roses: The
Most Dangerous Band in the World (UK Sidgwick & Jackson
Ltd 1991); Søderlind, Didrik and Moynihan, Michael
Lords of Chaos: The Bloody Rise of the Satanic Metal
Underground (US Feral House 2003); Mustaine, Dave
Mustaine: A Heavy Metal Memoir (US It Books 2011);
Rubio, Adriana Layne Staley: Angry Chair – A Look Inside
the Heart & Soul of an Incredible Musician (US Xanadu
Enterprises 2003); Arnold, Chris A Vulgar Display of
Power: Courage and Carnage at the Alrosa Villa (US MJS
Music & Entertainment LLC 2007); Manson, Marilyn
with Neil Strauss The Long Hard Road Out Of Hell (UK
Plexus Publishing 1998); Taylor, Corey Seven Deadly
Sins: Settling the Argument Between Born Bad & Damaged
Good (US Ebury Press 2012). The following sources
have also been invaluable: newspapers, periodicals
and documentaries: Metal Hammer, Kerrang!, Rolling
Stone, NME, Revolver, Terrorizer, Spin, Mojo, MK Magazine,
Extreme Magazine, Guitar World, Total Guitar, Drum
Magazine, Allmusic, Maxim, Decibel, Fuse, Axcess magazine,
Blender, the Daily Telegraph, Sunday Telegraph, New York
Post, Los Angeles Times, Sydney Morning Herald, Herald
Sun, the Guardian, Des Moines Register, Aquarian Weekly,
High Times, Convulsion Magazine, Alternative Press, AORTA
magazine, Antiquiet magazine, Empyrean magazine, the
Grimoire of Exalted Deeds, Metal Injection, TMZ, MTV
News, CNN, AOL, VH1: Behind the Music, The Decline of
Western Civilization II: The Metal Years, Motörhead: Live Fast,
Die Old, Death Metal: A Documentary, Bowling For Columbine,
Let There Be Rock: The Movie – Live In Paris, Celebrity Rehab
with Dr Drew. Websites: esoterra.com, orangeplaylist.
com, deadcentral.com, andpop.com, suicidegirls.
com, burzum.org, ultimateguitar.com, dmme.net,
blabbermouth.net, wired.com. artistdirect.com,
braveworld.com, invisibleoranges.com, exploremusic.
com, contactmusic.com

We would also like to thank the following agencies for
supplying photographs: Michael Ochs Archives Michael
Ochs Archives/Getty Images/Stringer; Redferns/
Getty Images/Fin Costello; Getty Images/Michael
Putland; Redferns/Getty Images/George De Sota;
Redferns/Getty Images/Fin Costello; WireImage/
Getty Images/Annamaria DiSanto; Getty Images/
Photoshot; WireImage/Getty Images/Jeffrey Mayer;
Nihil Archives; WireImage/Getty Images/Theo Wargo;
Redferns/Getty Images/Mick Hutson; Photoshot/
Getty Images/Martyn Goodacre; WireImage/Getty
Images/Chris Walter; Redferns/Getty Images/Krasner
Trebitz; Getty Images/Larry Marano; Redferns/
Getty Images/Ian Dickson; Redferns/Getty Images/
Robert Knight Archive; WireImage/Getty Images/
Jerod Harris; Redferns/Getty Images/Mick Hutson;
Photoshot/Getty Images/Steve Brown.

contents

Introduction: Symphony for the Devil   7

Saints

Ronnie James Dio   17

Bon Scott   29

John Bonham   41

Peter Steele   51

Cliff Burton   63

Dimebag Darrell   73

Paul Gray   85

Layne Staley   97

Dead (Per Yngve Ohlin)   107

Jimmy 'The Rev' Sullivan   117

Survivors

Lemmy Kilmister   129

Ozzy Osbourne   141

Nikki Sixx   155

Dave Mustaine   165

W. Axl Rose   179

Trent Reznor   191

Slash   203

Marilyn Manson   217

Varg Vikernes   233

Corey Taylor   243

Symphony for the Devil

'Faith Divides Us - Death Unites Us.'
- Nick Holmes, Paradise Lost

If New Year's Eve is nothing but a harbinger of what's to come, then 2010 was cursed before it even began.

For Jimmy 'the Rev' Sullivan (Avenged Sevenfold's fun-loving, borderline ADHD sticksman) there would be no more broken resolutions. On Monday, 28 December 2009, his partner Leana Silver woke to discover the body of her husband-to-be: cold, unresponsive, *gone*. With an age to match the date exactly, the Rev escaped the infamous 27 Club by a single year.

And the Rev's was only the first in a string of heartrending losses to come. Four months down the line, no fan of Type O Negative wanted to believe that Peter Steele – the band's huge-hearted frontman – had become the latest talent to slip silently through the cemetery gates. Famed for his unique sense of humour, Steele had announced his own death online once before, by way of an ominous grey tombstone. Etched into the granite was the short-and-sour inscription: 'Peter Steele – 1962-2005 . . . Free at last'. But it wasn't until 2010 that Pete's doom-laden lyrics finally came to pass. 'Peter Steele passed today,' tweeted *Fuse* VJ Juliya Chernetsky on the evening of 14 April. And this time, it was no hoax. As for the cause of death – to the minds of all those who'd danced to the self-deprecating grooves of Pete's ode to oblivion, 'I Don't Want to Be Me', it was a foregone conclusion. 'Without warning,' Pete croons in the song, 'heart attack' – accurately predicting the circumstances of his own lonely demise years later.

Though not wholly unexpected, news that Ronnie James Dio had finally succumbed to stomach cancer was no less devastating. The 67-year-old stalwart passed on 16 May. Yet, days before his memorial service, the spotlight shifted to Des Moines, Iowa, and the men of Slipknot. On this sombre occasion, the bare-faced band opted to leave their masks at home. Struggling to hold back the tears, a subdued Corey Taylor et al. called an emergency press conference to inform the world that Slipknot were nine minus their No. 2: Paul Gray. In fact, the bassist's body had been discovered by panicked hotel workers on 25 May – shot full of two kinds of morphine.

Beneath his ever-changing porcine mask, Paul Gray was as vulnerable as those who worshipped him. The same was clearly true of Adam Darski, a.k.a. Nergal, the darkened soul of Behemoth. On 8 August, fans were horrified to learn that the titanic frontman had been rushed to the haematology ward of Gdansk Medical University Hospital for the treatment of a mystery illness. On 24 August, the horror was named: leukaemia.

The response of metal fans worldwide – whether online or in print – was overwhelming. From *Revolver*'s end-of-year tribute to the 'fallen heroes' of the scene, to those who eagerly offered up their own bone marrow (each hoping that they might be the one to provide the genetic match needed to save their hero), to others who simply posted sincere condolences online. 'Umm, what in the blue hell, man!?' typed one user on *Metal Injection* news portal in the aftermath of Gray's passing. 'What the fuck is 2010 doing to our beloved community?' Irrespective of the usual scene snobbery, metal fans – whether their tastes ran to death, black, gothic or some more chart-friendly variant – were concluding that, 'like the band or not, respect should be shown'. Death unites us, indeed.

Unlike any other genre you could name, metal commands a uniquely obsessive fan base. As the Rev himself expressed it, 'The type of music we play, we have fans that are "lifers" – just like I'm a lifer for my favourite bands.' For Jimmy Sullivan and any other lifer you could name, there can be no half-measures or passing fads. 'Metal is my religion!' proclaimed more than 21,000 dogged campaigners in support of a 2011 bid to have 'Heavy Metal' added to the UK census. Thus – six feet under – the seeds were sown for the tome you're holding now.

When Lemmy Kilmister – the 'living, breathing, drinking and snorting fucking legend' (in the eyes of Dave Grohl) who held Motörhead together for more than three decades – named his band's third live album *Everything Louder than Everyone Else*, he inadvertently identified the sacrosanct creed by which many of the musicians covered in this book have lived. For if 'louder' is sinful shorthand for 'harder, faster, higher, sicker' – then the likes of the Rev, Pete Steele and Paul Gray have died by this very same adage of extremes.

While it's true that the curse of 2010 made for front-page news, this year constitutes but a brief chapter in the chequered history of heavy metal. *Live Fast, Die Old* may well be another of Lemmy's oft-quoted mottos, but the number of gnarled metal survivors who've built their lives around such a philosophy are part of an ever-dwindling fraternity. Indeed, even in such infamous company as you'll find in *Cemetery Gates*, Lemmy is arguably one of a kind – the ace of spades within this pack of sinners.

'People ask me how come I'm still alive and I don't know what to say,' a bewildered Ozzy Osbourne stated candidly, as the community waited eagerly for his riveting tell-all memoir, *I Am Ozzy*, to hit the shelves in summer 2009. 'It haunts me, all this crazy stuff. I took lethal combinations of booze and drugs for thirty fucking years. I survived a direct hit by a plane, suicidal overdoses, STDs. I have been accused of attempted murder . . .' more of which later. Yet even the Prince of Darkness has a second, more sheltered existence (albeit invaded by the occasional camera crew) as a husband and father-of-three. By Ozzy's own admission, it's the prospect of a future with his family that's finally enabled him to lay his hell-raising past to rest. Newly dried-out and cleaned-up, he paid tribute to the influence of his wife, Sharon. 'If it weren't for her, without a shadow of doubt, I would be dead.'

But the redoubtable Mr Kilmister outlived his own fiancée by decades and refuses to adapt his lifestyle for anything or anyone. Indeed, the only true change that's occurred is in his vital functions. Thanks to Lemmy's regular dose of Jack Daniel's – a bottle-a-day habit that would see lesser-livered individuals lying in a hospital bed if not the cold, hard ground – doctors have told him that the only substance that could finish him is an infusion of pure blood from a non-intoxicated donor. Yet, faced with stark medical evidence of just how far he's strayed from the 'norm', Lemmy remains philosophical. A bastion of hedonism, he's prepared to judge himself by no one's standards but his own (echoing the self-centred Satanist doctrine adhered to by the likes of Marilyn Manson and Watain frontman, Erik Danielsson). 'I still do exactly what I did, more or less. I don't see any reason to change it,' he simply shrugged when questioned by journalist Claire Dyer in 2001. 'If it works, don't fix it.'

And after all, if there's one thing that the varied cast of *Cemetery Gates* will prove, it's that the line between tragic saint and raucous survivor is perilously fine and arbitrary at best. Immersed in a scene of brutal extremes, these men are captivated by the *Sturm-und-Drang* melodrama of the fiercely electrified riffs that define the genre. Professor Adrian North of Heriot-Watt University is one psychologist who's long theorised that, 'it's as though [these musicians] are choosing the music to tell the world something about themselves'. Two headings within this book – 'From Cradle to Grave' for saints and 'On a Highway to Hell' for survivors – are devoted to deciphering precisely what that 'something' might be. From Pete Steele's maudlin meditations on mortality to Marilyn Manson's lyrical fixation with the lunchbox, it's at once blindingly obvious and easy to overlook that songs which serve as a soundtrack to the lives of millions are also deeply personal to the artists themselves – inspired by buried trauma and memories that will never quite be exorcised, even through the medium of music.

For every striking standout, you'll read other individual histories running along ominously parallel lines – leading to the wrong side of the cemetery gates all too often. You'll also learn some of the truths behind the tabloid headlines. Contrary to popular belief, Marilyn Manson and Mayhem's Dead were born victims rather than villains. Behind the hulking legend of their alter-egos, you'll discover two alienated teens – persecuted by their peers and desperately seeking like-minded bandmates – who never quite recovered from the intense emotional and physical abuse inflicted on them in their formative years. Testing the time-honoured maxim that 'we are but the sum total of our experiences' to its very limits, *Cemetery Gates* – and the metal fraternity in general – provides a fascinating insight into the darkest reaches of the human psyche. In a scene where supportive family networks are the exception rather than the rule, creative renown can be something of a double-edged sword. Precisely how many of the artists featured here have not been in thrall to the darkest kind of muse at some point in their lives is an intriguing question – and one that must surely give every fan pause for thought.

Pushing further, harder, faster and ever closer to the cemetery gates, the hell-raising cast of the book you're about to read are all casualties of the dangerously destructive ethos that drives their music, their brethren and their public. 'Anything worth doing is worth overdoing,' quips 'shattered rock star' Nikki Sixx by way of introduction to his tell-all book, *The Heroin Diaries*. Yet there's nothing original about this particular one-liner. Borrowed from Rolling Stone Sir Mick Jagger, his words are simply an echo of the decadent past. For in truth, sex, drugs and insanity are not only synonymous with metal music; they are the rules by which the scene lives. From Trent Reznor's downward spiral to Sixx's stuttering, stalling heart, from Axl Rose's histrionics to Dead's hankering for the hereafter, the crazed antics and darkest misdeeds collected here – in the guise of 'Deadly Sins' and 'Moments of Madness' – constitute the lethal inspiration behind many of the genre's most defining anthems of excess.

For Corey Taylor, at least, it seems there can be no creation without self-destruction of the most brutal kind. For the duration of the recording of *Iowa* – the follow-up album to Slipknot's brutal debut – the frontman remained stark naked. His favoured method for obtaining Slipknot's trademark cathartic primal scream? Self-mutilation. Covered in cuts and lacerations – as well as his own vomit – he laid down the vocals for such floor-filling tracks as 'Left Behind' and 'My Plague'. 'That's where the best stuff comes from,' Corey shrugged in an interview years later. 'You've got to break yourself down before you can build something great.'

The bitter flipside – expressed simply by Guns N'Roses survivor Duff McKagan – is as follows: 'Of course, no one sets out to be a junkie or an alcoholic. Some people can experiment in their youth and move on. Others cannot.' Implicit in the second syllable of this final word, *'cannot'*, is the stark finality of the divide between the two sides of *Cemetery Gates*. Presenting survivors and saints; the living alongside the dead; of all ages, sub-genres and settings – from Stockholm through to Seattle – what you're about to read will demonstrate precisely how these complex individuals have been shaped. Spotlighting shared experience, eerie coincidence and bitter irony (including the night when clean-living Metallica bassist Cliff Burton drew the death card, beating his hell-raising tour-mates to an early grave), it shows that all that's truly separating saint from survivor is a heady mix of chance, circumstance and luck. Or is it?

'People over the years have tried to soften the blow by saying maybe [my] being in Mötley Crüe turned me into an addict, but I don't think it did. That stroke of genius was all my own work,' reckons Nikki Sixx. 'Even as a kid, I was never inclined to dodge a bullet.' Indeed, back in the day, the bassist's self-destructive alter-ego (a.k.a. Sikki) had neither the will nor the inclination to stray from his own personal highway to hell. Mötley Crüe simply enabled him to buy a 'better class' of poison than what he'd otherwise have been reduced to. In light of this predilection for destruction, his achievement in banishing Sikki from his life once and for all is nothing short of inspirational – and well worth retelling here. And in this respect, Nikki's certainly not unique.

The secrets of how stoical survivors like Nikki dragged themselves back from the abyss are another key preoccupation of this particular study in sin. As always, Corey Taylor has his own theory on the subject. 'Slipknot is probably a more important part of who I am,' he reflected, 'because I let that out and tap that valve I can be myself . . . I think that's why a lot of people are drawn to what we do. My job is to give you that voice . . . it's the primal scream; it's more healthy a lot of people would admit, because I'm free. I'm a better person because I'm in a band like Slipknot.'

After all, there's more to Corey Taylor – husband, father, son, artist, frontman – than the mask he shields himself behind onstage. But, thanks in no small part to the crucial catharsis and creative freedom this disguise allows, it's possible for him to be all these things at once – without the risk of disappointing his fans, his haters and the myth-making journalists who've written his persona and his career to date. Tragically, the same did not suffice for Corey's bandmate. Behind masks, doors and barriers unspoken, the painfully introverted Paul Gray was – according to his widow, Brenna – fighting a losing battle. Though unaware of Gray's struggle in life, Corey has no intention of letting his friend's memory fade after death. 'For me,' he explained, 'it's important to celebrate life and not revel in death. Paul wouldn't want anyone want to do that, because he absolutely loved doing this . . . it helps me remember to embrace life. Don't spend too much time on the darkness; you have to live every single minute with every bit of spirit you have.'

A riotous epitaph to men who've lived every day as if it was their last (whatever their deadly sin – be it lust, greed or an act so heinous it warrants a category all its own) *Cemetery Gates* is a similar celebration of life – and a set of incendiary talents who should never be forgotten, whether they belong in heaven, hell, or the uncertain land between.

Laura Coulman

RONNIE JAMES DIO
PAUL GRAY
BON SCOTT
JIMMY 'THE REV' SULLIVA
JOHN BONHAM
DEAD (PER YNGVE OHLI
PETER STEELE
LAYNE STALE
CLIFF BURTON
DIMEBAG DARREL
PAUL GRAY
CLIFF BURTO
DIMEBAG DARRELL
BON SCOT
LAYNE STALEY
RONNIE JAMES DI
DEAD (PER YNGVE OHLIN)
PETER STEEL
JIMMY 'THE REV' SULLIVAN
JOHN BONHAI

Saints

Ronnie James Dio

Bon Scott

John Bonham

Peter Steele

Cliff Burton

Dimebag Darrell

Paul Gray

Layne Staley

Dead (Per Yngve Ohlin)

Jimmy 'The Rev' Sullivan

Ronnie James Dio

10 July 1942 - 16 May 2010

Born: Ronald James Padavona

Alter-egos: Ronnie James Dio; Leather Lungs (thanks to a temporary teenage devotion to the trumpet).

(Pre) occupations: Saviour of Black Sabbath; inventor of the devil horns; purveyor of leather-lunged vocals for Dio, Elf, Rainbow and Heaven & Hell, and patron saint of an array of worthy causes.

In memoriam: 'Well, you've caught me in the library. One of my favourite places in all the world, because it contains words [. . .] this is a place that I don't do any work in. It's strictly a library. Most of my writing is done in the dungeon.' – Ronnie James Dio

Deadly sins: Of all the unholy congregation assembled within these pages, the Bible-bashing bigots belonging to the Westboro Baptist Church – who actually held a rally denouncing Ronnie as a Satan worshipper on the day of his memorial service – seem most deserving of a roasting within the fires of eternal damnation. Though the late frontman no longer had a voice to defend himself, Ronnie's widow, Wendy, urged those attending the funeral to take a leaf from Christian doctrine when ignoring the protest: 'Ronnie hates prejudice and violence. We need to turn the other cheek on these people [who] only know how to hate someone they didn't know. We only know how to love someone we know!'

Of course, dismissing metal bands as 'devil-worshippers' has become a popular stereotype – especially with Mayhem's Dead and Varg Vikernes taking playful satanic inferences to their literal extremes. But the only connection Ronnie shared with the guitarist-killing Vikernes was a fondness for including swords and sorcery in his lyrics. And had these so-called 'do-gooders' – who belong to a church whose website is titled 'Godhatesfags.com' – bothered to read up on Ronnie, they would have been shamed by the realisation that they couldn't have picked a target less deserving of their asinine denigrations. For though Ronnie blatantly flirted with devilment while fronting God-bothering acts such as Black Sabbath and Heaven & Hell, as the man himself said, this is all part and parcel of being in a heavy-metal band. And isn't it ironic that they chose to ignore Ronnie's involvement in Hear 'n Aid, the metal equivalent of Band Aid and USA for Africa, which helped raise $1 million for famine relief?

One has to wonder what Ronnie would have made of the protests, for though he was raised a Catholic, he said he never agreed with the Catholic Church's message – a conviction he maintained until his dying day. 'I just disagree so much with the way the Catholic church says things like if you're not a good person you'll die and go to hell, there's a purgatory there,' he revealed during an interview with *HM* magazine in May 2010. 'If I was talking with a Holy Ghost, it would scare the living hell out of me. God's Son was nailed to a piece of wood up in the air . . . instead of really explaining it all, I think, at least from my perspective, they frightened us first, and then we're supposed to just believe everything, and follow the rules or you'll burn in hell or something. And I just totally disagree with that. I disagree completely with that idiom.'

His views on the validity of a first-century carpenter from Nazareth being the Son of God would have caused plenty of breast-beating amongst the Westboro Baptist Church faithful: 'I think that He was a prophet [but] I've had a difficult time coming to terms with Jesus Christ as the Son of God,' he elaborated. 'He was a great man for the time. He was the right man for the right time. Let's put it this way: I think He was a hell of a lot better than Michael Jackson. My feelings are that the [Christian] teachings were great, but in my mind, my religious beliefs are that you are God, and you are Jesus Christ, and you are the devil, and I am, and all the people I know around me are,' he continued. 'But I don't need to go to some place and listen to somebody else to tell me whether I'm good or bad, or whether I'm right or wrong. I am my shrine. You are your shrine. We are all Jesus Christ, and again, I have no problem with anyone thinking Jesus Christ is this deity, someone up there. It's cool. Well, I have yet to see that proof, and when I do, maybe I'll be a believer. How can anyone possibly prove to me that Christ rose from the dead? How can you prove it?'

From cradle to grave: While Ronnie never went so far as to actually lie about his age, he wasn't above deflecting such irreverent questions, retorting that the focus of the interview should be the music. In other words, if you're happy with the message why bother with the messenger? However, what we do know is that he was born in Portsmouth, New Hampshire, on 10 July 1942; the only child of Italian parents who later moved to Cortland, New York, shortly after the Second World War.

Young Ronnie began his musical career playing the trumpet and French horn, and performed in several rockabilly bands. He later played bass in a high-school band, the Vegas Kings, soon becoming their lead singer by virtue of his burgeoning vocal prowess. He would later attribute the power of his voice to the breathing discipline he acquired as a brass player: 'I started playing the trumpet when I was five years old, which was great training for me as a singer,' he told *Extreme* magazine. 'It taught me the correct way to do it, because I've not taken singing lessons from anyone.'

> 'It is a very sad day for the world of metal when an artist
> as unique and special as Ronnie James Dio leaves us.
> He will be forever imitated but never duplicated.'
>
> - Rob Zombie

On realising Ronnie was the star attraction, the band undertook a name change: firstly to Ronnie and the Rumblers, and then to Ronnie and the Red Caps. Under this name, they released their debut single 'Conquest' – backed with 'Lover' – on Reb Records in 1958. Somewhat bizarrely, given Ronnie's newfound status within the line-up, 'Conquest' was a Ventures-esque instrumental. Also, though his distinctive pipes can certainly be heard on the flip side, the main vocal was performed by the outfit's original singer, Billy DeWolfe. By the time of the follow-up single, 'An Angel is Missing' backed with 'What I'd Say' (Seneca Records, 1960), DeWolfe had been shoed away from the Red Caps' rehearsal room door, leaving Ronnie free to find his range.

Despite having recorded and released two singles by the time he graduated from the Cortland City School in the summer of 1960, Ronnie was reluctant to give the rockin' Red Caps his all and enrolled at the University at Buffalo in upstate New York, majoring in pharmacy. When subsequently asked by *dmme.net* whether his lifelong abstinence from drugs was influenced by the knowledge he acquired taking a pharmacology degree, Ronnie answered in the negative, saying he'd chosen his path simply because: 'I saw how destructive it was, and how it dulled your sensibilities and ate up your talent and your life.' Ronnie would quit his course after just one year in order to further his musical ambitions. But while medicine's loss was set to be metal's gain, his parents were not best pleased to hear that their only son was abandoning his studies in favour of rock stardom. Ronnie's mind, however, was made up, and being the private person that he was, he purposely kept this part of his life to himself for nigh on half a century. Indeed, the secret only came out when Heaven & Hell played a show at the Darien Lake Performing Arts Centre – which was only a 70-cent bus ride from his one-time alma mata – on 19 September 2007.

It was soon after he tossed his study books into the trash that the Red Caps morphed into Ronnie Dio and the Prophets. It's been alleged that Ronnie adopted his lasting stage name in homage to the renowned Italian-American organised-crime figure and labour racketeer, Johnny Dio. However, when viewed in conjunction with the 'Prophets', it becomes clear that Ronnie's chosen surname is a reference to 'Dio' being the Latin word for God.

> 'Most of it's been working; it's been a pretty normal life other than the musical part of it.'
>
> - Ronnie James Dio

Over the next five years or so the Prophets would record one album – *Dio at Domino's* for MGM – and a clutch of singles on a variety of labels before eventually disbanding in 1967. That same year, together with Red Caps/Prophets' long-serving guitarist Nick Pantas, Ronnie formed the Electric Elves, recruiting Ronnie's cousin, David Feinstein, keyboardist Doug Thaler and drummer Gary Driscoll. Specialising in broody blues-rock, they released a single – 'Hey, Look Me Over' backed with 'It Pays to Advertise' – for MGM, but tragedy struck the following year when Ronnie and his fellow Elves were involved in a car smash, which claimed the life of Nick Pantas and left Thaler seriously injured.

Though Ronnie walked away from the wreck with only minor cuts and bruises, it's reasonable to assume that in those terrifying seconds before the impact – no doubt with his life flashing before his eyes – he might have caught a glimpse of the cemetery gates opening. It's also safe to assume that the experience of seeing someone he'd been laughing and joking with a short while earlier being taken away in a body bag would have had a profound effect on his outlook. For here was proof of Ozzy Osbourne's claim that the edge is always closer than we think, and as such it's little wonder that Ronnie let his peers adopt rock'n'roll's clichéd 'live fast, die young' credo, while he got on with making music.

Deciding to go forward as a quartet rather than try to replace Pantas, the band truncated their name to the Elves and signed a deal with Decca Records, before abbreviating their name further, to the singular Elf. Thaler quit the band soon after the release of their 1971 bootleg album, *Live at the Beacon*, when he relocated to New York after landing a job as a booking agent. Having brought in replacement keyboardist Mickey Lee Soule, Elf signed a one-off album deal with Epic and headed into the studio with producers Roger Glover and Ian Paice – otherwise known as the rhythm section of Deep Purple. The experience of working with two of his longstanding idols clearly made a profound impression on Ronnie James. 'It was great,' he enthused in *Extreme* magazine. 'Two of our heroes were producing the album. It was just great to be around them. It was real quick. I played bass on that album, and we did almost everything live. We went in and I played and sang at the same time. We just did it and away it went! It wasn't like where each instrument was done separately in a different studio, you know, with that craziness. We were very well prepared; it was a good band. We played together for a long time, grew up together. So we just went in and "bang", did it! It was so much fun to do and a really good album as well.'

Nevertheless, Dave Feinstein soon decided it was time to strike out on his own and would go off to enjoy a modicum of success with his band, the Rods. Having recruited guitarist Steve Edwards as his cousin's replacement, Ronnie also brought in bassist Craig Gruber – leaving himself free to concentrate on vocal duties.

After bonding with Ronnie in the studio and on the road (Elf would often be invited to open for Deep Purple), Glover invited him to provide the vocals on his 1974 concept album, *The Butterfly Ball and the Grasshopper's Feast*. Indeed, Ronnie suddenly found himself much in demand, as Purple's disaffected guitarist, Ritchie Blackmore (who'd recently quit the band to work on his debut solo album, *Ritchie Blackmore's Rainbow*), had been equally impressed with his supercharged, quasi-operatic pipes. And it wasn't only Ronnie who accompanied Blackmore into the studio, for with the exception of Steve Edwards – for rather obvious reasons – the rest of Elf went with them. It was this coalition which eventually evolved into Rainbow, but no sooner was the album finished than Blackmore informed Ronnie that – though the microphone was his for as long as he wanted it – Mickey, Craig, and Gary simply didn't fit in with his master-plan.

Though he felt guilty about letting his friends down, Ronnie was astute enough to recognise that working with Ritchie Blackmore was a unique opportunity, and one he couldn't afford to spurn – especially as Blackmore would be bringing in drumming powerhouse Cozy Powell, who'd made his name playing with the Jeff Beck Group, before enjoying success with his first solo single, 'Dance with the Devil', in 1974.

Roger Glover also wanted Ronnie to accompany him on the road to promote his solo album, but Ritchie wasn't overly keen, as Ronnie subsequently explained: 'I didn't do the [*Butterfly Ball*] live show. At that time we'd just put Rainbow together, Ritchie and I, and he felt it was not something that I should do; that we should be concentrating on the Rainbow thing and not me [getting] side-tracked by that. It was his band, and he was another one of my heroes, so I figured he knew what he was doing. In retrospect I'm quite glad I didn't do the show.' He was, however, more than happy doing the Rainbow show, because the band's blistering onstage energy quickly established them as one of heavy metal's most compelling live acts.

Whereas *Ritchie Blackmore's Rainbow* narrowly missed out on the UK top ten, the band's 1976 follow-up, *Rising*, gave Ronnie his first taste of chart success, spotlighted in the first issue of *Kerrang!* (June 1981) as the number-one album of all time. A live album followed in 1977 (*On Stage*), along with a third studio album, *Long Live Rock'n'Roll*. Yet at the end of a gruelling year-long world tour to promote the release, Blackmore announced that he wanted to take Rainbow in a new direction, away from the swords-and-sorcery theme of their previous efforts. For once, Ronnie was not ready to fall in with the battle-plan outlined by his mentor, and promptly announced his departure.

Many years later – when quizzed as to the nature of his relationship with Blackmore – Ronnie would comment (showing a refreshing lack of animosity towards his former bandmate): 'Ritchie lives on the other side of the continent in New York, so I only get to speak to him through people that we both know. Roger, the same . . . I haven't seen him in a long while, but we've all remained friends. It's nothing like it's been blown up to be in the press, you know: "Ritchie's the most difficult man on earth to work with!" He probably is for everybody else, but he never was for me. I have nothing but the best to say about Ritchie. He's the one who gave me my first great opportunity and I learned a hell of a lot from him.'

Needless to say, Ronnie's lung capacity – which soon earned him the sobriquet 'Leather Lungs' within the industry – meant he wasn't going to be sitting idle for too long following his departure from Rainbow, and when Ozzy Osbourne was given his marching orders from Black Sabbath over his drink and drug intake, it was – on the recommendation of Ozzy's girlfriend and future wife, Sharon Arden – at Ronnie's door that Geezer Butler and Tony Iommi came a-knocking. Soon after Ronnie's initiation into Sabbath, Iommi would tell reporters that while 'Ozzy was a great showman, when Dio came in it was a different attitude; a different voice and a different musical approach.' And with hindsight, Sharon's choice seems almost prophetic, as *Heaven and Hell* is the album credited with stoking Sabbath's dying embers and revitalising the band. Indeed, Ronnie rated *Heaven and Hell* as his personal favourite of all the albums he worked on: 'And it's not just the music – it's all the things that went together with it,' he enthused to *Extreme* magazine. 'You know, the reason it was made,

'What I do keeps me sane . . . So I plan on doing it until people tell me I shouldn't anymore, or until I get to the point that my bones start creaking so much I just fall over!'
- Ronnie James Dio

how difficult it was to make it, the time it took, the people involved, the changes while we were doing it – that's what made the difference, I think. It was an album, again, that started a cycle for hard-rock music, and I'm very proud of that.'

Mob Rules – the second Sabbath album to feature Dio's epic pipes – followed in November 1981 (by which time Vinny Appice had been brought in as a temporary replacement for long-standing Sabbath drummer Bill Ward, who'd taken an absence of leave during the Heaven and Hell Tour). Yet, just one year on, the new line-up seemed to be teetering closer to hell than heaven. Given the alcohol-induced paranoia of certain crew members, the mixing of 1982's *Live Evil* became an all but impossible process. As Ronnie later explained: 'The first time I left [Sabbath] it was just over some stupidity about the live album we were doing. The engineer was drinking a bottle of Jack Daniel's a day and told Tony and Geezer he thought Vinny and I were sneaking into the studio and turning the vocals and drums up. As is their wont, they believed it, and that led to the break-up of that one. It was all completely untrue and absolutely stupid!'

Ronnie had been too long in the saddle to put up with such childish antics, and rather than risk similar temper tantrums in the future, he decided it was high time he took a leading role. Though Vinny dutifully followed when he announced his departure from Sabbath, Ronnie had made his mind up that there was only going to be one leader in his new project. And in choosing the name 'Dio', he removed all doubt as to who that was going to be.

Having recruited guitarist Vivian Campbell and bassist Jimmy Bain (whom Ronnie knew from his time with Rainbow), and secured a recording contract with Warner Bros, Dio went straight to the studio to begin work on their debut long-player, *Holy Diver*. The auguries appeared favourable when the album hit number thirteen on the UK chart, and a respectable number 61 on the *Billboard* chart, and Ronnie's status as one of heavy metal's most bankable artists was confirmed with the ensuing studio albums *The Last in Line* (1984), *Sacred Heart* (1985), and *Dream Evil* (1987). Though they only released two studio LPs during the nineties, Dio

'I don't dote on religion. Religion, I think, is something that you can never argue, and you can certainly never convince the other person, because even though there's a Bible . . . how concrete is it? It depends on the point of view.'
- Ronnie James Dio

would continue to be a driving force on the metal scene. So much so that in 2000, Century Media released the tribute compilation album *Holy Dio: Tribute to Ronnie James Dio*, featuring cover versions of Ronnie's best-known songs from his time with Rainbow, Black Sabbath and Dio.

Though 2004's *Master of the Moon* (Dio's tenth and final studio album), reached number seven on the US independent chart, it failed to land on the *Billboard* chart. Ronnie, however, remained unfazed, opting to take a well-deserved break from recording and touring to spend some quality time with his wife, Wendy, who, of course, also served as his manager. Aside from undertaking a tour of Siberia and Russia's Far East in September 2005, Ronnie's career appeared to be on hiatus. But in 2006, he was back in the news when it was revealed that he and Vinny Appice would be going out on the road with Tony Iommi and Geezer Butler as Heaven & Hell, playing a set-list of songs from their time together as Black Sabbath. The decision to go out under the Heaven & Hell moniker was influenced by Iommi and Butler having recently made their peace with Ozzy Osbourne, with whom they'd been touring as Black Sabbath.

While having both incarnations of Black Sabbath playing together again was music to the ears of every metalhead, it inevitably fuelled the debate as to whether Ozzy or Ronnie represents the true soul of the band. Such speculation was, of course, pretty much superfluous, because Ronnie and Ozzy – at least during Ozzy's first stretch with the band – were polar opposites in their approach to the job. Ozzy was the Dionysian hell-raiser, whereas Ronnie was discipline personified. And of course, the irony won't have been lost on every Sabbath fan that the sinner has outlived the saint.

Though the release of a double live album, *Live from Radio City Music Hall* – taken from Heaven & Hell's performance at the legendary New York venue on 30 March 2007 – was enough to whet the appetites of fans everywhere, it would be another two years before the band's debut studio album, *The Devil You Know*, finally hit the record shops. However, judging from its soar-away success both in the UK and the US, they deemed it well worth the wait. Alas, though plans were underway for a follow-up Heaven & Hell album, everything was put on indefinite hold in the aftermath of a shock announcement via Ronnie's official website in November 2009.

'Ronnie has been diagnosed with the early stages of stomach cancer. We are starting treatment immediately at the Mayo Clinic. After he kills this dragon, Ronnie will be back onstage, where he belongs; doing what he loves best, performing for his fans. Long live rock'n'roll, long live Ronnie James Dio. Thanks to all the friends and fans from all over the world that have sent well wishes. This has really helped to keep his spirit up.'

It appeared as though Ronnie would indeed be back doing what he loved best when Wendy posted the following update on Ronnie's progress on his website in March 2010: 'It has been Ronnie's seventh chemo, another CAT scan and another endoscopy, and the results are good – the main tumour has shrunk considerably, and our visits to Houston [cancer clinic in Texas] are now every three weeks instead of every two weeks.'

However, fans realised something was wrong when it was announced on 4 May that Heaven & Hell had been forced to cancel their forthcoming summer dates as a result of Ronnie's ill-health. And their worst fears were confirmed by Wendy just twelve days later. 'Today my heart is broken, Ronnie passed away at 7:45am, 16 May. Many, many friends and family were able to say their private goodbyes before he peacefully passed away. Ronnie knew how much he was loved by all. We so appreciate the love and support that you have all given us. Please give us a few days of privacy to deal with this terrible loss. Please know he loved you all and his music will live on forever.'

Aside from his musical legacy, Ronnie is assured immortality amongst metalheads the world over for having given them the 'cornu': the devil horns hand gesture, created by extending the index and pinky finger, with the middle and ring fingers held under the thumb. Whether or not it was ever Ronnie's intention, audiences picked up on it and began repeating the gesture, which led to it now serving as an internationally recognised sign between metal brethren.

When asked where he'd got the idea from, Ronnie, who was fronting Black Sabbath at the time, said it was an 'Italian thing' that he'd picked up from his grandmother. 'It was a symbol that I thought was reflective of what that band [Sabbath] was supposed to be all about. It's *not* the devil's sign like we're here with the devil. It's to ward off the Evil Eye or to give the Evil Eye, depending on which way you do it. It's just a symbol, but it had magical incantations and attitudes to it and I felt it worked very well with Sabbath. So I became very noted for it and then everybody else started to pick up on it and away it went. But I would never say I take credit for being the first to do it.'

It was undoubtedly in recognition of this massive contribution to the metal scene that Ronnie was given a cameo appearance in the 2006 film *Tenacious D in The Pick Of Destiny* starring Jack Black, which sees Ronnie spring to life from a bedroom wall poster and tell the young JB to go forth and follow his dreams before bellowing the immortal line: 'Now go, my son, and rock!'

However, Ronnie was right not to claim the credit, possibly because he was already aware of the psychedelic rockers Coven, whose frontman, Jinx Dawson, can be clearly seen giving the devil's horn sign on the back cover of the band's debut album *Witchcraft Destroys Minds & Reaps Souls*, which was released in 1969. And it's also interesting to note that the album's opening track was called 'Black Sabbath'.

Moments of madness: When Dio's 1990 album, *Lock up the Wolves*, failed to emulate the success of its predecessors, Ronnie suffered what can only be described as an incandescent moment of madness in agreeing to rejoin Black Sabbath – albeit on a temporary basis. 'When we did reform in '92 the apologies went all the way around,' he explained in *Extreme* magazine. 'The second time was because of the shows I was told we were going to do. We had all our shows booked in LA, and now we were going to change that to become the opening act for Ozzy . . . which I refused to do! I didn't do it out of a personal thing with Ozzy; I couldn't care less about him. But it was . . . here we were trying to get this band back on the road together, trying to reform this band and make it special again . . . and now, suddenly, we were going to be the opening act for the ex-lead singer! And I also knew that when that show came that they were going to announce the reunion between the four of them . . . which did happen! So what was the sense of my doing the show to bolster their careers, they obviously didn't care less about mine. So that was the end of that!'

When asked if he still felt that he'd been maligned and misunderstood by the music press at the time of his second bite of the Black Sabbath cherry, Ronnie added: '"Misunderstood" isn't the word. The thing is that everybody continually believes the things that they hear about me . . . that I'm some kind of "Hitler" figure. People who know me will tell you absolutely different. You know, I don't need to defend myself. Was I misunderstood? Yes, I think so, because of the perception people have that of course it's my fault, that two unassuming gentlemen – Geezer and Tony – couldn't possibly make any kind of wrong decision, that it had to be Dio who was wrong. Those are my beliefs. My beliefs were that I gave up the Dio band and they gave up nothing! They had Black Sabbath and were lucky enough to get Vinny and I to come back and do it! And at the end of the day our preferences weren't given any credibility. When that happens you have no communication, which is what we didn't have and spelled the break-up. I can only tell my version of the truth and I believe what I know is correct.

'Others will hear other things. I think a lot of it was the Ronnie versus Ozzy thing that cropped up for some reason or another. I don't know why, because it's never really bothered me what Ozzy does . . . I'm happy for his success, but it was that more than anything else, you know, that "I disrespected Ozzy" or something . . . like I really care!'

Bon Scott

9 July 1946 - 19 February 1980

Born: Ronald Belford Scott

Alter-egos: Bon Scott; the Bonnie Scot

(Pre) occupations: Frontman and songwriter with AC/DC.

In memoriam: 'I'm a special drunkard . . . I drink too much.' – Bon Scott

Deadly sins: Perpetually thirsty Bon was an old-school rock'n'roller with an incurable weakness for good drink, 'bad food and nasty women'. As for his one backstage requirement: 'I don't give a fuck what else is on the rider,' he's reported to have roared, 'as long I've got Jack Daniel's.'

By the time he'd replaced Dave Evans as the frontman of AC/DC in October 1974, he was 28 years old, and though he'd already packed a lot of hard living into the latter half of his life – including a near-fatal motorcycle accident while under the influence, which saw him a mere ambulance's reaction time away from an even earlier demise – his macho need to match or outdo his younger bandmates in the drinking stakes saw his already considerable alcohol consumption steadily rise, until it reached the point where his body clock was permanently set to cocktail hour.

From cradle to grave: Ronald Belford 'Bon' Scott was born at the Fyfe-Jamieson Maternity Hospital on 9 July 1946, to Charles and Isabelle Scott – known to all as 'Chick' and 'Isa', respectively – and until the age of six was raised in Kirriemuir, in the county of Angus in south-east Scotland. Prior to Bon's rise to fame with AC/DC, the sleepy Scottish market town, which lies nestled within the foothills of the Grampian Mountains – the 'gateway to the glens' – was famous for being the birthplace of Peter Pan creator, J.M. Barrie, but in recent years a memorial plaque to Bon was unveiled in Cumberland Close, where he and his family resided.

By all accounts, young Bon was a mischievous handful who preferred to run with his mates rather than return home after school to do chores, which often resulted in Isa having to go out in search of her wayward son. As music ran in both sides of the family it was perhaps inevitable that Bon would show an interest, even if the instrument on which he chose to express himself left plenty to be desired – both in the family home, and in those of his immediate neighbours. 'He was mad on drums,' Isa explained in *Highway to Hell*. '[He] played on a biscuit tin, or the bread board. He loved it. People heard him practising.' Kirriemuir's residents had ample opportunity to monitor Bon's progress on the biscuit tin, as each and every Saturday he would dutifully fall in line behind the Kirriemuir Pipe Band with the makeshift drum hanging about his neck on a piece of twine when the pipers marched through the town square.

Though a welcome addition to the Scott Clan came with Bon's younger brother Derek's arrival in 1949 (Chick and Isa's first-born son, Sandy, died aged just nine months in 1943), his parents were beginning to get itchy feet. Isa was receiving regular updates from her sister in Melbourne – where she and her husband and baby daughter were living, having taken up the Australian government's 'Populate or Perish' scheme, whereby British citizens were offered a new life Down Under for the subsidised fee of just £10 (with children under the age of sixteen going free) – and in the summer of 1952 the Scotts packed up their meagre possessions and waved a fond farewell to Scotland.

Upon their arrival in Melbourne, the Scotts temporarily moved in with Isa's sister and her family in Sunshine, a suburb in the Victoria state capital's industrial west (which was home to immigrants from all over Europe), before they were able to procure their own home after Chick landed a job as a window-framer at a local factory. Despite its idyllic-sounding name, however, Sunshine – with a myriad of rundown terraced housing specially built for its migrant workforce – was situated on the wrong side of the divide and had its fair share of local troublemakers, who were keen to give the incoming 'whinging Poms' a not-so-warm welcome. And it seems their sons were equally frosty when it came to new arrivals at school, as Bon later explained: 'My new schoolmates [at Sunshine Primary School] threatened to kick the shit out of me when they heard my Scottish accent. I had one week to learn to speak like them if I wanted to remain intact. Course, I didn't take any notice. No one railroads me, and it made me all the more determined to speak my own way.'

It was at Sunshine that he was to receive his lasting nickname. As there was already a Ronald on the class register, his new friends took to calling him 'Bonnie' – as in Bonnie Scotland – which was inevitably truncated to Bon. According to Isa, Bon also attended Sunday school until deciding early on that learning scripture got in the way of doing more enjoyable things – especially when Chick and Isa purchased a beautiful piano for their new home. Though Bon was happy to tickle the ivories at his own pace, he was unwilling to take lessons. And when the accordion became the latest instrument to catch his musical eye, his bemused parents sold the piano and bought him an accordion with the proceeds. This time Bon got as far as taking a few lessons, but as his true passion was for the drums, the accordion soon went the way of the piano to make way for a set.

In 1956, the Scotts were on the move again as Bon's youngest brother, Graeme – who'd been born three years earlier – had been diagnosed with asthma. On their doctor's recommendation, the family relocated to Fremantle, some 1700 miles away, as the hot and dry climate would be better suited to Graeme's condition. Having relatives in Melbourne had helped the Scotts acclimatise to their new life Down Under, and though Chick would be working for the same company he'd worked for in Melbourne, when they arrived in Fremantle they didn't know a soul.

As Fremantle is a port, the local populace was made up of all nationalities so, as a means of making new friends, Chick joined the Caledonian Society, whose members were also ex-pats. On hearing his dad had joined the Fremantle Pipe Band, Bon, sensing an opportunity to show off his drumming technique, joined the band as a side-drummer. But while donning a kilt and cap and playing the side-drum with the pipe band on big occasions – such as the opening ceremony of the Empire Games in nearby Perth in 1962, which saw Bon get his photograph in the *Fife Free Press* back in Scotland – was considered a huge honour, his ear was most definitely cocked towards the rock'n'roll music emanating from the family's valve radio. In *Let There Be Rock: The Movie – Live in Paris* (filmed at the Pavillon de Paris on 9 December 1979, but not released until 1997), Bon recalls his mother's reaction to his new vocation: 'Back in about 1957 or '8, I used to sing in the shower, and [she] used to say, "Ron, if you can't sing proper songs, shut up; don't sing this rock'n'roll garbage."'

With school coming in a poor second to having fun, Bon got out of high school – John Curtin College of the Arts – as soon as he turned fifteen. With no qualifications, the only job he could find was working as a farmhand on a market garden, which was low-paid, but he at least got to drive a tractor. Living in a port town meant there was always plenty of work on the docks, and his friend got him work on a Cray-fishing boat, but

Bon quickly realised he wasn't cut out to be a fisherman and he returned to the land, taking a job with Avery Scales as an apprentice weighing-machine mechanic.

Music, of course, was still very close to Bon's heart, and at weekends he could be found tearing it up with his mates at Port Beach dances. Needless to say, it didn't take much persuasion for Bon to get up onstage and belt out a gutsy version of his rock'n'roll idol Little Richard's 'Long Tall Sally' or 'Tutti-Frutti'. It was at one of these dances that Bon's world ground to a juddering halt. Embroiled in an altercation there in March 1963, he was sentenced to nine months at Fremantle's Riverbank Juvenile Institution after pleading guilty to charges of supplying the local police with a false name and address, escaping police custody, having unlawful carnal knowledge with an underage girl, and of stealing twelve gallons of petrol. Though Bon rarely spoke about this unsavoury episode in his life, we know that he had 'gone for a walk' with the girl in question, and that when they'd returned to the hall some of the other boys decided they wanted a piece of the action. Bon had naturally stepped in, only to then foolishly give a false name and address to the officers called in to quell the disturbance, before making off in a friend's car.

Upon Bon's release shortly before Christmas, the parole officer assigned to him suggested the best thing he could do was apply to join the Citizen Military Forces (CMF), but nothing ever came of his application. However, as Australia had become embroiled in the rapidly-escalating Vietnam War, Bon had to register for National Service. Thankfully, he was not one of those called up for duty, but he would subsequently claim in an interview with a German magazine that he was rejected for service after being labelled 'socially maladjusted'. Having secured another dead-end job as a store man with the National Egg Board, Bon began concentrating all his efforts on becoming a rock'n'roll drummer, and devoted his free time to pounding away on the drum kit he'd set up in the bay window of his parents' living room.

Within a couple of months he'd formed the Spektors with a couple of guys he'd befriended who worked at the local oil refinery –Welsh-born guitarist Wyn Milson and singer John Collins – and another friend called Brian Gannon roped in to play bass. Though the Spektors gave Bon his first taste of being in a band, in the grand scheme of things they were little more than a weekend show band trawling the Perth club circuit, playing various rock'n'roll standards and Beatles and Stones covers. They made their live debut in early 1965 at the Medina Youth Club, and it was here that Bon first set his eyes on a striking seventeen-year-old blonde called Maria Van Vlijman with whom he would embark on a tempestuous on-again-off-again four-year relationship, despite the fact that she was dating Brian Gannon when they met. The Spektors, however, would soon be reduced to a shadowy memory when Bon and Wyn jumped ship to join forces with the more musically proficient members of their Fremantle rivals, the Winstons – including their singer, Vince Lovegrove – to form the Valentines. 'I was a drummer in those days, and I used to play half the night on drums and spend the other half singing,' Bon later explained.

There was no vocal training in my background, just a lot of good whisky, and a long string of blues bands - or should I say "booze" bands?'

- Bon Scott

'The singer [Collins] also played drums, but not as good as me. Then I got an offer from the Valentines as drummer. But I wanted to be a singer so I joined as singer. It wasn't because I wanted to be up front, it was because the singer used to get more chicks!'

Having established themselves on the Perth scene, the Valentines headed into the studio and recorded their debut single 'Everyday I Have to Cry', which gave them a Top Five hit in the Western Australian charts. Though the follow-up single, 'She Said' – penned by George Young, Scottish-born songwriter/guitarist with the Sydney-based Easybeats – failed to trouble the charts, the band got through to the prestigious state final of the Hoadley's 'Battle of the Sounds' competition, staged in Melbourne. While they didn't win, they impressed several prominent local music bigwigs and decided to relocate to Melbourne to further their chances of mainstream success. However, despite further trips into the recording studio, the only newsworthy event came when the band were arrested for possession of marijuana, and in the summer of 1970 the Valentines went their separate ways.

Bon's path took him to Adelaide, where he threw in his lot with progressive rockers Fraternity, who – when they weren't recording albums and touring – were happy living the hippie dream in a communal farmhouse out in the wilds outside of Adelaide. Fraternity would record two albums – *Livestock* and *Flaming Galah* – but while the movers and shakers on the Aussie music scene were touting them as the next big thing, the band repeatedly failed to capture their live sound on vinyl. Though Bon quickly tired of living a nomadic existence and moved back into town, he was obviously still required to make frequent forays to the farmhouse in order to write songs and rehearse, and it was during one of these weekly sojourns that he met his future wife, 21-year-old Irene Thornton. Bon and Irene tied the knot in a civil service on 24 January 1972, but the honeymoon was put on hold as Fraternity were about to embark on a tour of the Australian outback before travelling to England.

Bon was understandably thrilled at the prospect of touring England, as it would give him the chance to take Irene to Kirriemuir, as well as reconnect with his Scottish roots. What no one had taken into consideration, however, was that while England was in the grip of one of its periodical economic meltdowns, glam rock was in the ascendancy. Britain's teenagers couldn't get enough of T Rex, David Bowie, Sweet and Gary Glitter, but they had no interest in what a bunch of bearded Aussie hippies had to offer. Somewhat amazingly, Fraternity would remain in England for eighteen months, though for the first six months they did nothing other than sit around their rented house smoking dope and waiting for something to happen. When it became patently clear that nothing was likely to happen, the interpersonal relationships within the band began to sour, as did Bon and Irene's marriage. Even a band name change – to the unimaginative Fang – failed to stop the rot, and following an outdoor show in Windsor in August 1973, the fragmented band returned to Adelaide under a cloud – one that was largely of their own making. (In one of those ironic quirks of fate which wouldn't become evident until later, while in England Fraternity/Fang had played a couple of shows with a Newcastle-based band called Geordie, whose singer Brian Johnson would take Bon's place in AC/DC following his death.)

Bon and Irene made the return trip to Adelaide together in time for Christmas, but though Bon was hoping that being back on home ground might help to heal their rift, Irene knew in her heart that their marriage was over. As if worrying about his estrangement from Irene wasn't bad enough, Fraternity appeared no nearer to resolving their problems than they had been in England, and Bon was forced to take a regular job loading trucks at a fertilizer plant to make ends meet. With nothing happening on the Fraternity front, he kept his hand in musically by jamming with a ramshackle local outfit called Peter Head and the Mount Lofty Rangers.

With his first wages Bon bought himself a second-hand Triumph motorcycle so that he could get to and from work, make the Rangers' rehearsals, and drop in on Irene in the hope that seeing him might erode her resolve. Irene, however – though still in love with Bon – had seemingly made up her mind. Bon couldn't accept that the marriage was over, and sometime in late February 1974, having yet again failed to convince Irene to give him another chance, he arrived at the Rangers' rehearsal space in a fit of drunken rage. In a classic case of Freudian 'transference', he took his frustrations out on the band before storming out and purposely riding the Triumph at high speed into the path of an oncoming car.

While his external injuries included a broken jaw and collarbone, and a nasty cut to his throat, his internal injuries were rather more serious, and for three days his life hung by a thread as he drifted in and out of consciousness. On hearing about the accident, Irene rushed over to the hospital and never left Bon's side. 'I remember being there once, sitting there with my sister,' she recalled in *Highway to Hell*. '[I was] looking at the screen, you know, the heartbeat monitor, and the line stopping, and yelling for the doctor. The doctor came and banged him on the chest. It started again. He was terribly sick; he looked like a thin, frail old man. He was hunched from the broken collarbone, his throat was cut and his jaw was wired up. He was virtually skin and bone.'

When he regained consciousness and saw Irene maintaining a vigil at his bedside, Bon's hope was renewed – especially when Irene agreed to allow him to stay with her after he was discharged a few weeks later. But, of course, Irene was simply doing what any friend would do under the circumstances: 'He made a bit of an effort then but it [the marriage] was already stuffed,' she says. 'But it was probably like the friendship was a lot better after it was all over, when the bullshit and bitterness was out of the way.'

Although he was bedridden, Bon still had the use of his arms and was able to ease the pain with a steady supply of joints. And as he'd left several of his front teeth embedded in the tarmac at the scene of the crash, he was forced to sip his medicinal Jack Daniel's through a straw. Bon was soon on his feet and seemingly back to his fighting best, but the truth is he never fully recovered and suffered severe pain in his upper body for the remainder of his life. However, the physical scars he was carrying from the accident were nothing compared to the mental anguish he was suffering over his failed marriage, coupled with him now being considered just another washed up has-been by the movers and shakers on the Melbourne music scene. And one cannot help but wonder what might have become of Bon had it not been for AC/DC.

Easybeats guitarist George Young's younger brothers, Malcolm and Angus, had formed AC/DC the previous November, some ten years after they'd arrived in Sydney from their native Glasgow. However, while having an older brother in the Easybeats opened a few industry doors that might otherwise have remained closed – as well as securing them a support slot with Lou Reed on the former Velvet Underground frontman's Australian tour – they might well have been left to flounder in the Sydney surf if it hadn't been for Bon. Because while Malcolm and Angus's twin-guitar attack was incredible to behold, it was undoubtedly Bon's guttural vocal that provided the missing link they'd been searching for. Yet it was a link they came within an E string of passing up.

According to Vince Lovegrove, it was he who put Bon's name in the frame after inadvertently discovering – during a casual conversation with George Young – that AC/DC were fed up with their singer Dave Evans, and on the lookout for a new frontman. Lovegrove was astute enough to recognise the serendipity of the moment, because with Fraternity/ Fang on enforced hiatus, Bon was at a loose end. In fact, with nothing happening on the musical front, he'd resorted to doing odd jobs for Vince

'Bon moulded the character and flavour of AC/DC.
He was one of the dirtiest fuckers I know.'
- Angus Young

simply to survive. Vince had his work cut out in convincing Malcolm and Angus that Bon wasn't 'too old', and cajoled them into giving him a chance to prove that he could rock their arses off. Despite this, when Vince gave Bon the news that he'd secured him an audition, Bon was less than enthusiastic about the proposal, going so far as to dismiss AC/ DC as 'a gimmick band'. And even though the chemistry between Bon, Angus, and Malcolm was obvious enough for the band's manager, Dennis Laughlin, to offer Bon the gig on the spot, he was in no immediate hurry and went away to weigh up his options. Being a classic Cancerian, Bon was a bundle of contradictions, for while he'd dreamed of rock'n'roll stardom since the first day he'd served as a self-appointed Kirriemuir Pipe Band auxiliary, and knew in his heart that joining this happening young band would lift him out of his mundane existence, he also knew that joining AC/DC would mean abandoning any hope of getting back together with Irene – even though Irene had already made her feelings known.

While Bon is remembered for his onstage rock'n'roll machismo, beneath his gruff exterior lay the heart of a hapless romantic. Bon certainly wasn't the only *Cemetery Gates* inductee to give his all to the woman he loved – as Axl Rose's ill-fated affairs with Erin Everly and Stephanie Seymour, and Pete Steele's attempted suicide after a failed romance readily testify. Indeed, it was the only way he knew how to love, and it's certainly nothing to be ashamed of. Yet, in holding nothing back, Bon left himself with nothing to cling to in the aftermath of the break-up.

Though fools rush in where angels fear to tread, Bon would have plenty of time to ponder his decision, because Laughlin was happy to wait until AC/DC had completed a six-week residency in Perth before he stopped off in Adelaide en route back to Sydney to reiterate his offer. It was well worth the detour, because the following day Bon called at Vince's office and gave his friend notice that he would need to advertise for another handyman.

Bon's debut with AC/DC came a few weeks later on 5 October 1974 at the Brighton Le-Sands Masonic Hall in Sydney, and such was his confidence that he didn't even see the need to rehearse the songs, as Angus explained: 'The only rehearsal we had was just sitting around an hour before the gig, pulling out every rock'n'roll song we knew. When we finally got there Bon downed about two bottles of bourbon with dope, coke, speed, and says, "Right, I'm ready," and he was too. He was fighting fit. There was this immediate transformation and he was running around with his wife's knickers on, yelling at the audience. It was a magic moment. He said it made him feel young again.'

Within a month of Bon's arrival, AC/DC had recorded their debut album *High Voltage*, which included Bon's ode to Irene, 'She's Got Balls' (the first song he wrote after joining the band), and was unleashed on a largely unsuspecting Australian public via the EMI-distributed Albert Productions the following February. The band's follow-up album *T.N.T*, which was released in December 1975, and opened with the anthemic 'It's a Long Way to the Top (If You Wanna Rock'n'Roll)', was also only available in Australasia. The LP did, at least, further establish AC/DC as Australia's premier rock band, and it was surely only a matter of time before the rest of the world sat up and took notice.

Somewhat surprisingly, given that EMI had been given ample warning from their man down under that AC/DC were the hottest ticket in town, it was the American label Atlantic Records that secured the band's signatures in early 1976. With the ink barely dry on the contract, Atlantic re-released *High Voltage* – this, unlike the original debut, consisted of tracks lifted from both Albert Productions albums – and sent the band on a tour of Europe to promote the compilation album. The Lock Up Your Daughters Summer Tour, as it was called, not only introduced AC/DC to a wider audience, it also gave them a taste of what it was like playing on the big stage. And on subsequent tours promoting *Dirty Deeds Done Dirt Cheap*, *Let There Be Rock*, *Powerage*, and *Highway to Hell*, both the stages and audiences got bigger and bigger.

While Malcolm and Angus's drive, determination and dedication – not to mention their seemingly effortless knack for coming up with kick-ass riffs – was enough to ensure that the outside world would hear of AC/DC, both brothers readily acknowledge that they got to the top a whole lot quicker rockin' and rollin' with their 'brother from another mother'. And even now, three decades on, their love and respect for Bon has not diminished. 'I think it's just something that is part of you. It's like you lost someone close to you, in your family or a very close friend,' Angus told *braveworld.com* on the thirtieth anniversary of Bon's death. 'You've always got that feeling they're there but you just, I suppose, miss them in the physical sense. There's always memories that keep coming back to you, and it doesn't matter what the situation is. You could be travelling; you could be relaxing somewhere, or going to play or being in the studio, there's always something that reminds you.'

Angus also told the website how their journey with Bon had eerily come full circle: 'Just before he died, he'd come down with me and Mal, he got behind the kit and Mal said to him, "Ah Bon, get on the drums, we need a drummer," and that's what he loved. Bon wanted to be the drummer in the band. It was kind of funny, the first time we ever sat down, here's this guy saying, "I'm your new drummer." Mal convinced him to sing, to get up to the front of the stage. Then he was there at the end again. The last time you saw him, there he was behind the kit.'

Though Angus was a strict teetotaller, he and Malcolm were well accustomed to Bon's inability to stop at just one bottle, and would have said their goodbyes expecting to hear about another crazy night on the town the next time they met up, but Bon's uncanny knack for pulling away from the Grim Reaper's scythe was about to desert him.

Moments of madness: Sometime during the early evening of Monday, 18 February 1980, Bon, having tired of drinking alone and trying to come up with song ideas for the follow-up album to *Highway to Hell*, accepted an invitation from an acquaintance called Alistair Kinnear to check out a new band who were making their live debut at London's Music Machine. However, as Kinnear didn't pick Bon up from his flat until approaching midnight, the show was over by the time they arrived at the Camden Town venue. The aftershow party, of course, was in full swing, and as Kinnear admitted in *Metal Hammer* magazine in 2005, he and Bon both partied hard into the early hours. When the party came to an end Kinnear – with apparent scant regard for being way over the legal limit – drove Bon home. By the time they arrived at Bon's flat in Ashley Court, Bon had drifted off into unconsciousness, and as Kinnear couldn't rouse him from his slumber he took Bon's keys and let himself into the flat, fully expecting to find Bon's current girlfriend, Anna, tucked up in bed. However, on finding the flat empty, Kinnear staggered back down into the street for another fruitless attempt to wake Bon. On realising that he'd inadvertently left Bon's keys in the flat, and no doubt wanting to get to bed himself, he went in search of a phone box and called a mutual friend who suggested he take Bon back to his own flat in East Dulwich.

Though this solved one problem, Kinnear was still faced with what to do with Bon once he got home, as there was no way he was going to be able to assist Bon up three flights of stairs – especially in his sorry state. He made a second call to the same friend, who, having had plenty of experience of Bon passing out at inconvenient moments, told him to wrap Bon in a blanket, and suggested that as Bon had never been to Kinnear's place before, he should leave a note indicating which flat was his so that Bon would know where to go once he came to. After bundling Bon up in a blanket, Kinnear lowered the passenger seat to make his friend as comfortable as possible. Little could he have known, however, as he placed a note bearing his address and phone number on the dashboard before staggering off to his bed, that he'd unwittingly signed Bon's death warrant.

Kinnear says that it was somewhere between 4:00 and 5:00am before he got to bed, and he didn't stir until sometime around 11:00am, when a friend called. As his head was pounding, he asked his friend to go back outside to check on Bon, and when the friend returned to say the car was empty, he simply assumed that Bon had woken up at some point and made his way home. It wasn't until 7:30pm that Kinnear realised his mistake in not telling his friend that he'd lowered the seat. In a state of panic, Kinnear drove Bon to King's College Hospital in nearby Camberwell, but he knew from Bon's clammy skin and distorted features that the singer was already some way along the highway to hell he'd so often sung about.

Bon may be long gone, but his memory will continue to be saluted by those about to rock.

John Bonham

31 May 1949 - 25 September 1980

Born: John Henry Bonham

Alter-egos: Bonzo, la Bête (French for 'the Beast').

(Pre) occupations: Powerhouse drummer with Led Zeppelin.

In memoriam: 'After a few nights out with Zeppelin, I worked out that their drummer, John Bonham, was as fucking nuts as I was, so we'd spend most of the time trying to out-crazy each other. That was always the way it was with me, y'know? I'd try to win people over like I did in the playground . . . of course, behind the mask there was a sad old clown. Bonham was the same, I think. He'd just drink himself to fucking bits.' – Ozzy Osbourne

Deadly sins: As Disney would have it, *la belle* and *la bête* belong together . . . yet there was nothing pretty about John Bonham's reaction to the culinary delights on offer at a Led Zep gig in Nantes, circa 1973. As anyone present would surely testify, the wrath of Bonham (the legendary sticksman who once declared, 'If it moves, I hit it. If it doesn't move, I still hit it') was a sight to behold. Indeed, his destruction of three backstage trailers that day was enough to cement his awesome, elemental reputation for life. He'll be forever remembered as 'la Bête' – a nickname bestowed on him by record company executive Benoit Gautier. And little did Gautier realise how pertinent a moniker this was to become.

Later that same evening, the Frenchman could only look on in horror as Bonham single-handedly laid waste to his Volvo. 'He could be the most generous guy and the worst guy,' he observed years later. Significantly, he believes that Bonham's Hyde side would manifest at moments when his Doctor Jekyll was missing his family the most. 'He would cry talking about his family,' Gautier explained. 'Then the band or roadies would push him to do something and he'd go crazy.' As an example of Bonham's on-the-road lunacy, Gautier cites the time the drummer offered him 'cocaine', knowing full well that it was a dose of heroin. 'He thought that was the funniest thing. He would take a chance on killing you.'

Up until then, Bonham's tailspins into deep depression had been primarily booze-induced, but with each enforced separation from his loved ones, he sought more potent chemical distractions. Onstage he would pound away at the kit with a plastic bag nestled between his knees. Holding an ounce or more of cocaine, the secreted bag meant he never had to be separated from his stash. Indeed, the sticksman was forever reaching down for not-so-covert handfuls of his favourite poison as he played. Such was his intake that, after the show, roadies knew to dismantle the drums over another bag. Bonham's leftovers would be more than enough for them to throw a party of their own.

Another memorable incident (for all the wrong reasons) occurred while Led Zeppelin were over in LA, laying down tracks for *Presence*. Strolling into the Rainbow Bar & Grill on Sunset Strip, Bonham plonked his considerable bulk down on a stool at the bar and proceeded to order twenty Black Russian cocktails – half of which he downed one after the other. Glancing about the room he espied Michelle Myer, a long-time associate of producer Kim Fowley. On seeing Bonham, Myer, who was dining alone in a booth across the room, acknowledged him with a smile that Bonham didn't return. Instead he lumbered across to where she was sitting, leant across the table and punched her full in the face. The force of his fist knocked her clean off her seat. 'Don't ever look at me that way again!' he bellowed before returning to his seat, ready to continue his one-man party as though nothing had happened.

From cradle to grave: For John Bonham – or 'Bonzo' as he was known throughout his adult life, for no particular reason other than the nickname seemed to suit him – the urge to drum began maddeningly early. 'I used to play on a bath salt container with wires on the bottom, and on a round coffee tin with a loose wire fixed to it to give a snare-drum effect. Plus there were always my mum's pots and pans,' he said of his first 'kit', which his dad rigged up at their Kidderminster home. 'When I was ten, my mum bought me a snare drum. My dad bought me my first full drum kit when I was fifteen. It was almost prehistoric. Most of it was rust.'

Amidst a cloud of rust, Bonzo would pound the kit for all he was worth, until the cacophony resolved itself into an altogether slicker sound. Though he never took a single formal lesson, he was playing in two local bands by the time he left school. While working with his dad as a hod-carrier on various building sites, Bonzo supplemented his wages playing in outfits like Terry and the Spiders (who insisted he wear a tight-fitting purple jacket with a velveteen collar) and the Nicky James Movement – whose career juddered to a halt when their gear was repossessed after a show – before finally deciding to commit full-time to a band called Way of Life.

By this time, he'd married his sweetheart, Pat, who was expecting their first child. When Way of Life went into temporary hiatus, he accepted an offer from his pal Robert Plant, who was fronting a struggling blues outfit called Crawling King Snakes. Though Bonzo would return to Way of Life in order to be closer to his family following the arrival of his son, Jason, he kept in touch with Plant, and the pair teamed up again for a while in Band of Joy. Their paths would cross again in Oxford in the summer of 1968, while Bonzo was touring as part of American singer-songwriter Tim Rose's backing band. Plant was working with ex-Yardbirds guitarist Jimmy Page. Session musician to London's rock royalty, Plant had already provided riffs for the Rolling Stones, the Who, and the Kinks.

Though he listened politely while his friend gushed about Page's prowess, and let it be known the drum stool was as yet vacant for the 'New Yardbirds' (as they were considering calling themselves), Bonzo was already earning £40 a week with Rose – an amount which had allowed him and Pat to upgrade from the fifteen-foot caravan in which they'd begun married life to a council house in Dudley. He also knew that Pat viewed Plant with a slightly jaundiced eye. For while she hadn't forced Bonzo to honour the pledge he'd made to give up drumming if she married him, she'd always looked upon Plant as a disruptive influence, and wouldn't be best pleased by the prospect of the pair joining forces; because she'd learned from experience that every time the two got together he'd be out till the early hours, pouring whatever money he was earning down his throat before staggering home with half a crown (12½p) in his pocket.

What Pat hadn't counted on, however, was that Plant had been bigging up Bonzo's drumming prowess to Page, and on Plant's recommendation Page went along to the Country Club in Hampstead, North London, on 31 July 1968, to see Bonzo playing with Rose. 'He [Bonzo] did this short five-minute drum solo, and that's when I knew I'd found who I was looking for,' Page told Mick Wall for his 2008 Led Zeppelin tome, *When Giants Walked the Earth*. After Page informed his manager, the formidable Peter Grant, of his find, Grant began bombarding Bonzo with telegrams inviting him to join. Bonzo, however, remained unfazed, and there were others clamouring for his services, including Chris Farlowe and Joe Cocker.

But it was the music that mattered most to Bonzo. 'It wasn't a question of who had the best prospects, but also which music was going to be right,' Bonzo recalled. 'I thought the Yardbirds were finished, because in England they had been forgotten. Still I thought, "Well, I've got nothing anyway so anything is really better than nothing." I knew Jimmy was a good guitarist and that Robert was a good singer, so even if we didn't have any success, at least it would be a pleasure to play in a good group.'

Exceeding Bonzo's mildest dreams for the future, the band's first two eponymous albums – *Led Zeppelin I* and *Led Zeppelin II* – were a raging success, and the weekly £40 he'd given up on parting company with Tim Rose was replaced by near-monthly six-figure royalty cheques, the first of which enabled the Bonhams to relocate to a fifteen-acre farm on the outskirts of Birmingham – not that Bonzo himself was able to appreciate the country air.

Zeppelin's punishing tour schedule meant Page, Plant and Bonzo were away from their respective homes for months at a time, with little to alleviate the tedium of life on the road but small pleasures, such as hurling television sets out of hotel-room windows. Displaying a most creative approach to 'rearranging furniture', they paid managers to trash their own rooms when the mood took them. And then, of course, there were the girls. Though Bonzo was a married man (as were Plant and Zeppelin bassist, John Paul Jones), he wasn't above taking his pick from the bevy of groupies backstage. Lingering behind after each of Zeppelin's shows, these women would do pretty much do anything, just to be allowed to remain in the presence of the band. And, after all, what happened on tour stayed on tour. Mere ports in a storm, these girls were usually treated with the same tenderness shown to Bonzo's kit during 'Moby Dick', Bonham's epic, 30-minute, spotlight-stealing solo. And indeed, these were not the only occasions on which Bonzo would find himself centre stage . . .

While Zeppelin were relaxing in Los Angeles during their second US tour in 1969, the band's road manager, Richard Cole – who was fast becoming Bonzo's partying partner-in-crime – cajoled him into screwing a notorious LA groupie known as the 'Dog Act', owing to her habit of bringing along her Great Dane. Having tried repeatedly – and unsuccessfully – to get the dog to perform cunnilingus on its willing mistress by dangling strips of fried bacon from her vagina, Cole had Bonzo take the animal's place. While Bonzo was going hell for leather, Peter Grant came into the room and dumped an industrial-sized can of baked beans over the couple before spraying them with a magnum of champagne.

Fish would be on the madcap menu when Zeppelin returned to the States the following year, and once again Bonzo and Cole were at the centre of the incident, which would subsequently be voted number one on *Spin* magazine's list, '100 Sleaziest Moments of Rock'. Following their appearance at the Seattle Pop Festival on 27 July 1970, the band returned to their hotel, the Edgewater Inn, which, as its name implies, overlooked the Pacific Ocean, and had a unique selling point in that its residents could literally fish from their balconies. With the following day a designated day off, Bonzo and Cole rented a couple of rods from reception and ushered in the dawn drinking heavily and fishing for sharks with champagne-soaked bait. However, rather than release their haul of mud sharks and red snappers, the pair – rather inventively, it has to be said – threaded coat-hangers through the gills and hung the fish in the closet.

> 'Bonzo was the main part of the band . . .
> I don't think there's anyone in the world who could replace him.'
> - Robert Plant

Later that same evening, when one of the gaggle of local teenage girls the band were entertaining teasingly enquired if they were 'into bondage', Bonzo and Cole led the procession to their room, stripped and then tied the girl to the bedposts with rope ordered from room service. Then – with their pal, Vanilla Fudge drummer Carmine Appice, capturing the moment for posterity on his Super 8 camera – they proceeded to insert the long snout of a dead red snapper into her vagina, and the head of an equally-dead mud shark into her anus. Aside from gaining Bonzo and Cole a lasting place in the rock'n'roll hall of sleaze, their antics were further immortalised by Frank Zappa – himself no stranger to offstage debauchery – in the song 'The Mud Shark', which appeared on the album *Fillmore East – June 1971.*

On 23 July 1977, while Zeppelin were playing the first of two nights at the Oakland Coliseum in San Francisco during the third leg of their latest US tour, Bonzo became embroiled in a rather unsavoury incident which landed a security guard in hospital and saw the drummer and several other members of the Zeppelin entourage being carted off to jail by a SWAT team. It all started when Peter Grant's son, Warren, was stopped from removing a hand-painted sign saying 'Led Zeppelin' that was affixed to the backstage trailer serving as the band's makeshift dressing room, as it was needed for the following night. According to Richard Cole, another of those arrested, the security guard had shoved Warren away, and it was on seeing the youngster being so brusquely treated that Bonzo – who happened to be offstage taking a breather, presumably during one of Jimmy Page's solos – had gone in search of Grant Sr. to inform him of what had occurred, and over-egged the pudding somewhat by saying the guard had slapped Warren. When the bear-like Grant heard what had happened, he, together with Bonzo and the renowned London gangster, John Bindon (a pal of Grant's who was along for the ride serving as the band's unofficial enforcer), went in search of the guard, Jim Matzorkis, dragged him inside the nearest production trailer, and proceeded to teach him a lesson in etiquette while a pipe-wielding Cole stood guard outside.

Nothing untoward occurred when Zeppelin returned to the Coliseum the following night, as the legendary Bay Area promoter, Bill Graham, had signed a letter of indemnification absolving anyone connected with Led Zeppelin from responsibility for the previous night's incident – which Grant had insisted on before allowing his charges onstage. However, the following morning, while Cole was overseeing the logistics in advance of their departure, he happened to glance out of the window and was astonished to see a SWAT team moving into position around the hotel. Cole barely had time to stash the band's cocaine supply before the officers stormed the building. Though Grant flashed his letter of indemnity, the disclaimer literally wasn't worth the paper it was written on, because aside from Graham having signed it under duress, the promoter had no legal right to act on behalf of Matzorkis.

The following day, 25 July, Bonzo and his fellow accused were brought before the court and charged with assault, while the security guard's lawyers filed a $2 million civil suit on behalf of their client. Despite having filed a collective plea of *nolo contendere* when the case was heard six months later, Bonzo and the others were all found guilty and given varying fines and suspended jail sentences. However, as none of the four was required to appear personally in court, Matzorkis's civil suit was never heard.

Very little was heard from Led Zeppelin during this same period, due to the tragic death of Plant's five-year-old son, Karac, who'd died suddenly from a mystery viral infection the day following Bonzo's court appearance. Though Led Zeppelin had redefined rock, and by default given birth to heavy metal, the advent of punk and its attendant countercultural revolution had caused a seismic shift in how rock music was perceived. If long hair and flared denims were considered passé, then so were the long-haired, denim-wearing musicians – regardless of their respective past glories. And while Led Zeppelin had weathered the storm better than most of the other 'dinosaurs' – playing two sell-out shows at Knebworth in May 1979, and hitting number one in both the UK and America with their latest album, *In Through the Out Door* – by April 1980, the very same English music press which had championed them through their decade of decadence was now dismissing them as an extinct species.

Regardless of what the fickle music press was writing about them, Led Zeppelin still had a loyal hardcore fan base – particularly in America which, aside from embracing the Clash, had remained largely unmoved by punk rock. A stripped-down US tour had already been set up for the

'Almost the moment he died, they put him in Playboy as one of the greatest drummers, which he was - there's no doubt about it. There's never been anybody since. He's one of the greatest drummers that ever lived - John was the greatest rock drummer ever, as far as I'm concerned.'
- Jimmy Page

Autumn, but in April 1980 the band embarked on a fourteen-date tour of Europe – their first European dates in seven years. It was also their first outing without Richard Cole.

Having decided that Cole's rampant drug use had made him a liability, Grant asked Bonzo's personal assistant, Rex King, to oversee the European jaunt. Cole, in a fit of pique, had made a vague threat against Grant's kids. When this got back to Grant, Cole was out through the back door – and not even an intercession from his drug buddy Bonzo was going to save him.

Moments of madness: Owing to the unforeseen cancellation of a series of shows in France, Zeppelin hadn't played live since the beginning of July, but with the US tour creeping up on them, the band convened at Jimmy's house on Old Mill Lane in Windsor – a rambling former mill which the guitarist had recently purchased from Michael Caine – to blow off the collective cobwebs from their two-month hiatus. The date was 24 September 1980, a date that was to pass into Led Zeppelin legend, as it would be the last time they were all in the same room together.

While the rest of the band were looking forward to the tour and getting back to doing what they did best – and still better than anyone else –

Bonzo was becoming more and more anxious as the 21-date tour – set to commence in Montreal, Canada, on 17 October – drew inexorably nearer. The reason being that their last visit to the States had been something of an unmitigated disaster, and on a personal level, he still had the three-year-old, Sword of Damocles-esque $2 million lawsuit hanging over him in California.

Though he'd weaned himself off heroin, he was over-compensating with alcohol, and was also taking Motival, a mild anti-depressant designed to lift the patient's spirits, but which carried numerous side effects such as restlessness, agitation, panic attacks and hostility, as well as the risk of tremors and paraesthesia of extremities – hardly the most suitable medication for someone who earned their corn as a drummer.

On that fateful morning, Bonzo was picked up by Rex King, who'd been hired by Grant because of his tough, no-nonsense attitude. However, while en route to Berkshire, Bonzo insisted they stop off at a pub, where he proceeded to knock back four quadruple vodka and oranges, helped down with a couple of ham sandwiches. Sixteen measures of vodka would have put the Russian Bear to sleep, but this was merely a typical 'breakfast' for Bonzo, and upon arriving at Jimmy's he continued drinking until he was no longer capable of maintaining the beat. This was something hitherto unheard of, but Bonzo's capacity for alcohol was legendary, so there was little cause for concern – even when he passed out on Jimmy's sofa sometime around midnight.

Like Rex King, Jimmy's assistant, Rick Hobbs, had been part of Led Zeppelin's entourage for the past three years, and was therefore well-versed in Bonzo's drinking habits. Having half-carried, half-dragged Bonzo's not inconsiderable bulk up the stairs and into one of the guest bedrooms, he laid the comatose drummer on his side and supported his frame with pillows. This wasn't so much for Bonzo's comfort, but rather to prevent him choking on his vomit should he be sick during the night – a fate which had befallen Jimi Hendrix a decade earlier.

As the Old Mill House was a hive of activity the following morning, with everyone getting on with their duties, no one paid any attention to Bonzo's failure to appear. When he still hadn't put in appearance by mid-afternoon, however, John Paul Jones and Robert Plant's attendant, Benji Lefevre, went upstairs to rouse him. On opening the door and being hit by a pervading unpleasant smell, they knew something was very wrong, but they instinctively rushed to the bed and tried shaking their friend awake. An ambulance was summoned, but with Bonzo's body already ice cold and showing signs of discolouration, the attending paramedics deduced that he'd been dead for several hours. The police had also arrived, but having found nothing to rouse suspicion, went away to file their report.

Robert Plant went to break the news to Bonzo's family, while John Paul Jones returned home to grieve with his own family, leaving Jimmy Page alone to ponder what the press – which had long been fascinated with his obsession with the occult – would make of the latest tragedy to befall Led Zeppelin. For one of rock'n'roll's more enduring myths is that the band – with the exception of John Paul Jones – entered into a Faustian pact with the Devil by signing away their immortal souls in exchange for earthly success and its attendant pleasures. Yet while notions of satanic pacts are the realm of fantasists, that's not to say the myth is not without its requisite kernel of truth. For Jimmy Page's interest in the occult – especially the writings of Aleister Crowley, the self-styled 'Great Beast 666' – went way beyond that of the casual layman. Indeed, the origins of heavy metal's ongoing fascination with Satanism and Devil worship can be directly traced to Led Zeppelin: be it Black Sabbath's decision to plough a darker furrow in their music; Trent Reznor recording *The Downward Spiral* at 10050 Cielo Drive, where Sharon Tate and her friends were slain in August 1969; Marilyn Manson and Varg Vikernes's fixation with Anton LaVey, founder of the Church of Satan, and the spate of Norwegian stave church burnings Vikernes was convicted of. Of course, while much of this is simply posturing for publicity's sake, as nothing attracts attention quite like dipping a toe into the darker side of the human psyche, there are certain elements within the metal community – most notably the Scandinavian black metal scene – who regard pushing the boundaries as their *raison d'être*. And, of course, therein lays the danger. Because singing about the 'De Mysteriis Dom Sathanas' (as Mayhem did) is one thing, but once you step onto the Left-Hand Path, there's no guaranteeing you'll find your way back.

However, regardless of whether John's death was retributive karma or a tragic consequence of his hedonistic lifestyle, his drums had now fallen forever silent. And with Bonzo's absence as insistent as his formidable presence had been, Robert, Jimmy and John Paul decided it was impossible for them to carry on as a band, and issued the following, typically ambiguous statement to the press: 'We wish it to be known that the loss of our dear friend and the deep respect we have for his family, together with the sense of undivided harmony felt by ourselves and our manager, have led us to decide that we could not continue as we were.'

Peter Steele

4 January 1962 - 14 April 2010

Born: Petrus Thomas Ratajczyk

Alter-egos: Peter Steele, Lord Petrus of Vinland.

(Pre) occupations: The Green Man of NYC Parks Dept; bassist and frontman for Carnivore and Type O Negative.

In memoriam: 'Human nature never fails to disappoint me . . . you want to blame someone go look in the fuckin' mirror. It's not the church, it's not the schools, it's not your parents – it's fuckin' you, man, everyone has a choice.' – Peter Steele

'My views on virtually everything have changed radically. People ask me about how I used to fuck around on the road and abusing my body and writing songs like "Christian Woman". I turn around and say, "God loves his lost little lambs the most. Especially those that return to the flock. So flock you."' – Peter Steele

Deadly sins: Till his dying day, Pete Steele never forgot the blue-eyed harbinger of his own debauchery. 'In the past I was immature, dishonest and, most of all, I was a sneak,' confessed a penitent Pete, speaking with *Terrorizer* in 2003. 'That's one of the things I hate the most in people. It's a crazy thing. When I was a kid I used to walk home from school with my nieces and there was this old Italian woman who used to sit outside her house every afternoon. She was around seventy years old and every time she saw me walk past she would point at me and say "You will become what you hate!" She'd never say it to anybody else. She'd look right at me with those really light blue eyes. Her hair was black and she had olive skin – she was a very interesting-looking person, like a witch. I'll never forget her pointing at me with her bony finger saying that.'

In sharp contrast with quintessential good-time guys like Jimmy 'the

Rev', Pete Steele's penchant for oceans of wine and blizzards of coke was never about hedonistic abandon, but rather the abandonment of hope. 'I'm not the life of the party, I'm the death of it,' he once shrugged. And in hindsight, it's painfully clear: Pete was not so much using as self-medicating.

Whether administered as 'liquid courage' (a temporary antidote to the crippling self-doubt he was never quite able to shrug off), or his ticket to the blessed state of 'Anaesthesia', Pete's substance abuse couldn't have been further from recreational. And though he's the perpetrator of many a misdemeanour, perhaps Peter's greatest sin is a failure to keep a (velvet-lined) lid on the unbridled violence of his emotions. 'What's the difference between a criminal and a non-criminal?' quipped Peter back in 1991 in interview with *MK* magazine, firing back his punch-line within the same breath. 'A criminal gets caught. I mean, I have gold platinum criminal records – how many people can say that? I mean, I get the big breaks.'

'No, I'm not a vampire, I'm a fucking alcoholic!'
- Peter Steele

More than a decade on, Pete found himself serving time in Rikers Island for an offence unlike any other within these pages. Whereas the *NME* decried the singularly detached acts of black metallers Varg Vikernes and Euronymous Aarseth as indicative of some 'chilling moral vacuum', Pete was imprisoned for what seems a textbook crime of passion in comparison: the beating of a love rival he'd threatened to kill.

Incarceration in the maximum-security prison made a lasting impression on Pete. 'To be white in jail and to have long black hair and fangs is not an advantage,' he revealed. 'I was in maximum security, and there were some pretty scary people in there who are never gonna get out, so they had nothing to lose by fucking with me. Fortunately, I'm six-foot eight and I weigh 260 pounds, so I'm not exactly a target.'

Yet, Peter's confinement didn't end with his release from Rikers. Fearful for the sanity of their younger brother (there'd always been a shred of reason and wit in Pete's madness – for example, the signing of his exploitative record deal with a mixture of bodily fluids rather than ink; his insistence on driving a gleaming hearse round town instead of a conventional car – but when Pete took to installing cameras in light switches for his own protection, they could no longer turn a blind eye), his family staged an intervention, insisting he check into Kings County

Hospital psych ward, where he could finally begin to work through the baffling contradictions of life on the very threshold of the cemetery gates.

In his 48 years on the planet, Pete Steele was a self-loathing *Playgirl* centrefold, a philandering Lothario dreaming of 'children, responsibility . . . McDonald's', a lapsed Catholic who got born again – and so much more in the eyes of his fans. His chequered history is living proof that: 'God loves his lost little lambs the most. Especially those that return to the flock.'

𝔉**rom cradle to grave:** The face that launched a thousand copies of *Playgirl* magazine, Peter Steele suffered a long and torturous relationship with the looking glass. 'When you're seven feet tall, 350 pounds with long black hair, dark green eyes and fangs,' quipped Type O's less-than-jolly green giant, 'you are a caricature.' Though his gift for self-deprecation proves he was anything but, Pete's enigmatic origins are enough to satisfy even his most imaginative disciples.

A Capricorn by birth, 4 January 1962 marks the beginning of Petrus Thomas Ratajczyk's earthly torment. Proud 'creators' ('parents' was never part of Pete's vocabulary) Nettie and Peter Ratajczyk had already welcomed five daughters to their home on East 18th Street, Brooklyn, but Peter was to be their only son. Weighing in at a hefty ten pounds, baby Peter was a surprising addition to the clan to say the least. 'My mother said it was like giving birth to a pumpkin,' he later quipped.

More tangled than the interlacing branches featured on Type O's landmark release, *October Rust*, Pete's rich European heritage was a source of perpetual fascination. 'I'm into my past, so I definitely read up on [it],' the baritone proudly proclaimed in interview with *The Grimoire of Exalted Deeds*. However, Pete's insatiable thirst for literature of all varieties was often overshadowed by his other more literal one . . .

With an exotic cocktail of Russian, Polish, Icelandic, Scottish and Irish blood coursing through his veins, the Type O Negative lyricist seemed almost fated to succumb to the time-honoured addictions of his ancestors. 'All these nationalities are known for their drinking,' sighed an older, wiser Peter in one of the last interviews of his life (*Metal Injection*, 2009). Keen to share his hard-won experience with a new generation of hedonistic young stars, Peter spoke of the curse of his obsessive personality with disarming humour, articulating the struggle of countless other artists to be found within these pages. 'I'm an addict,' he reasoned simply. 'I can't moderate. There is no such thing as just one drink for me. I just can't have one glass of wine before going onstage – no. I drank the whole vineyard!'

Yet the most illustrious skeleton in the Ratajczyk family closet is that of his grandfather's cousin, Joseph Stalin – who bewitched an entire nation of Soviet rebels into submission in the early twentieth century. Were it not for the chequered past of his infamous relative, Pete Ratajczyk Jr. may never have come up with a stage name to suit him. In fact, 'Stalin' was an alias, borrowed from the Russian word for 'steel'. Decades later and worlds away, the same moniker worked for Peter like a lucky talisman . . .

To the minds of his sisters, Pete's gift for music and lyrics was no less evident than his towering stature. His peers, however, were harder to convince. 'As a kid, I was kind of heavy,' Pete admitted. 'I was the perfect punching bag. I was big, but didn't know how to fight back. I looked fifteen but I was ten. I was completely introverted playing with HO trains in the basement.' Pete's memories of playing to a lunchroom crowd at high school were anything but rose-tinted. 'My first performance ever,' he reminisced in a chat hosted by AOL, 'I was twelve years old [and] on the first note of the first chord I was hit in the head with an apple.'

Though he was destined to be hit with far worse – a used tampon being the most 'fucked up' example of all ('I stopped the song, pulled it up and said, "No, it's not type O negative," and threw it back') – this fateful piece of fruit was enough to cement Pete's fear of the stage for life. Decades later, the frontman confessed, 'I haven't played soberly in about ten or fifteen years. I'm actually a shy person believe it or not. This whole stand-up comedy routine is really just an act because I'm just a little boy in a big body. I've always gotten stage fright and I found that wine or vodka gave me some liquid courage, you know? So a couple of sips before a show turned into a couple of bottles. And my record was twelve bottles of wine – I drank four before the show, four during the show and four after the show and I did not fall down. I just stayed up and annoyed the fuck out of everybody!'

Nonetheless Pete Jr. formed his first band at the tender age of twelve, 'to escape the insanity prevalent in my family'. Devoted to maintaining the aura of gentleman vampire, Pete press-ganged his sister's dentist into filing his incisors down to points. But even the obliging Dr. Wasserman had some qualms about carrying out the cosmetic work that Pete was demanding: 'Pete didn't exactly disclose the "tooth problem" he was having, and Pat [Pete's older sister] didn't ask,' explains Pete's niece via her blog ('For the Love of Peter Steele'). 'But then about a month later, Dr. Wasserman called Pat very perplexed. He thanked Pat for her recommendation, but he was worried . . . Peter wanted to do something to his teeth and the doc didn't understand why. Now, Pat just assumed that when Pete said he had a tooth problem, he was talking a cavity [. . .] What she didn't realise was Dr. Wasserman's call was more about fear of what Pete's mother or sister would do to him if he carried out Peter's request for *fangs* to be implanted into his mouth.'

That same year, Pete signed up for guitar lessons, only to switch to bass six months down the line. Fast-forward to his fifteenth birthday and 'something' happened to change high school as Peter knew it: 'My balls got really big,' he explained. 'I grew a foot and gained a hundred pounds – but it wasn't fat. The people who picked on me became best friends.' Yet Pete himself remained nonplussed. 'With friends like that, who needs

'How would I like to die? I don't know. It wouldn't really matter so long as I thought I'd made a difference in the world.'
- Peter Steele

enemies?' he shrugged, voicing the same question that haunted him to the end, resonating through hours of doom-laden lyrics yet to be penned, sung and immortalised by Type O.

Cutting his fangs in garage bands Hot Ice and Northern Lights, 1979 marked a turning point for the seventeen-year-old Pete, as well as another gifted young musician named Josh Silver. Type O's future master of the keys, Silver was the pianist destined to bring Pete's hauntingly beautiful melodies to life – though they could hardly have guessed as much when they first hooked up to form a twisted metal outfit named 'Fallout'.

Ironically enough, Fallout wasn't to last. And so, strapping on studded armour, bloodstained pelts and ropes of heavy artillery, Pete threw himself headlong into Carnivore – a brutal new three-piece specialising in anthems of unadulterated 'fucking, feasting and fighting', played at break-neck speed and ear-shattering volume. In the company of his bandmates – the same 'guys who he ate with, played ball with, picked up girls with, hung out with' – Peter quickly concocted the concept behind the band's first opus, *Carnivore*. Released by Roadrunner Records in 1986, this muscular beast of an album unveils the brutal sound of a world that should have ended. The concept of said album is as follows: forced underground in the aftermath of a third world war (and a thermo-nuclear one at that), it's hard to credit that life could get any tougher for those sun-starved survivors who dare to drag themselves back to the surface. But this is reckoning without Peter Steele's lawless barbarian horde. Red in tooth and virtually everywhere else you care to mention, they'd take to the stage dressed to kill – quite literally – leaving a crimson trail of animal entrails in their wake.

Two years, one album (1987's *Retaliation*, influenced by Pete's 'discovery of hardcore') and countless gore-laden live shows later, Carnivore's fierce flame was all but burned out. Wherever Pete's barbarian butchers weren't banned from playing, their grisly appearance and controversial lyrics had drawn mobs of outraged listeners. Left with little else to occupy his time, Pete was reduced to 'hanging out in bed in my underwear, eating pretzels and watching *Seinfeld*'.

Pete's decision to sign his first ever record deal (with Roadrunner in the run up to Carnivore's debut) with a mixture of his own blood and semen turned more than a few stomachs. Yet, as Pete always maintained, 'we don't care what you think'. More than just a gimmick, Pete's novel use of bodily

'I think people do drugs because they have too much time on their hands. Lately, with technology, the quality of life's improved. Two-hundred years ago you tended fields for twelve hours, drank wine, and went to sleep.'

- Peter Steele

fluids can be read as a most eloquent act of defiance. When Carnivore finally split, Pete's bandmates were released from their contract without question. However, for Peter, blood – and his semi-Faustian pact with the record company – proved more binding than ink. 'I was withheld,' Peter told the makers of *Death Metal: A Documentary*. 'I like that term. "Withheld" . . . it makes me feel like my balls are soaked in ice-water.'

Though still searching for a day job ('I cut off all my fucking hair, because I was going for a job as a police officer and then I realised, "Man, I'd have to lock up my whole fucking family and my friends!"' he deadpanned), Pete realised the only way forward was to seek out three more 'fucking hippies, put out a demo and shop it to other record companies'. The 'fucking hippies' who completed the 'Drab Four' were Josh Silver on keys, Kenny Hickey on guitar, and Sal Abruscato on drums. They settled on the moniker of 'Repulsion', only to be threatened with legal action by a German grindcore outfit of the same name. Second choice 'Subzero' was also taken, despite Pete having acquired a tattoo of a minus sign within a zero (the band's would-be logo). His inking wouldn't be in vain, however. Half-listening to a radio appeal for donations of 'type O negative' blood, Pete realised there was a powerful alternative . . .

Melding Carnivoresque thrash with dragging, dirge-heavy riffs more typical of the doom genre, Type O Negative's debut, *Slow, Deep and Hard*, was released in 1991. Pete claimed to have written the entire album during a single sleepless night. Inspired by a bitter break-up with a cherished lover turned cheat, it seethes with a plethora of conflicting sentiments: heartbreak, thoughts of revenge and even suicide. In this respect, Pete's lyrics were based on more than just a fleeting impulse. 'On 15 October 1989,' stated Pete. 'I slashed my wrists. All I can say is that I fell in love with the wrong person.' In a later interview, he was more forthcoming: 'All my songs are like my children. Some are bad, but you love them equally because they all stem from myself. The whole first record, I exposed my weaknesses to the world. I told them I got fucked over. It was therapy. I didn't think that album would actually be pressed. It was a demo the record label gave us $30,000 for. Capitalist that I am, I took the money and handed them the tape. For awhile, people thought I was a psychopath.'

When Pete removed his tongue from his cheek long enough to speak, the results were both charming and disarming. Yet apparently his wilfully warped humour was not to everyone's taste. Out on the road promoting *Slow, Deep and Hard*, Dutch activists went so far as to brand him a misogynist, and a Nazi sympathizer – despite Josh Silver being Jewish. When confronted, Pete shrugged the accusations aside. 'You need a working knowledge of English to even pick up on [my humour],' he quipped in *Aquarian Weekly*. 'When I'm sarcastic with people in Europe, they print it as I say it and it looks very strange. It's all a mind game.'

Yet, when it came to mind games, Peter was the greatest player of them all. In response to Roadrunner's demand for a Type O live album (as per their contract), the band simply retired to Silver's basement and – fuelled by vodka – re-recorded *Slow, Deep and Hard* before dubbing in added sound effects, including a 'fight' between Type O and their imaginary crowd.

Though less than impressed, Roadrunner had little option but to release the resulting opus, *The Origin of the Feces*, with an accompanying caveat printed on its casing: 'Not Live At Brighton Beach.' Though it's doubtful anyone stopped to consider the warning label in view of the artwork: a close-up image of a man's anus (reported to be Pete's own) being spread by his hands.

While Type O Negative's (TON to their fans) 1993 follow-up, *Bloody Kisses*, didn't stray from the band's darkened focus on love, sex, and death, Pete couldn't resist taking a swipe at those who still believed him to be a racist with the tracks, 'We Hate Everyone' and 'Kill All the White People'. *Bloody Kisses* would prove to be Sal Abruscato's swansong with TON, as shortly after its release he departed to join fellow New Yorkers Life of Agony. Rather than go through the tedious rigmarole of auditioning drummers, the band simply gave the gig to their drum tech, Johnny Kelly. Kelly's inclusion was something of an enigma to fans, for though he occupied the drum stool whenever the band played live, and was credited on the albums, by Josh Silver's own admission in an interview with *deadcentral.com*, all the drum parts on all subsequent TON albums until 2007's *Dead Again* were programmed.

Bloody Kisses was the first Roadrunner long-player to achieve gold – and subsequently platinum – certification, and the label's bosses began exerting pressure on the band to repeat the formula with their next album. Yet while the songs on 1996's *October Rust* were undoubtedly penned in a similar gloomy rhapsodic vein to those on *Bloody Kisses*, the album's sales subsequently fell away. One reason could have been the switch from punk-metal to lush instrumentation, but Pete remained undaunted: 'Reverb drowns out all the errors,' was his tongue-in-cheek response during promotional interviews in the wake of the album's release. 'What people think is Goth and genius and depth is just layers of mistakes. The reason we cover those songs is because being born in 1962 with five older sisters, each with their own stereo, I was always subjected to different music. The light sounds of the sixties and seventies became some childhood favourites. When you hear these songs on the radio, I think of fond memories and good times. Like Frank Sinatra said, I wanna do it my way . . . I'm going against the wishes of the record company and sometimes the band, [but] I'd rather prostitute myself and be to blame for my own destiny,' he candidly explained. 'The record company wants more sensationalism, more sex, perhaps a pornographic booklet. I'm on a small label thriving on sensationalism. They need shock value to sell albums. I hope I'm passed that. The highest form of art is civil engineering and architecture. It's not just something that looks good, but also is functional as well. Art should have function. It shouldn't sit on the wall and do nothing. When I find myself useless by my own standards, I'll take my life. I will take a swan dive off the World Trade Centre, hopefully on top of someone I hate.'

As the new album contained the fans' live favourite 'My Girlfriend's Girlfriend', it was perhaps inevitable that Pete would be asked to reveal the true experience behind such polyamorous lyrics. 'First, there's the lesbian snicker. Then, there's the comically absurd statement about what people's beliefs are and what the true situation may be,' Pete responded somewhat enigmatically, before revealing that the song was based on 'a few true-life experiences which turned out to be quite pleasant. There are no philosophical implications,' he added, 'It's purely flesh and fantasy. You definitely have to be up for a [ménage à trois].'

On a back of another successful, lengthy world tour, the band returned to the studio to begin work on new material. However, as Pete had suffered several deaths within his family in recent months – including his father – the subject matter of the songs which made up *World Coming Down* understandably took on a more sombre tone. Whereas *Bloody Kisses* and *October Rust* celebrated love, sex and romantic trysts, the new lyrics focused on death, depression, and suicide, with self-explanatory song titles such as 'Everyone I Love is Dead' and 'Everything Dies'.

> *'If I wanted to, I could make my life one continuous party schmoozing. But I'm not the life of the party, I'm the death of it.'*
> *- Peter Steele*

With Pete having chosen to seek solace at the bottom of the bottle, his melancholic mind-set hadn't improved any when it came to penning songs for 2003's *Life is Killing Me*. Aside from containing tracks dedicated to his parents – 'Todd's Ship Gods (Above All Things)' and 'Nettie' – the title track is an overt attack on the medical profession, which he blamed for his father's death eight years earlier, coupled with the shoddy treatment he believed Nettie was receiving at the hands of the doctors who were treating her. 'My mother's been in the hospital with diabetes, they take another piece of her foot every month just because there's no end in sight,' he raged during an interview with *Terrorizer* magazine. 'It just seems to me that the care she's receiving is adequate but it shouldn't be adequate, it should be fucking great!'

Pete's loathing for the medical profession was so deeply ingrained that, rather than visit a doctor for his own ailments, he preferred to let the local vet examine him. 'The only difference between myself and a Great Dane is that they walk upright on all four legs, and generally they're much smarter than I am,' he joked. Pete also chose the *Terrorizer* interview to explain to TON fans the reason behind his drinking: 'Most times I was drinking, that stems from low self-esteem and shyness – basic stage fright. No one thing can turn a person into an alcoholic. I'm making this a statement; I'm not blaming the band for it. I wound up with a drinking problem because of a psychological need to drink something before going onstage from nervousness.'

Having disingenuously said that he'd drunk alcohol as it allowed him to 'open doors to other things' because it lowered his resistance and inhibitions, and warning the readers of the perils of substance abuse, he then proceeded to offer an unreserved apology for his intemperate behaviour. 'What asshole starts to drink and use drugs every day when they are 36 or 37? It's a real fucking disgrace. I'm kind of shocked at myself, I'm embarrassed and I feel that I owe all my band members, all my family, the record company and, most of all, the fans some kind of an apology for not doing my job. That slump of doing too much drinking and cocaine is becoming a thing of the past and I'm starting to get myself back a little bit. 'I'm sick and tired of being sick and tired. I'm tired of feeling sorry for myself, of complaining and not doing anything about it – tired of isolating myself and not going out. This is all drug and alcohol induced. The more I did, the more depressed I became so the more drugs and alcohol I would do – it just becomes this horrible cycle.'

In May 2005, TON fans were left reeling when the band's website posted an image of a tombstone bearing Pete's name and the dates 1962-2005. It would later transpire that that the posting had been meant as a joke in relation to TON having parted company with Roadrunner Records and signed with the independent German label, SPV's heavy metal subsidiary, Steamhammer. At the time, however – especially as Pete had seemingly dropped off the earth – the rumour mill went into overdrive with varying reports that he was suffering from a terminal illness. It wasn't until the release of the *Symphony for the Devil* DVD the following year that fans discovered the true fate that had befallen their hero. It seemed Pete's family were so concerned about his drink-and-drug-ravaged mental state that they'd feared he might take his own life and insisted that he seek professional help – help which included involuntary commitment on Rikers Island, and 'the psych ward at Kings County Hospital'.

'I was suffering from drug-induced psychosis, and I was doing some pretty insane things, like putting cameras in light switches and in shower heads,' he subsequently revealed. 'The paranoia was because of all the cocaine I was doing.' It was the ensuing clear-headedness of sobriety that brought the realisation that Roadrunner Records' interests in Type O Negative differed greatly from his own, and that in order to take the band forward he would need to remove the millstone from around his neck.

However, Pete bore no personal animosity towards his former paymasters and even appeared on the *Roadrunner United* album to help celebrate the label's twenty-fifth anniversary in October 2005.

Having signed with SPV, TON headed into the studio to work on their seventh studio album, *Dead Again*. By the time of the album's release in March 2007, Pete had seemingly come full circle in resurrecting Carnivore – which included long-time Type O Negative collaborator Paul Bento in the line-up – to perform at the 2006 Wacken Open Air Festival.

Following the senseless slaying of his close friend Dimebag Darrell in December 2004, Pete had begun to question his deeply ingrained atheism. 'There are no atheists in foxholes, they say, and I was a foxhole atheist for a long time,' he revealed to *Decibel* magazine in April 2007. 'But after going through a midlife crisis and having many things change very quickly, it made me realise my mortality. And when you start to think about death, you start to think about what's after it. And then you start hoping there is a God. For me, it's a frightening thought to go nowhere. I also can't believe that people like Stalin and Hitler are gonna go to the same place as Mother Teresa.'

In the early hours of 14 April 2010, just three years on from the interview – despite having been clean for five years and enjoying his newfound life of sobriety – Pete would, alas, find the answers to his ponderings. The following day, the band issued a statement via the TON website:

> *It is with great sadness that we inform you that Type O Negative frontman, bassist, and our bandmate, Peter Steele passed away last night of what appears to be heart failure. Ironically Peter had been enjoying a long period of sobriety and improved health and was imminently due to begin writing and recording new music for our follow-up to* Dead Again *released in 2007.*
>
> *The official cause of death has yet to be determined pending autopsy results. The funeral services will be private and memorial services will be announced at a future date. We'd like to share our thoughts and those of Peter's family below. We are truly saddened to lose our friend and appreciate the tremendous outpouring today from around the world.*
>
> *Sincerely,*
> *Josh, Kenny and Johnny.*

CLIFF BURTON

10 February 1962 - 27 September 1986

Born: Clifford Lee Burton

Alter-egos: While Cliff preferred to play under the name he was born with, Dave Mustaine perhaps came closest to bestowing an alter-ego upon him when he hailed Cliff as the 'major rager' and 'four-string motherfucker'.

(Pre) occupations: Bassist with Metallica.

In memoriam: 'Cliff was the man who had that wild spirit that . . . made Metallica reach the sky. After his death, Metallica sold their souls for fame and fortune – things that he would never [have] wanted to deal with.' – Lars Ulrich

'He was a wild, hippie-ish, acid-taking, bell-bottom-wearing guy. He meant business and you couldn't fuck around with him. We gave him shit about his bell-bottoms every day. He didn't care. "This is what I wear, fuck you!" He loved music. He was really intellectual, but very to the point. He taught me a lot about attitude.' – James Hetfield

'As a player and as a person, Cliff was not afraid to be different. We could all learn something from that.' – Alex Webster, Cannibal Corpse

Deadly sins: Cliff is something of a rarity within *Cemetery Gates*, as he committed no deadly sins, but was instead imbued with heavenly virtues.

From cradle to grave: Clifford Lee Burton was born on 10 February 1962 in the semi-rural surroundings of Castro Valley, California. His mother, Jan – a Californian born and bred – was a specialised teacher, while his father, Ray, who hailed from Tennessee, worked as a highway engineer. With elder siblings Scott and Connie to show him the ropes, young Clifford – or Cliff, as he was known to his family – was already getting wise to the ways of the world, as dad Ray subsequently revealed in Joel McIver's *To Live is to Die*: 'Cliff was 22 months old before he started walking on his own, and we were quite concerned about it. But the doctor said: "There's nothing wrong with him. He's just smart enough to know that mom and dad will carry him around." When we look back on it, it's quite humorous. He damn near broke Jan's back!'

Jan would often point to his brother and sister playing with the other kids on the avenue and suggest that he go and join in the fun. But even at this tender age, Cliff seemed tuned to some alternate frequency. 'I used to say, "All the kids are playing outside, why aren't you out there playing with them?" And he [would say] "They're not playing, they're just sitting around talking – that's boring." Then he'd go in the house and read his books or put on his music. Even when he was a tiny little kid he would listen to his music or read. He was a big, big reader, and he was very bright. In the third grade they tested him and he got an eleventh-grade comprehension. He just heard a different drummer; he never went with the crowd if he didn't want to. He was always popular and had a lot of friends. He was a very kind, very gentle kid, but always his own person.'

While Cliff preferred to keep his own counsel at Earl Warren Junior High, where his mom taught students requiring special attention, in reality he was merely biding his time. Like-minded souls often find a way of connecting regardless of the physical distance between them, and the first such individual to enter Cliff's orbit was an aspiring drummer named Doug Teixeira (currently drumming with thrash-metal outfit Blitzenhamer). Though Doug lived in a neighbouring city, the fates conspired to bring the two together, as he explained: 'We were at high school together. Cliff was a year older than me, I was living in Hayward, the next city over from Castro Valley, and because I was born with blindness and hearing loss I went to Castro Valley High School because they had a programme for the blind.' Having recruited another of Cliff's classmates who happened to play guitar, the trio would get together and jam the whole evening. 'We had good camaraderie because Cliff was a bass player and I was a drummer. He was a very mellow, down-to-earth person. Everybody I talked to loved him.'

Despite his passion for classical music (inspired by his parents' extensive record collection), Cliff was also a keen aficionado of country rock – notably the Eagles and Lynyrd Skynyrd, as well as their more blues-inspired cousins, Aerosmith and Blue Öyster Cult. Though he'd progressed to the bass by the time Doug Teixeira arrived at Castro Valley High, Cliff started out on piano. With his parents' help he sought out a reputable piano teacher, and paid for the lessons with the money he earned doing odd jobs around the neighbourhood.

Life was so good that Cliff could surely taste it on the balmy breeze drifting down from the San Leandro Hills, but tragedy struck the close-knit Burtons when, in May 1975, sixteen-year-old Scott suffered a cerebral aneurysm and died after being taken to hospital. Needless to say, the loss of his older brother affected Cliff deeply, and while no one can pinpoint the defining moment when he decided to pick up the bass and devote his life to music, those closest to him feel he was driven to succeed in memory of Scott. 'Cliff didn't take music lessons until he was thirteen, after his brother died,' Jan Burton explained. 'He said to a couple of people, "I'm

'When Metallica lost their bass player, they also lost their soul.'
- Lars Ulrich

gonna be the best bassist for my brother." We didn't think he had much talent at all. We had no idea. We just thought he'd plunk, plunk along . . . which he did at first. It was really not easy for him at first. About six months into the lessons, it started to come together. I thought, "This kid's got real potential." And I was totally amazed, because none of the kids in our family had any musical talent. He took lessons on the [Castro Valley] Boulevard for about a year, and then he totally outgrew the teacher and went to another place for a couple of years and outgrew him, too.'

Thankfully, it was a case of third time lucky, as Cliff's next teacher, Steve Doherty – who worked at ABC Music – was the guy with all the grooves. ABC Music was a tiny store with studios attached, and each and every Wednesday afternoon his dad would drive Cliff to the studio and sit outside reading a book until it was time to drive him home again. Unsurprisingly, Steve Doherty remembers his pupil with genuine affection: 'The one thing I remember most about Cliff was that he always came prepared for the lesson. He wasn't one of those kids that I had to drag through the exercises and make them do the lessons over again – he came prepared, ready for what we were going to do next. He had a lot of discipline, and I also remember that he already had the mark of a player.'

Aside from painstakingly studying and mastering alternate time signatures (such as the 3/4, 6/8, 5/4 and 7/8 signatures he would subsequently use to great effect with Metallica), Cliff was happy to play along with whatever was hip on the radio at any particular time. He and his friends – including future Faith No More stalwarts 'Big' Jim Martin and Mike 'Puffy' Bordin – would pack their gear into a truck and head up to a remote forest cabin called the Maxwell Ranch. As Cliff himself revealed a decade or so later, 'I got together with these guys who called themselves EZ Street, named after a strip joint in San Mateo . . . it was all kinds of weird shit. It was pretty shit, actually. We did a lot of covers, just wimpy shit. But I was with them for a while, for a few years.'

'The bass player we had wanted to quit, but he [said], "I know some guy who might be pretty good for you,"' Jim Martin explained of his initial encounter with Cliff. 'We jammed together a lot. We'd go out into the hills and fire up the generator. Me and Cliff, and another fella named Dave [Donato]. We were the only guys around for miles. We'd play this really weird shit and record it. We'd experiment with crazy, weird music. We'd play whatever came up, stuff right from the top of our heads, some Faith No More and Metallica songs that [people] are familiar with were germinated during these sessions.'

Cliff quit EZ Street immediately after graduation from Castro Valley High, when he enrolled at Chabot College to further his four-sting education. He did, however, remain good friends with Big Jim and Dave Donato, and the trio got up to all the usual teenage mischief, as Jan Burton revealed. 'He [Cliff] used to stay up all night. He didn't want to change his lifestyle: it was too hard on his body. Dave and Jim would come over and they'd play Dungeons and Dragons or watch videos, and he'd fix these huge meals, like omelettes – and he'd seldom wake us up. He was exceptionally considerate and loving.'

Dave Donato, however, remembers there were times when they tested Ma Burton's patience to its limits: 'We'd come back to Cliff's house at like three or four in the morning, and Cliff would start cooking huge food in the kitchen [. . .] I have a loud voice, and the first thing that usually happened was Jan would say, "Cliff, come here." Cliff would look at me and say, "You're a dick!" He'd walk down the hall, and I'd hear [Jan telling him to keep his friends quiet]. The second time she just came right out and said, "David! I don't want to have to ask you to leave . . . but your voice!" There were a lot of times like that. She used to laugh about it.' Jan and Ray Burton were thrilled that Cliff had managed to secure a place at such a prestigious college as Chabot, and generously offered to pay his rent and buy his food during his tenure there. However, this show of support came with a caveat: if, after four years of college, he hadn't reached the stage where he could comfortably make a living from his music, then he would have to get a regular job to pay the bills.

It was while studying at Chabot that Cliff joined his first serious band: the San Francisco-based Trauma, who by this juncture were making something of a name for themselves on the Bay Area circuit playing what has since been described as straight-up, Judas Priest-esque heavy metal and LA-style glam. However, while those who knew Cliff around this time had varying opinions of Trauma, all are agreed that Cliff didn't so much give the band a new dynamic as take the music to a different plane.

In their attempt to tempt record company execs along to their shows, the band put together a five-song press kit that included a promotional video, filmed in Los Angeles the night before a show at the legendary Whisky a Go Go. One of the more enduring myths surrounding Cliff's induction into Metallica is that it was upon hearing him shredding his Rickenbacker bass during the Whisky a Go Go show that a disorientated Lars Ulrich

'He is the Hendrix of bass for his groundbreaking style.'
- Jason Newsted

and James Hetfield – bewildered by the sound of Cliff's wah-wah pedal, which was enough to trick them into thinking they were listening to a lead-guitar solo – sought him out after the performance and offered him the vacant bassist role in the then relatively unknown Metallica.

Metal Blade's Brian Slagel – whom Trauma's management had approached with a view to him signing the band – confirmed this sequence of events, revealing that he'd tipped Lars off about Cliff after hearing that Metallica were contemplating getting rid of their incumbent bassist, Ron McGovney. 'At this point, Trauma were gonna play the Troubadour again. I said, "You've got to come and see this bass player, this guy is incredible." He and Hetfield came to the show and watched it. Lars came up to me right after Trauma had finished and said, "That guy's gonna be in my band."'

However, according to Trauma guitarist, Mike Overton, Lars and James spoke with Cliff at a practice session, which took place the evening prior to the shoot. 'Cliff was a little frustrated [and singer] Don Hillier and I both knew this,' Overton told the news portal *Blabbermouth*. 'Cliff had always wanted [Trauma] to be a little heavier in sound and so did I. The drummer wanted to be a lot more commercial, so there was some infighting going on as to what direction we needed to head [in]. We met

Lars and James at the practice session. They were cool to talk to, although I did at the time wonder why they talked to Cliff so long.'

When asked for his memories of that day as part of *Revolver* magazine's twenty-fifth anniversary coverage of Cliff's death, Lars said that he'd never seen anyone quite like Cliff before. '[He] was just unique and so original. And there was just this incredible stage presence and this uniqueness to the whole vibe. I had just never seen anything like it. It was new, it was different. And obviously you could tell there was an incredible ability, and there was a stage presence, and all this type of stuff wrapped up in this incredible type of personality. And I think we were a little intimidated by him in the beginning because he was just so unique.'

'We heard this wild solo going on, and [I] thought, "I don't see any guitar player up there,"' James said in another interview. 'It turned out it was the bass player, Cliff, with a wah-wah pedal and this mop of hair. He didn't care whether people were there. He was looking down at his bass playing.'

'As a player and as a person, Cliff was not afraid to be different. We could all learn something from that.'
- Alex Webster

Though Cliff was flattered by Lars and James's offer, it was no secret that he held the LA scene in contempt. Ergo, he was ready to accept on the proviso that James, Lars, and their guitarist Dave Mustaine relocate to San Francisco. Fortunately, uprooting a little way up the Pacific Coast Highway proved no great hardship. Indeed, the existing three Metallica men weren't exactly enamoured of LA themselves – especially considering what they were getting in return, as Cliff's use of quirky jazz timing, psychedelic melodies, and distorted solos gave Metallica the hitherto unimagined dynamic that Trauma had enjoyed. However, the trio's stay in the Bay Area would prove short-lived, for while their original demo tape (recorded prior to Cliff's arrival) had impressed Jon Zazula – owner of the independent Megaforce Records – their new material was enough to inspire him to sign them outright. And since Megaforce was based in Old Bridge, New Jersey, Metallica were forced to relocate accordingly.

The band initially wanted to call their debut *Metal Up Your Ass*, with gross-out cover art to match. However, Megaforce's marketing team – horrified by the sight of the dagger-wielding hand emerging from the toilet bowl – urged the band to rethink their concept. Utterly disgruntled by the collective timidity of the label's suits, Cliff jokingly told his bandmates that they should 'kill 'em all, man' – little realising that he'd just come up with the alternate title they were desperately seeking.

Yet, despite the hyper-charged riffage of the band's muscular debut, it was the increased musicality of Metallica's sophomore effort, *Ride the Lightning* (released via Megaforce the following year), that truly brought Hetfield and co. to the attention of the majors. Tellingly, Cliff scores songwriting credits for six out of eight tracks on this career-defining recording. In the wake of *Ride the Lightning* Metallica duly signed with Elektra, for whom they recorded their breakthrough, *Master of Puppets* – which in turn led to Ozzy Osbourne inviting them onto his Original Sin Tour later that same year.

Moments of Madness: Cliff was once quoted as saying that we, as human beings, don't burn out from going too fast, but rather from going too slow and getting bored, which aside from being a telling philosophical take on the human psyche, also served as his personal maxim on how to live life. Alas, Cliff was denied the chance to put this theory to the test.

In the early hours of 27 September 1986, while Metallica were wending their way through the rural landscape of the Ljungby municipality in southern Sweden, during the European leg of their Damage Inc. Tour in support of *Master of Puppets*, the band's tour bus skidded off the road and flipped over onto the grass after allegedly hitting a patch of black ice. The accident occurred just outside the sleepy town of Dörarp, and while Lars, James, guitarist Kirk Hammett (who replaced Dave Mustaine in April 1983), and everyone else aboard miraculously came away from the crash with a few minor cuts and bruises – and in Lars's case a broken toe – Cliff was hurled through a window and crushed to death when the bus rolled over on top of him.

While the survivors stumbled around in a state of shock, James, who was naked except for the underwear he'd been sleeping in, stalked up and down the fatal stretch of road frantically searching for the black ice that the driver was claiming had caused him to lose control of the bus. And having found none, he returned to the scene with murder in his eyes. 'The bus driver [. . .] was trying to yank the blanket out from under him to use for other people. I just went, "Don't fucking do that!" I already wanted to kill the driver. I don't know if he was drunk or if he hit some ice. All I knew was, he was driving and Cliff wasn't alive anymore.'

James's distrust of the driver's story was given more credence by the testimony of Lennart Wennberg, a local photographer who'd attended the crash scene the following morning. Wennberg said that the formation of ice on the road that morning – black or otherwise – was a meteorological impossibility. In fact, the temperature had been around two degrees Celsius. This was subsequently confirmed by the Ljungby police who, like James, failed to find any ice on the road, with one detective going so far as to inform a reporter on the local newspaper that the tyre tracks at the accident site suggested that the driver – whose name has never been publicly revealed – had indeed fallen asleep at the wheel. However, when called upon to testify at the inquest, the driver stated under oath that he'd been wide awake at the time of the tragedy, as he'd slept during the previous day. As his testimony was backed up by the driver of the second tour bus, which was following behind carrying the band's crew and equipment, the driver was exonerated and no charges were brought against him.

According to his testimony in *To Live is to Die*, Lars only became aware of Cliff's death while being treated for his injuries at the hospital: 'I remember being at the hospital and a doctor coming into the room . . . telling us that our bass player had died. We couldn't grasp it, it was too hard, it was too unreal . . . It's not new that people in rock'n'roll die, but it's self-inflicted in terms of excessive drink or drug abuse. Cliff had nothing to do with it. It's so useless. Completely useless.'

In the wake of his guitarist Randy Rhoads's death in March 1982, Ozzy Osbourne would observe that we go about our daily lives never knowing how close we are to the edge. And Cliff's death serves as an even more illuminating example of how each and every one of us lives within the shadow of the grim reaper's scythe, because had it not been for a turn of the cards, it could have been Lars, James, or Kirk lying dead at the side of the road. The tour bus's no frills, utilitarian furnishings meant that there was only one comfortable bunk, and each night the band would draw cards to lay claim to the coveted cradle. The previous night Kirk had enjoyed a restful slumber, but that night, having drawn the ace of spades, Cliff had claimed the prize. And while some have dismissed this as an apocryphal tale intended to add an ethereal edge to the story of Cliff's demise, Kirk has always insisted that this was the way it played out: 'It absolutely happened, yeah,' he reiterated in *To Live is to Die*. 'Just another weird, ironic sort of thing that destiny kind of spits at you. It was almost a harbinger of what was to come.'

Cliff's funeral service was held on 7 October 1986, in his hometown of Castro Valley, California, where he was cremated and his ashes scattered at the Maxwell Ranch where he'd spent so much time. 'Orion', the instrumental track from *Master of Puppets*, which was Cliff's favourite Metallica song and features two of his finest solos, was played during the ceremony, and as a lasting tribute to their fallen comrade, Metallica refrained from playing the song again in its entirety for the best part of a decade. Indeed, immediately following Cliff's death it was uncertain whether Metallica would even continue as a band.

Of course, Metallica are far from unique in having to face such a scenario. But whereas the surviving members of Led Zeppelin and Pantera couldn't face taking to the stage again, and the likes of Marilyn Manson and Mayhem adopted something of a laissez faire attitude to death within their ranks, others such as AC/DC, Def Leppard, Alice in Chains, Slipknot and Avenged Sevenfold opted to honour the dead at the setting of the sun before looking to a brighter tomorrow. And after careful deliberation, Lars, James and Kirk decided they owed it to themselves and their fans to carry on, as Kirk Hammett explained in a February 1987 interview: 'Right after the accident happened, we individually decided that the best way to get rid of all our frustrations would be to hit the road, and get all the anxiety and frustrations out onstage, where they should go. We were very traumatised and felt a lot of emotional distraught over the situation. The worst thing we could do is just sit in our room and sulk over the matter and wallow in our pity. The more you think about it, the deeper you sink. We each thought individually, we have to keep going; we have to work because it wouldn't be fair to Cliff to just stop. Also, if he were alive . . . and like, y'know, he couldn't play bass, he wouldn't tell us to stop. That's the way he would've felt. He would've wanted us to carry on.'

Later that same year, the band released *Cliff 'Em All* as a further mark of respect − a retrospective documentary featuring live footage of the Cliff-era Metallica shot professionally or by the audience, while Ulrich, Hetfield and Hammett reminisce about the bassist who'd been so crucial to their development and subsequent success. Dave Mustaine also paid tribute to Cliff with the song, 'In My Darkest Hour', which featured on Megadeth's 1988 album *So Far, So Good . . . So What!* On 3 October 2006, to mark the twentieth anniversary of Cliff's passing, a memorial stone − featuring a close-up image of the bassist and a line from the Metallica song 'To Live is to Die' − was unveiled close to the scene of the accident: 'Cannot the kingdom of salvation take me home.'

Dimebag Darrell

20 August 1966 - 8 December 2004

Born: Darrell Lance Abbott

Alter-egos: Diamond Darrell, Dimebag Darrell.

(Pre) occupations: Beloved, shaggy-haired shredder with Pantera and Damageplan. In life, Darrell's tastes ran to 'shit that moves you; shit that has heart and soul'. As the writer of the monumental riffs of 'Cemetery Gates' – the epically evocative (anti-) ballad that inspired the title of the book you're holding now – he achieved nothing less.

In memoriam: 'Ah, man, the last thing that really matters to me is the last thing we [Dime and me] said to each other before we went onstage. We were warming up on the side of the stage like we always did and we were both really excited . . . Our code word to let it all hang out and have a good time was "Van Halen", man. And that's the last two words we ever said to each other . . . and we high-fived each other and went on the deck to do our thing . . . and a minute and a half later I'll never see him again.' – Vinnie Paul Abbott (brother and Pantera/Damageplan bandmate)

Deadly sins: While Darrell's chosen *nom de guerre* inevitably ruffled more than a few feathers – most notably in Indiana, where disgruntled school officials prohibited the wearing of his fan shirts – 'Dimebag' being the street term for a $10-baggie of marijuana, Darrell himself was only known to use the drug when he was a Kiss-obsessed high-school student. Whether Darrell would have gone on to commit any of the fabled deadly sins will never be known, because he was the victim of that most cardinal of sins: murder.

'There's been a shooting! Somebody's shooting! He's shooting the band . . . oh shit, he's still shooting!'

At around 10:20pm on the evening of Wednesday, 8 December 2004 – the same date that John Lennon was gunned down in New York

24 years earlier – the above 911 call from a traumatised audience member inside the Alrosa Villa in Columbus, Ohio, alerted the outside world to the fact that another musician had been targeted by a deranged gunman. And while Darrell wasn't as high-profile as the former Beatle, his senseless slaying sent a seismic shockwave rippling through the metal community.

Just as Mark Chapman (the former marine turned killer) will forever be synonymous with Lennon, the name Nathan Gale will be indelibly linked with that of Dimebag. But whereas Chapman, who is currently serving a 'twenty-to-life' sentence, might someday reveal the twisted thought processes that led to him keeping vigil outside the Dakota Building, waiting for his target to return from the recording studio, we can only speculate as to what possessed Gale to leap up onstage wielding a Beretta 92FS semiautomatic pistol and begin the killing spree that left four people dead and three others wounded. In fact, Gale exited Alrosa Villa in the same manner as his victims. Gunned down by the police, the killer was also destined for the county morgue.

Something that has never been properly explained is the rapid response time of Columbus' finest – again shades of Lee Harvey Oswald's arrest in a downtown Dallas theatre. True, there'd been a flurry of 911 calls from hysterical civilians claiming to have witnessed gunshots being fired, but this was a rock'n'roll concert and the 'madman jumping up onstage and shooting the band' could all have been part of the act – hadn't Alice Cooper faked his own execution live onstage?

According to Hertz's NeverLost Plan, it would take the average driver some nineteen minutes to cover the 13.31 miles from the police station to the Alrosa Villa out on Sinclair Road, and yet six officers were at the venue within a fraction of this time. Whether Darrell's killing was a conspiracy, as some fans have claimed, or merely the actions of a deranged lunatic, will never be known for certain, but it's worth remembering that there's no smoke without gunfire . . .

At a press conference held the following afternoon, a spokesman for the Columbus Police Department revealed that, in response to a call over his radio, patrol officer James D. Niggemeyer was able to slip into the Alrosa Villa unnoticed, through a backdoor. Guided through the dimly lit chaos by a couple of hysterical fans, he was able to approach the stage from behind, and was greeted by a horrifying spectacle. Amidst the bodies of his victims, the shaven-headed Gale – sporting jeans and a blue and white-striped sweatshirt bearing the logo of the Columbus Blue Jackets hockey team – had taken a living hostage: Damageplan drum technician, John 'Kat' Brooks.

According to the official report, Gale – who fired fifteen shots and calmly stopped to reload – had been focused on the five-strong team of officers who'd rushed in through the front entrance. This had allowed Niggemeyer, who was armed with a 12-gauge Remington 870 shotgun, to surreptitiously approach Gale from the opposite side of the stage. Only in the sickening seconds when Gale pressed his gun to the hostage's head did it become (in Niggemeyer's own words) a 'now-or-never scenario. Do I let him shoot the hostage in front of everybody? Or do I take what I feel is the best shot to try to keep the hostage from being killed?'

Instinctively, Niggemeyer pulled the trigger: striking Gale in the face with eight out of nine buckshot pellets and killing him instantly. After Gale was 'neutralised' – in euphemistic police parlance – several shell-shocked fans jumped up onto the stage. In a collective fit of rage, they began kicking his lifeless corpse.

Though the imposing six-foot three-inch Gale – who lived with his mother in Marysville – was known to the police, his previous arrests were for minor crimes of a non-violent nature, including driving with a suspended license and trespassing. Aside from Darrell, Gale's other victims were 40-year-old Jeff 'Mayhem' Thompson, who was head of Damageplan's security team; 29-year-old Erin Halk, who worked at the Alrosa, and 23-year-old audience member Nathan Bray, who was callously gunned down whilst trying to perform CPR on Darrell. Tour manager Chris Paluska was also among the injured.

The fact that Gale had had a clear shot at any of the musicians onstage – Darrell's brother Vinnie Paul was a literal sitting duck behind the drum kit – coupled with the number of shots he fired at Darrell's head (the third and final time at point-blank range), left the team of detectives assigned to this particular case in little doubt that, in the mind of this homicidal ex-marine, there'd only ever been one true target. Indeed, with the possible exception of Nathan Bray (Dimebag's would-be resuscitator), Gale's subsequent killings could be deemed defensive as he only fired on those attempting to disarm him.

While Alrosa Villa was lacking surveillance cameras of any kind – which had to be something of a rarity in the post-9/11, homeland security-obsessed USA – the investigating officers could watch Gale's five-minute rampage frame-by-frame thanks to several audience members who'd been filming the show for bootlegging purposes.

Among the early theories put forward regarding his motive was that Gale – who had supposedly yelled, 'You broke up Pantera! You ruined my life!' before opening fire – was a deranged fan reacting violently to the break-up of his favourite band (or else the much-publicised rift between the Abbott brothers and Phil Anselmo, due to the latter's struggles to kick his heroin habit), but given that Pantera hadn't played or recorded together in over three years, such a scenario was swiftly ruled out.

Gale had served with the 2nd Marine Division at Camp Lejeune in North Carolina until November 2003, when he was discharged after serving less than half of his four-year enlistment. Whilst the Marine Corps themselves were legally prohibited from disclosing the reasons why, Gale's mother, Mary Clark, didn't hold back, revealing in an interview with local TV station WCMH that her son had suffered from paranoid schizophrenia. Known locally as 'Crazy Nate', Gale had been prescribed medication to help manage his condition. However, the autopsy which was carried out by the Franklin County Coroner's Office revealed there to be no trace of drugs – antipsychotic or otherwise – in Gale's system at the time of the attack. According to his mother and friends, he'd been obsessed with Pantera since his high-school days and would usually have had one of their albums blasting on his headphones to psych himself up before football games. However, towards the end, Gale's behaviour became so erratic that even his closest friends eventually began to distance themselves.

While it was Gale's finger on the trigger, Vinnie Paul believes that former Pantera frontman, Phil Anselmo, is at least partly responsible for his brother's murder because of a comment Phil made during an interview with *Metal Hammer* magazine. '[Dimebag] would attack me, vocally,' Phil claimed, a matter of weeks before Gale's twisted plan came to fruition. 'And just knowing that he was so much smaller than me, I could kill him like a fuckin' piece of vapour. You know, he would turn into vapour . . . his chin would, at least, if I fuckin' smacked it. And he knows that. The world should know that. So physically, of course, he deserves to be beaten severely.'

It was a remark he'd live to regret. Despite Phil's later insistence that he'd been speaking with his tongue firmly in cheek, *Metal Hammer* chose to take him at his word. Splashing the throwaway comment across the front page of their December 2004 issue, along with a confrontational shot of Phil himself – tattooed biceps flexed for action – they ensured that the world knew it.

'The guy who asked me that – it was supposed to be off the record,' Phil told *Antiquiet* ezine in November 2008. 'He asked me straight out what would happen if [we] got into a fight – a physical thing. First of all, that never would have happened. Second of all, theoretically, once again – obviously, I would have the advantage over them. So I put it in a [certain] way, like a million motherfuckers do every day – boxers, etcetera – you know, they say they're going to do terrible, horrible things to each other, and then after everything clears, they shake hands and hug each other and it's done.'

Of course, it was only a matter of days after the incendiary interview was published that Phil received a phone call about Dime, the memory of which he's never quite been able to repress. 'I was laying down upstairs in my house,' he recalled, when quizzed by *Metal Hammer* in 2010. 'Matter of fact, I was sleeping. The phone rang and I picked it up and I didn't remember

> 'Let's for a second forget that I even knew him,
> and focus on just the fact that this was allowed to happen.
> If somebody can jump onstage with a gun and shoot one of the most
> influential guitarists of my generation, what's next?
> If this is allowed to happen, what the hell
> - what does that say?'
> – Corey Taylor

for about two years who had told me the news [of Dimebag's murder]. I remembered and found out years later that it was Rex . . . and I guess it was numbing, and yes, I was lying down upstairs . . . I was in a lot of pain and then the ultimate pain dropped the fucking hammer on the world.'

Vinnie Paul, however – along with the rest of Dime's family – remained largely unmoved by the 'pain' that Phil professed to be suffering. Despite the frontman's best attempts to heal the rift ('I love Dimebag Darrell because there was not one motherfucker like him; I love him like a brother loves a brother . . . Vinnie Paul, my other brother, I'm so sorry,' he gushed in the aftermath of Dime's shooting), he was tellingly banned from the guitarist's star-studded memorial service in Arlington, Texas.

From cradle to grave: Sons of the celebrated country singer/songwriter/ producer, Jerry Bob Abbott, musical dexterity was all but written in the Abbott brothers' DNA. And while Dimebag's elder sibling, Vincent 'Vinnie' Paul, picked up dad's finely-tuned ear for production (as well as being adroit behind a drum kit), young Darrell took to playing guitar like a true-life Johnny B. Goode.

Indeed, it was the strains of Kiss and Black Sabbath that set Dimebag's own bell ringing. 'I went back to my old man and asked if I could trade my bike back for the guitar,' he told *Guitar World* in September 1994. 'Actually, I didn't ask him that, but if I was slick, that's what I would've done! I didn't get my first guitar until my next birthday. I was about eleven, and he gave me a Les Paul copy and a Pignose amp.'

As well as his father, Darrell could also call on advice from renowned blues guitarists such as Bugs Henderson and Jimmy Wallace, both of whom were regular visitors to his dad's recording studio. Indeed, Wallace was happy to let the youngster jam with him on occasion. 'He would hang out at this music store about 45 minutes from my house,' Dime enthused in *Guitar Magazine* in September 1995, after being named as their 'Best Breakthrough Guitarist'. 'Whenever I could get a ride down there, Jimmy'd let me plug in with him in the amp room when I was like, fifteen. He'd show me a lick and we'd wail away.'

With such expert help on tap, as it were, Darrell had already won a score of local competitions in and around Dallas by the time he and Vinnie Paul formed Pantera Metal Magic ('Pantera' is the Spanish word for 'Panther') in 1981. Having honed their craft on the underground circuit within their home state, as well as in neighbouring Oklahoma and Louisiana – building up a cult following of hardcore fans along the way – the quartet gradually boosted their profile by opening for the likes of Metallica and Megadeth, as well as old masters Black Sabbath, Iron Maiden and Motörhead. The band's output was prodigious during this period and they released four albums on their own label, Metal Magic, yet despite this, each and every major record label deigned to pass on their unique brand of groove-metal.

Commercial success would continue to elude Pantera until the release of their fifth, *Cowboys from Hell* – which, of course, includes 'Cemetery Gates', the blistering, seven-minute epic that earned the band a Grammy nomination in 1998 – during the summer of 1990. 'I got home, picked up my axe, turned on the four-track and just played it. I played three solos back to back on "Cemetery Gates",' Dime revealed of the song's pseudo-mystic origins. 'The next morning, the second and third solos weren't bad, but the first had that first-take magic! I didn't touch it.'

The success of *Cowboys from Hell* raised Pantera's profile to the point where they were invited to appear on the 'Monsters in Moscow' bill alongside AC/DC and Metallica in September 1991 – where they played to a crowd of over 500,000 in celebration of the new freedom to perform Western music in the Soviet Union, shortly before its collapse three months later – but it was, of course, their follow-up Atco album, *Vulgar Display of Power* (released in February 1992), which served as a watershed and finally propelled the band into the metal major league. Indeed, *Allmusic* would subsequently hail it as 'one of the most influential heavy-metal albums of the 1990s'.

It had been a long and arduous journey, but Darrell and Vinnie Paul's steadfast determination had finally paid off. 'I grew up a heavy-metal kid and we are a heavy-metal band,' Dime told *Guitar World*. 'I know it's not fashionable, but I'm proud to say that's what we are and that's what we do. It kills me when I see some metal band trying to pass themselves off as an "alternative band". Well, dude, they can join the pack, but we'll remain true to our roots while shit keeps twisting around us.'

While said shit twisted in the breeze, *Vulgar Display of Power* entered and peaked at number 44 on the US *Billboard* 200 and spent a total of 77 weeks on the chart, culminating in it achieving double-platinum status in July 2004, having accrued sales of two million. Yet Pantera were only just hitting their stride. Indeed, their 1994 follow-up, *Far Beyond Driven*, slammed onto the *Billboard* chart at number one – this despite the album's original artwork (based around a drill bit impaling an anus) being deemed obscene. The album's artwork wasn't the only thing in Pantera's world to undergo an overhaul, as Darrell changed his name to 'Dimebag Darrell', which had apparently been his nickname back in high school owing to his prodigious weed habit – even though he no longer smoked cannabis.

However, by the time their seventh studio album, *The Great Southern Trendkill* (which peaked at number four on the *Billboard* chart), was released in May 1996, ominous cracks were beginning to appear within the Pantera veneer. One reason for this could simply have been the domineering dynamic created by Dime and Vinnie Paul's band strategy, with their decisions coming as a block vote within Pantera. Or it could have stemmed from Phil's frustrations at still being considered the outsider – even though he'd been in the band for nigh on a decade by this juncture. However, a more realistic cause for the in-house squabbling lay in the problems brought on by Phil's steady progress up the painkiller ladder: he'd moved from Anadin to using heroin in order to ease his chronic back pain. On being informed by doctors that his years of crazy onstage antics – which included clambering atop the PA system and diving headfirst into the crowd, or the concrete floor, depending on the crowd's mood – had finally caught up with him, he kept the news to himself. Instead of telling Dime and Vinnie that he'd ruptured three discs in his lower back, and that Pantera would need to take upwards of twelve months off while he underwent corrective surgery – which would involve slitting his stomach open, removing his intestines and replacing missing bone and cartilage with chunks of his own hip – he foolishly remained silent, and continued throwing himself about the stage as though nothing was amiss. While a back-brace, painkillers, and retardation-inducing muscle relaxants helped to some degree, as bone scraped bone and the nerve damage worsened, he was forced to seek stronger, 'street corner' medication.

Had it not been for Dime's senseless death, it's fair to say Phil would have been a worthy *Cemetery Gates* survivor, for as with Nikki Sixx, Slash, Izzy et al., his dalliance with heroin started out with him doing a little, only for the little to become more and more, until the hollow-eyed guy staring back from the bathroom mirror was a full-blown addict. And though he managed to keep his addiction a secret from the rest of the guys for a couple of years, following a homecoming show at the Coca Cola Starplex in Dallas, Texas, on 13 July 1996, Phil's heart reportedly stopped beating for almost five minutes before paramedics wrenched him back from the hereafter with a shot of adrenaline.

In an interview at Loyola University in March 2009, by which time he'd been clean for four years, Phil attempted to set the record straight regarding his drug problems. Far from recreational, it seems Phil's relationship with Nikki Sixx's one 'true love' gives new meaning to the term 'bad medicine'. 'It was about the time when the record [*Far Beyond Driven*] came in at number one,' he recalled. 'I was pretty terrified. I was happy as hell; don't get me wrong, man – I was like, "Oh, my God, yes!" At that point, I had just gotten back from the doctor – from having my second MRI done – and I realised I had two blown-out discs. Now, in order for me to be this superman that the media had built me up to be, I had to quell that pain. So I started off with regular painkillers and muscle relaxers [sic]. Eventually, you climb up the painkiller ladder, because painkillers lie to you; they will magnify that injury. And that's all that's on your mind – the injury and painkillers.'

When the *Invisible Oranges* website subsequently asked Phil to elaborate on what had caused him to kick his habit and get his life back on track, he said that he'd 'learned some insane fucking lessons from pain', and added:

'With pain comes the drugs. With drugs come more drugs, if you don't watch your ass. With more drugs comes death if you don't really watch your ass. I've hit all those motherfucking plateaus, or sinkholes, whatever you want to fucking call them. But with each one, you learn a lesson. And if you take the lessons to heart, like I did, then you pull out of it.'

However, at the time, instead of taking care of himself away from Pantera, Phil exacerbated his back problems by getting involved with various side projects such as Viking Crown and Eibon. And although Dime, Vinnie Paul and Rex Brown had their own ongoing side project, Rebel Meets Rebel (with outlaw country singer David Allan Coe) to occupy their spare time, when Pantera headed back into the studio to begin work on what would prove to be their eighth and final studio album, *Reinventing the Steel*, it wasn't only Phil's vertebrae that were rubbing each other the wrong way. But, irrespective of the internal problems the band were having, they were still capable of making sweet music together, and

'His influence will be felt forever. And he was the most genuine, kindest guy you ever met. Dime would give you the shirt off his back. The good Lord put him down here to whoop some ass and make everybody happy, and now he needed him, so he took him. I've never had a brother, but he was as close to blood as possible. My love for him is unconditional and beyond forever.'
- Zakk Wylde

Reinventing the Steel equalled the position of its predecessor on the *Billboard* chart when it was released the following March. Further affirmation came when the LP's lead single, 'Revolution is My Name', secured Pantera their fourth Grammy nomination in 2001.

Though there was no official break-up as such, with Phil seemingly committed to other projects (most notably recording Down's second album, *Down II: A Bustle in Your Hedgerow*, on which Rex Brown played bass), Darrell and Vinnie Paul eventually tired of waiting for him to return to the fold, and started focusing on a new project that would become Damageplan. Their decision try new ventures came from their Alice in Chains pal Jerry Cantrell, as the guitarist knew first-hand the futility of trying to keep a band together when heroin has become the singer's sole motivation. 'We'd made several attempts to reach out to Phil. In the end, we felt it had gone too far and we really needed to do something,'

Vinnie Paul told *Metal Hammer* in January 2008. 'I remember, Dime had made some demos, and Jerry was over. We were just hanging out, pretty depressed. Dime took Jerry out in the car and played him the demo – which later became Damageplan – and Jerry said, "You need to move on and do your own thing." Dime came back into the house and said, "Fuck this shit, we're not waiting around anymore. Let's just start our own band and do our own thing."'

Though the band's legion of fans ultimately blamed the breakdown in relations between Phil and the Abbott brothers, Dime and Vinnie Paul played down any bitterness during an interview with CNN, which was broadcast at the beginning of April 2004. Ever the diplomat, Dime explained: 'It just kind of got narrow-minded, and we just wanted to bust it open a little bit more and just broaden it up, go for the Baskin-Robbins 31 flavours instead of the one, you know what I mean?'

'We had thirteen years of really, really good success,' Vinnie Paul added. 'And basically the singer wanted to move on, do some other things and really lost his focus.'

Damageplan's debut album, *New Found Power* – featuring guest appearances from Corey Taylor, Jerry Cantrell and Zakk Wylde – was released in the US in February 2004 and, while not reaching the dizzy heights of the brothers' career with Pantera, peaked at a very respectable number 38 on the *Billboard* 200, selling nearly 45,000 copies within the first week of release.

On being asked during a January 2008 interview with *Metal Hammer* magazine whether Dime got the recognition he deserved, and whether people were perhaps too quick to see him as a party animal rather than a gifted guitarist, Vinnie Paul answered by saying Dime had accepted that these things tend to go hand in hand. 'He knew he was the life of the party and a character and that kind of came along with everything he did. That was okay with him and okay with us.'

On the evening of Tuesday, 14 December 2004, family, friends and fans alike gathered within the Arlington Convention Centre in Arlington, Texas, to raise a glass of Black Tooth Grin – Dimebag's favourite drink – and give him a final send-off, as well as celebrate his life and music. Among the celebrity guests at the three-hour service, which ran from 9:00pm to midnight, were Zakk Wylde, Jerry Cantrell and his former Alice in Chains buddy Mike Inez, Slipknot trio Corey Taylor, Jim Root and Paul Gray, and Dime's ultimate guitar hero, Eddie Van Halen. When paying tribute to Dime, Eddie held his cell phone to the microphone to replay a message an exuberant Dime had left after Pantera had played with Van Halen, in which Dime had thanked his hero for 'the most awesome, uplifting, euphoric, spiritual rock'n'roll extravaganza ever'. Aside from screenings of Pantera and Damageplan promo videos and home movies, the mourners were treated to performances from Jerry Cantrell (who, with Inez at his side, played the Alice in Chains songs 'Brother' and 'Got Me Wrong', which they'd also performed at the funeral service earlier in the afternoon), Rex Brown and a teary-eyed Vinnie Paul, who took to the stage with a life-size cardboard cut-out of his brother.

In accordance with the stipulations set in Dime's will, he was laid to rest at the Moore Memorial Gardens Cemetery in Arlington in a special edition 'Kiss Kasket' made of twenty-gauge steel, and featuring iconic Kiss images both inside and out. This, however, was no ordinary Kiss Kasket, as the band's frontman, Gene Simmons, explained. 'There were a limited number made, and I sent mine to [Dime's] family. He requested in his will to be buried in a Kiss Kasket, as he sort of learned his rock'n'roll roots by listening to us for some strange reason.'

While delivering his touching eulogy, Eddie Van Halen recounted that Dime – having learned from one of his industry contacts that Charvel guitars would be producing a limited-edition series of models bearing Eddie's trademark 'Bumblebee' tape-striping – called him asking if he could purchase one of the guitars before they went on general sale. Explaining that he'd promised Dime one of the guitars the next time they met, he then, to the surprise of his fellow mourners, produced the original Bumblebee guitar – as seen on the back cover of *Van Halen II*, which Dime had always said was his favourite of all the guitars in Eddie's collection – and laid it in Dime's casket to be buried with him.

Watching with a tear in his eye was Terry Glaze, who'd remained friends with Dime since leaving Pantera back in 1986. 'When Eddie put the black-and-yellow guitar in the casket with Darrell, I remembering thinking, you know what? If back in the old days, when we first started, if you would have told Darrell that, when you die, Van Halen is going to put that guitar in your casket, Darrell would have said, "Kill me now,"' he told Dime's biographer Zac Crane for his book: *Black Tooth Grin: The High Life, Good Times, and Tragic End of 'Dimebag' Darrell Abbott*.

This was a truly touching gesture on the legendary axeman's part, and on certain nights, if you believe hard enough, you just might hear Dime's tattoo-needle-sharp riff from 'Cemetery Gates' lilting on the midnight air . . .

PAUL GRAY

8 April 1972 - 24 May 2010

Born: Paul Dedrick Gray

Alter-egos: Paul Gray, a.k.a. Slipknot's #2, was a man forever changing faces. Yet, in all his crazed carnival of masks – from the shattered Hannibal to the mouth-less mutant – there was a single avatar that stuck. Lips wired shut, padlock shoved sadistically through his snout, Gray's mutilated pig mask screams wordlessly of death, suffocation, oppression – the very embodiment of Slipknot's tortured lyrics.

'It's definitely an Iowa thing,' drawled Paul – in tones that conjured the dust-choked cornfields of his hated home county. 'I know it is because that's where we got our work ethic . . . because – fuck! No A&R guys want to come out here. Dude, it was impossible, getting anyone to come and see a fucking show . . . there was no chance. So we had to work and work and work – actually prove ourselves. Just the way people were brought up; people in the band, just their moral structure made this band what it is . . . Iowa: that's it.'

(Pre) occupations: If Corey Taylor gave Slipknot its 'great big mouth', then Paul Gray surely constitutes the band's blackened soul. Bassist and primary songwriter, Gray was a natural-born introvert who craved anonymity rather than attention. *Guardian* scribe Ben Myers observed: 'While confrontational – and occasionally hilarious – singer Corey Taylor and his bandmates were happy to hog the mic to get their message across . . . "the Pig" was more enigmatic, seeming happier onstage behind his ever-changing mask than talking into tape recorders.' Yet in the years since Gray was ushered through the cemetery gates, the resulting silence speaks of his blistering contribution to the band more eloquently than the man himself ever could.

In memoriam: 'He was kind of the person in the band that really wanted everybody in the band to always get along and just concentrate on the band. He was a really great friend and a really great person. He's going to be sadly missed, and the world is going to be a different place without him.' – Shawn 'the Clown' Crahan

'Life is the same for everybody. You're born. You grow up. You go to school. You get a job. Then you meet whoever you're going to meet and you start some kind of family life. Then you die. There's a lot of horrible shit in between all that. All of the bullshit in between is what drags you down and holds you back. If you hold onto that, keep it inside and let it take over, it'll eat you up. We put that on record, and we get it out there. It helps us get through to the next day.' – Paul Gray

> *'Are the masks a fetish thing? Des Moines*
> *definitely has more than its fair share of freaks . . .'*
> *- Paul Gray*

Deadly sins: During a 2008 interview with *Revolver* magazine, Paul revealed how he'd chalked up not one, but several near-death experiences – all of them stemming from his addiction to heroin. Some may question why a guy who'd already gazed down the barrel of a gun would continue playing Russian roulette with such carefree abandon – especially when his wife Brenna was expecting their first child. Yet Brenna herself is less incredulous. 'He just wanted to be done with it,' she told *Revolver* in May 2011. 'It was a lifelong disease that even if he'd stayed clean for the rest of his life, he'd still have had it. It was a full-time job for him. He had to completely rearrange his life and it's hard. And people just don't want to get it. They're close-minded, and they can just fuck off in my book.'

In the beginning, only those closest to Paul were aware of his struggle. But by June 2003, the secret was most definitely out, with news that Paul had been arrested while in possession of undisclosed amounts of cocaine, marijuana and various drug paraphernalia. He'd been stopped by a Des Moines Police patrol car after a string of risky manoeuvres on the road. Having jumped a red light in his Porsche, Gray went careering into another vehicle. Of course, the head-on smash instantly attracted the watchful eye of the DMPD. Seconds into their questioning, the officers began to suspect that something was amiss with the decidedly 'mellow' Mr. Gray. Recognising the tell-tale signs – slurring uncontrollably, Gray could barely even grasp what was being asked of him – the officers opted to search his car. Results of 'field sobriety tests' on Gray were similarly damning. '[Gray] was found to have impaired balance, slurred speech and dull behaviour,' revealed Sergeant Tony Steverson. 'When he failed, he was arrested and taken to jail.'

According to the *Des Moines Register*, Paul attempted to exchange insurance details with the driver of the other car. The lady in question could not even read his writing. He proceeded to excuse himself with stories that he was on medication and that his brakes had failed, before attempting to write a $1,000 cheque to cover the damages. Needless to say, the woman's husband turned the aforementioned slip over to police. Though Paul was duly charged with possession, as well as failing to obey a traffic signal, he was released from custody after posting a $4,300 bond. However, before leaving the station he was warned that a charge of 'driving whilst intoxicated' could well be added to the list should results of a voluntary urine test come back positive. As no one was seriously injured, Paul's lawyers offered the court a plea agreement, whereby their client would plead guilty to reckless driving provided the prosecution agreed to drop the charges of possession of marijuana, cocaine and syringes.

Bleary-eyed mug shots of a dishevelled Gray began to surface in the aftermath of his arrest. Providing a rare glimpse of Gray's unmasked countenance (back then the faces of the 'Knot's nine-strong fraternity were a fiercely guarded secret within the metal community – to the envy of the considerably more exposed, one-man metal machine Trent Reznor), these candid shots should have been intriguing. In fact, Paul's shadowed eye sockets, bloated features and deathly pallor were nothing but the first indication that, whatever his addictions, they were rather more serious than hitherto suspected. Indeed, court records are said to include a note from a Dr. Joseph Takamine describing his discussions with Paul. In his own words, they'd been 'very frank and open about his sporadic use of various drugs and of the long periods of abstinence in between'.

𝔉rom cradle to grave: Paul was born in Los Angeles, but moved to Des Moines, Iowa, following the death of his father. Seeking comfort in sound, teenage Paul set about teaching himself guitar. And though it was in the guise of Slipknot's fearful porcine-headed bassist that Paul was destined to make his name, his decision to make the switch from six strings to four came about by fortuitous happenstance. 'I think I started playing bass in 1990, which is what? Nineteen years ago . . . wow, I'm getting old!' Paul joked with *Total Guitar* magazine during a backstage breather at Download

Festival in 2009. 'Actually I played guitar first and never picked up a bass – wasn't interested in it at all. Then I moved to Iowa and I didn't have any friends there. I didn't know anybody, and I was in this music store and I overheard this dude talking about needing a bass player . . .

'I was listening in on their conversation, eavesdropping, they were talking about doing covers of Slayer and Metallica – all these songs that I knew how to play on guitar. So I was like, "maybe I should jump in and say I play bass and try to meet some people?" I went over and said, "Dude, I play bass," even though I [had] never picked one up. I figured that it couldn't be that different to playing guitar, but later on I found out it's a totally different thing. It was weird because when I started practising these songs on bass, I didn't know any of them . . . I was like, "Fuck!" I had to go back and listen to them. Doing that actually made me fall in love with bass guitar.'

Having grown weary of playing covers in outfits like Vexx, Body Pit, Inveigh Catharsis and Anal Blast, Paul sought out like-minded souls amongst his new friends on the Des Moines scene and, together with drummer Shawn Crahan, guitarist Donnie Steele and Anders Colsefni, formed the Pale Ones. Thinking it might give them an edge, Paul invited another drummer buddy of his, Joey Jordison, along to rehearsals. They were pleased with the results. So much so that Jordison would soon take over full drumming duties. Crahan moved over to custom percussion. Indeed, such was their percussion obsession that Colsefni would grab whatever instrument came to hand to augment the backbeat during live performances. While some bassists might have balked at the prospect of having to accommodate impromptu tub-thumping, Paul simply rose to the challenge. 'We have three drummers, there's a lot of low end,' he chuckled to *Total Guitar*. 'You gotta find your pocket. It's definitely a different thing compared to if I was playing in a punk band with only one guitar player and I could fucking, y'know, noodle around and do lots of stuff.'

Having recruited second guitarist Josh Brainard to further flesh-out their sound and changed their name to 'Meld', the six-piece made their live debut on 4 December 1995. However, by the time they headed into SR Studios a couple of weeks later to work on some demos, at Jordison's suggestion they'd changed their name yet again to Slipknot – the title of one of the compositions they'd be recording. These demos would eventually make up the track-listing of *Mate. Feed. Kill. Repeat*, which the band self-released on Halloween 1996.

Of course, the volatile line-up of early Slipknot fluctuated, as new members either found their feet or had the rug pulled out from under them. In summer 1997, Stone Sour frontman Corey Taylor took over vocal duties. Yet, owing to a rather ingenious idea whereby the band adopted a collective identity – donning matching red boiler suits, garish face masks, and numbers as aliases – only those close to the band could ever be sure of just *who* was in the line-up at any given time. 'When we go to radio stations for interviews, we wear the masks and never fail to freak people out,' Paul revealed gleefully. 'Are the masks a fetish thing? I'm definitely into that stuff. Des Moines definitely has more than its fair share of freaks.' According to Slipknot folklore, the idea behind the masks came from Crahan having brought a clown mask along to early rehearsals. 'It's our way of becoming more intimate with the music,' Corey Taylor explained in 2002. 'It's a way for us to become unconscious of who we are and what we do outside of music; a way for us to kind of crawl inside it and be able to use it.'

'It's our way of becoming more intimate with the music. It's a way for us to become unconscious of who we are and what we do outside of music; a way for us to kind of crawl inside it and be able to use it.'
– Corey Taylor

Clearly, there's always been a strong element of method in the 'Knot's staging of the crazy. In July 1998 (by which time Slipknot had bolstered its line-up to nine with the initiation of DJ Sid Wilson), the band inked a $500,000, seven-album deal with Roadrunner Records. Their eponymous debut was unleashed the following June. Though the album and its attendant singles received minimal airplay, by the time they returned to the studio to begin work on the follow-up, *Iowa*, their fan base had swelled considerably. With *Iowa* reaching number three on the *Billboard* 100, many of the industry movers and shakers who'd thus far remained impervious to the peculiar charm of the 'Knot, suddenly began to sit up and take notice. Yet, just when it seemed Slipknot had planet metal firmly within its noose, some long-festering internal squabbles rose to the fore. When several members went off to concentrate on varying side projects, fans were left wondering whether there would be another Slipknot album. And they certainly weren't alone in their anxiety. 'Slipknot is my life,' Paul told website *Artistdirect* in August 2008. 'It's everything. Without Slipknot I'd probably be sleeping on someone's couch, working at the old bar I used to work at.'

Not long after Gray's arrest in June 2003, news hit the grapevine that Slipknot had gone back into the studio with renowned producer Rick Rubin to start working on song ideas for the much-anticipated third album. If Roadrunner had been fretting about Slipknot's popularity waning during their enforced hiatus, they needn't have. The resultant album, *Vol. 3: (The Subliminal Verses)* went one better than its predecessor on the *Billboard* chart upon its release in May 2004. 'It was the rebirth of Slipknot, it was like us coming back together, pushing out the vibe that had gotten in there and kinda started pulling people away,' Paul said of the album. 'But we figured out that, you know, we do have to get space . . . we do need to let people be sometimes.'

And those fans who'd long been clamouring for an official Slipknot live album finally got their wish with the release of the two-disc *9.0: Live* – a compilation of 24 songs culled from various shows during their mammoth two-year-long Subliminal Verses World Tour.

Though the band went into temporary hiatus for the remainder of 2005, during which time Paul became involved with *Roadrunner United: The All-Star Sessions* (a compilation album to celebrate the label's twenty-fifth anniversary), Slipknot's stock rose significantly the following year when they picked up a Grammy Award for 'Before I Forget' in the Best Metal Performance category. And their stranglehold on the metal scene was complete when their fourth studio album, *All Hope is Gone*, slammed onto the *Billboard* chart at number one in August 2008. 'It's definitely a sign of us maturing, we never let anyone guide us or tell us what to do, but this time we went right for how we were feeling,' he told *Artistdirect* backstage at a show in Atlanta, Georgia, shortly after the album's release. 'Everybody in this band has been playing forever – we know what we're doing. We threw caution to the wind, and we wrote this record for us.'

It seemed their record label bosses had learned it was best not to meddle with Slipknot when they were in the zone, as Paul explained: 'We had none of the LA people in our ear. The record label wasn't coming out there saying, "We need a single" or "We need a song that's like this". We didn't have any of that shit. We got to do our own thing. We were left alone, and the record came out great because of it. I think it's our best. It's definitely the most well-rounded and most cohesive record we've done.'

In a subsequent interview with *Andpop*, recorded shortly before his death, Paul commented on how happy he was that Slipknot's music had continually matured with each album: 'They've all gone in different directions,' he explained. 'Not one of the albums sounds totally the same, like we're rehashing the last album or anything, even though you can tell all of our albums are Slipknot albums. I think that's a good thing. We never wanted to be painted into a corner.'

Paul also hit back at the naysayers who've branded the 'Knot a band of fame-hungry sell-outs. 'It's weird because Slipknot's at the level now where it became cool not to like Slipknot,' Gray mused. 'We got a little bit of backlash. Kids that are sixteen or seventeen will say we're "nu-metal". These kids try to tell me what true metal is, when I was at the fuckin' *Powerslave* concert in 1984. They weren't even born yet! I don't care. Dude, I know metal. I'm 36 years old; I've been in metal bands for 23 years. I was doing Metallica and Slayer covers when I was thirteen. I've paid my dues and I've paid my respects to the metal gods for that shit. I'm not going to be told by some teenybopper motherfucker that we're

'He was always very optimistic and dealt with the cards that life dealt him.'
- Brenna Gray

"mall metal" when I know what the fuck we're doing. People can say whatever they want, but when we play, we're playing in front of 20,000 people every night. Slipknot's bigger than ever. I'm so fucking proud and happy to be in this band. I'm so thankful for the fans that have stuck by us through all these years. We have the most loyal fans in the world, and we're gaining new ones every day. If any detractors can do it better, they should start a band and write a record, man. I'll buy it from them.'

2009 marked the tenth anniversary of the release of *Slipknot*, and with Roadrunner intent on re-releasing the album complete with bonus tracks, the band hit the road once again – with every intention of paying a few more dues to the 'metal gods'. However, after the tour wound up with a show in Las Vegas on Halloween 2009, the band was put back on hiatus, to allow numbers 0-8 time and space to focus on their respective side projects. And of course, it was while Paul was standing in for Megadeth's Dave Ellefson in the super-group Hail that tragedy struck.

Moments of madness: Sometime around 10:50am on the morning of Monday, 24 May 2010, a hotel worker at the TownePlace Suites in Urbandale, Iowa, entered room 431 and got the shock of his life. In the next few seconds, he took in the hypodermic syringe discarded near the bed; the carpet strewn with 'all kinds of pills' and finally the room's sole occupant . . . slumped lifeless in a corner. These were the grim details reported by celebrity news site *TMZ*, which managed to obtain the transcript of the proprietor's panicked 911 call. While such tragic finds are not unheard of in the hotel business, this was clearly no ordinary death and no ordinary guest. The name of Paul Gray was guaranteed to inspire a frenzy of unsolicited media attention.

Hence, when the time came, hotel spokesman Chris Diebel was more than prepared to face the press. His painstakingly-worded statement explained how a member of staff had gone to check on the bassist – who'd booked into the extended-stay hotel on Saturday and been due to check out that day – in response to a call from his relatives, who were becoming increasingly concerned that he wasn't answering his cell phone. Diebel finished by emphasising that the staff had neither seen nor heard anything out of the ordinary coming from Paul's room before the discovery of his body. Over at Des Moines Police Department HQ, Sergeant Dave Disney told those same reporters that, as there was no evidence of foul play at the scene, no official statement would be made until after the autopsy and toxicology tests – both of which were scheduled for later that day.

'Paul's spirit is still with us, in so many different ways. I mean, there's not a day that goes by that at least once every hour I don't think about him.'
– Corey Taylor

The findings of said toxicology tests were as follows: Paul died from an accidental overdose of morphine and a synthetic morphine substitute called Fentanyl – both of which had been self-administered intravenously. According to the US Drug Enforcement Administration, Fentanyl is hundreds of times more potent than morphine and therefore highly sought-after by dealers and addicts alike. Like morphine, Fentanyl is commonly used for anaesthesia and pain relief. However, the DEA's website also states that Fentanyl's manufacture in illegal labs has caused thousands of deaths by overdose in recent years. The autopsy also revealed that Paul had been suffering from heart disease. Yet a more pressing concern for the investigating officers was their failure to establish where – or from whom – Paul had obtained the Fentanyl in the first place.

'I knew something was going on, but I couldn't put my finger on it. Because he would be fine one day, and the next he wouldn't,' Brenna told *Revolver*. 'So I was kind of unsure, like, "Hmm, something's not adding up here." And it wasn't till that Saturday that I realised what was going on when I found things in my home. Then he passed away that Sunday.

So I really had no time to really make a move. That Saturday I said, "Hey, we need to do something. We need to fix this." And he agreed, and he was getting ready to go out on tour with Hail. And he said, "I'll go get help after I come back from this tour." And I just said, "You're not going." And I called his manager, and I said, "You need to cancel this tour. He's not going." And I just think it was a little too late. I think there's nothing anyone could have done. Paul was my husband. He was an amazing person and I just want people to remember him for just that, and his daughter will remember him for the way he was.'

Echoing Nikki Sixx's theory that 'Mötley gave me the resources to be an addict . . . but if it hadn't I'd have found some other way to do it,' Brenna remains convinced that Paul's drug problems went beyond the occupational hazard of being in a successful metal band. In accordance with step one of Nikki's three-point descent into all-consuming addiction, Paul Gray could lay claim to having suffered an equally 'shitty childhood'. Yet, contrary to the title of the third single to be culled from *All Hope is Gone*, Paul's own recollections of the past were anything but 'Dead Memories'. Indeed, Brenna has never stopped believing that everything that was wrong with Gray's present stemmed from a terminal inability to shake off the emotional baggage of his past. 'His father committed suicide when he was a child. And his father also was an addict,' she revealed. 'It weighs a lot on your shoulders. I mean, he looked up to his dad. He had a really shitty childhood, moving here to there, here to there. The death of a father or the death of any family member is not easy. I never pushed him to talk about [it] because it was such a burden to him. And I don't know if he was embarrassed or just sad. But he would talk about it and get really upset. And I think a lot of that did contribute to his problem. I don't know. I wish there was more I could've done. I tried to get him into counselling and to talk about it. But when they're not ready to do that, you can't push somebody. So I never pushed him. I let him talk about it on his own terms, but he was never like, "Wow, my life was like this so I'm bitter," or anything like that. He was always very optimistic and dealt with the cards that life dealt him.'

When Paul first got together with Brenna his drug habit was already taking a heavy toll. 'He wasn't doing very well at all. And I really had no idea because I had never been in a situation like that,' Brenna said. 'I knew something was wrong, but I just didn't *know*. And of course I was forewarned by friends, but I loved him. And as soon as I did realise what was going on, we moved back to Iowa. And as soon as we came here, it was like day and night. I mean, he did great. He was awesome. And he worked really hard on his sobriety, and he did really well. And I think it was just getting him out of the "toxic city", as they say out there, and I know it's such a cliché, but that's exactly what it was. I felt like if he stayed out there, he would have perished way sooner.'

In the tragic aftermath, the 'Knot's legion of 'maggots' finally glimpsed the faces of their heroes unmasked, when Corey, Shawn, and the rest of the band – together with Brenna and Paul's brother, Tony – paid tribute to their fallen brother-in-harm at a private press conference held at Wells Fargo Arena in Des Moines, the day after Paul's death. Black-clad and overcome with grief, the bandmates were barely able keep their voices from breaking, with Corey extending a tattooed arm to comfort numbers five and six (the distraught Mick Thompson and Shawn Crahan) at regular intervals. When Corey finally stood to leave the table – with a simple, 'thank you very much, that'll be it' – the press maintained a respectful silence. Despite the question mark now hanging over the future of Slipknot, this was clearly not the time to begin pushing for answers.

But when conflicting statements as to said future began appearing in the media, fans really did begin to fear the imminent unravelling of the 'Knot. Thankfully these claims would prove groundless and – following in the footsteps of AC/DC, Def Leppard and Metallica – the band eventually reached a unanimous decision. Believing that Paul would have wanted the show to go on, Corey et al. made up their minds to soldier on even without the man who'd helped to set them on their path.

Yet anyone expecting the 'Knot to remain as they'd been was to be left somewhat confused. 'He's gonna be sadly missed. The world is gonna be a different place without him,' promised Crahan on the day of the band's emotional press conference. And, as a mark of respect to their fallen brother, the 'Knot's trademark masks will never again be worn onstage, but forever consigned to Slipknot history.

Another tribute came with the decision to invite Donnie Steele back to fill in on live duties rather than bring an outsider into the fold. 'There were a handful of names that were thrown about, but we all mentioned Donnie's name, and once we realised we were all on the same page, we were like, "Right – he's the one. He's the guy,"' Corey Taylor told *Ultimateguitar* e-zine in January 2011. 'He's the type of person that we were able to kind of put our emotions in his hands, and he kind of just walked with it. It's been really good to know that we still have the backbone of this band, because Paul's spirit is still with us, in so many different ways. I mean, there's not a day that goes by that at least once every hour I don't think about him, so it's just knowing that someone who had Paul's back has ours now. It makes it infinitely easier.

'Paul's style was so distinctive, and his sound was so distinctive, that not hearing it took me a while to get used to, and I still don't think I'm fully used to it,' he continued. 'But . . . soldiering on is really what it comes down to. I'm just really happy that we have Donnie. He's one of the most selfless people I've ever met. He was like, "You know what? I'm only going to do this if it feels right," and we all got together and it felt good. It felt right. We were all so close that there was really only one person who was going to be able to fit those [Paul's] shoes.'

Despite the 'Knot's return to the stage, Corey confesses he's still struggling to come to terms with the loss of his friend. 'It's been over a year now [sic], and I've been slowly but surely talking a little bit more about it,' he said. 'Obviously, it's still with me, and it's still hard to talk about it. But I've found the more I talk about it, the easier it is to deal with it. Paul was one of those guys who really lived it. He lived it right to the hilt. He fought his demons, but he didn't let his demons control his personality. If you had just met him, you wouldn't have thought that he was fighting those demons.

'He was such a sweetheart, and there were times that I forgot that he had issues that he was fighting against, and it really kind of made him almost indestructible in my eyes. So when he passed, it fucked me up, to be honest. It was hard, and it is still hard, but it taught me that you have got to cherish every day and cherish every moment. I don't mean to be overly sensitive or anything like that, but you just have to take a minute in every day, and just reflect on where you are, and just realise what you've got, because you just never know where the next huge change in your life is going to come from. That's the biggest lesson I've taken from it.'

If only he'd been able to let the mask slip – providing the likes of Corey and Brenna with just a glimpse of the man beneath – then who knows how the story of Paul Gray could have ended.

Layne Staley

22 August 1967 – 5 April 2002

Born: Layne Thomas Staley

Alter-egos: Tragically confined 'man in the box'.

(Pre) occupations: 'I'm Layne Staley and I sing like a lark,' Alice in Chains' tortured frontman once quipped. And, drawn to the siren-like strains of his harrowing vocals, Jerry Cantrell (the Alice axeman who says that he loved Layne like 'a brother') was certainly hooked in a heartbeat. 'I knew that voice was the guy I wanted to be playing with,' he recalls in interview with *Rolling Stone* scribe, Charles R. Cross. 'It sounded like it came out of a 350-pound biker rather than skinny little Layne. I considered his voice to be my voice.' And the talented Mr. Staley was happy to lend his voice to Alice's anthems of despair, channelling the anguish of a generation, as well as the men who became his brothers and bandmates. 'We don't stuff our personal demons [down] inside us; we get them out,' stated Staley, circa 1992. And, thanks to the blistering legacy he left behind, Layne will always be more than just the sum of his earthly sins.

In memoriam: Jerry Cantrell: 'Our music's about taking something ugly and making it beautiful.'

Layne Stayley: 'I do that every day when I'm dressing . . . I take an ugly face and make it beautiful.'

'Layne wore his soul on the outside. He was luminous . . . too tender for this world.' – Ann Wilson (backing vocals; *Sap*)

'Layne had an amazing voice that had such a beautiful, sad, haunting quality about it. He was different because his heaviness was in that voice.' – Billy Corgan

𝔇eadℓy sins: 'My bad habits ain't my title; my strengths and talents are,' Staley once ranted in an interview with Jon Wiederhorn, the *Rolling Stone* scribe who dared to mention Staley's lifelong addiction to heroin. Yet, as *Dirt* (Alice in Chains' master opus and the sonic equivalent of Nikki Sixx's *Heroin Diaries*) proves beyond a shadow of a doubt, in Alice's tripped out wonderland, there'd have been no creation without self-destruction; no inspiration without addiction, and no strength without Staley's terminal weakness. Compassionate and imaginative by nature, Layne was a highly susceptible personality whose powers of empathy extended to certain breeds of livestock. 'I started writing about censorship,' explained Staley in interview with Jeffrey Ressner. 'Around the same time, we went out for dinner with some Columbia Records people who were vegetarians. They told me how veal was made from calves raised in these small boxes and that image stuck in my head. So I went home and wrote about government censorship and eating meat as seen through the eyes of a doomed calf . . . ' And how better to exorcise this particular demon than with the masochistic 'Man in the Box'?

Years later, Paul Rachman – the director charged with capturing Layne's nightmare on film – recalled the filming of the video that made Alice in Chains the toast of MTV. The 'baby-faced' Layne he remembers was 'very, very magnetic', 'inspiring' and absolutely committed to bringing his vision of a bad trip down on the farm to life. Rachman reminisces: 'Layne's idea for the video and song were based on images of a rainy drippy barn and a baby with his eyes sewn shut. I took those ideas on board and came up with an animal farm, but used an adult for the eyes-sewn-shut idea [. . .] It was easy to visualise his ideas because there really was truth in them. [Layne] was very sweet, talented, sensitive and inwardly emotional. He was very comfortable and confident with his ideas and his art and music [. . .] I don't remember him as ever hesitant or asking too many questions. He just did it [. . .] I mean, look at the video. I asked the frontman to sit in a corner of a real dirty barn tied up and sing. To most frontmen that would seem demeaning and negative; Layne just did it and you can see he is in that moment. There is a vulnerable sadness in his eyes [. . .] in that scene.'

As for the blind man – whose eyes are puckered mounds of flesh – he's never far from the shadows at the periphery of Rachman's camera, haunting Alice's barnyard performance from start to finish. Part-grim reaper, part-sadistic saviour (Staley howls repeatedly for deliverance from 'Jesus Christ'), the true identity of the man beneath the cowl is imbued with eerie significance. In fact, he was played by Staley himself.

When twenty-year-old Layne (glam-rock band Sleze's super-charged, drag-clad frontman) announced the name of his newest project, his mother couldn't help but voice her disappointment. In interview with Adriana Rubio (author of *Angry Chair*, a respectful 'look inside the heart and soul of an incredible musician'), the lady herself, Nancy McCallum, reveals that 'Jerry [Cantrell] and Layne started asking, "What should we call ourselves?" Lots of names were thrown out . . . Layne said "Alice in Chains" and the room went completely quiet. Everybody was quiet and the boys said, "Well, that must be it."'

Nancy, however, was less than impressed. 'I was very upset with Layne for using that name,' she continues. 'I said, "That's a female bondage name . . . Honey, it makes me feel really upset. Could you please come up with something else?"' Though he wasn't about to reconsider, Layne

> '*At the end of the party, when everyone goes home, you're stuck with yourself.*'
>
> *- Layne Staley*

did all he could to put his mother's mind at rest. 'He made up a story that was supposed to make me feel better,' recalls Nancy wryly, 'about how Alice in Chains had broken her chains. The band was named for a woman who had been caught up on drugs, but gotten free.' Yet while Alice broke free of her bonds, the gifted young artist who dreamed her into existence never did.

When interrogated as to his greatest regret, Corey Taylor (of Slipknot shame) doesn't hesitate. 'My biggest mistake,' he muses, 'is to allow myself to give in to my addictive personality.' And this could just as well be the epitaph of Alice's tragic frontman. 'When I'm not doing drugs, I eat,' raved a restless Staley in interview with *Rolling Stone*'s Jon Wiederhorn. 'And I binge and I fucking gain twenty pounds. And I work out. And when I start working out, I go crazy on it. I can't do anything in small doses.' Yet whereas Corey's tale ends in (relatively) contented sobriety – 'it used to be [. . .] that I needed to fucking drink every moment because I just didn't want to deal with the shit I was dealing with. Now I can take it or leave it,' explained Slipknot's former 'disaster-piece' – Layne succumbed to the wrong addiction.

'It's not the newest story,' sighed Alice drummer Sean Kinney at Staley's memorial service, held in April 2002. 'It's the fucking rock'n'roll cliché and I wonder if it will ever stop.' For, in keeping with the tragic blueprint set by Andrew Wood back in 1990 (aged just 24, Mother Love Bone's frontman became grunge's first sainted icon, foreshadowing Staley's own overdose by more than a decade), it seemed almost a foregone conclusion that Staley should be hopelessly in thrall to heroin – the most addictive substance he could have procured on the gloomy city streets. 'The sky is always crying in Seattle,' wrote *Guitar World's* Jeff Gilbert. And given the track record of his peers (Mother Love Bone's Andrew Wood, Kurt Cobain of Nirvana), the outlook for Staley was no less grim than the ashen Seattle skies.

Staley may have been the first to lose the game, but back in 1992, his chained bandmates were all gambling with their lives. 'We partied like demons,' Kinney finally admitted in interview with *Rolling Stone*, adding ominously that 'it took a toll. From 1991 on, it was getting pretty ugly' – as the harrowing testimony of bandmate Mike Starr corroborates.

> 'It's like one of the world's longest suicides . . .
> I'd been expecting a call for seven years, but it was still
> shocking and I'm surprised at how devastated I am.'
> - Sean Kinney

Barely recognisable as the band's charismatic young four-stringer, a tearful Starr made one of the last appearances of his life on 2010's *Celebrity Rehab with Dr. Drew*. His cheekbones obscured by jowly layers of fat and stubble, he could scarcely look Layne's mother in the eye as he recalled some of Alice's wildest backstage antics. On one particular occasion, he asked Layne and Kurt Cobain (of Nirvana) to 'shoot him up', with terrifying consequences.

'I was twenty,' he began, with downcast eyes and a tremor in his voice. 'We were just casually using except for Layne. He was using heroin. I died, like, eleven minutes. Dead for eleven minutes, Layne said. Woke up I was all wet and I was in a different room, I was in the bathroom and Layne was punching me in the face crying. I let him die too and he saved my life, isn't that terrible? On my birthday . . .' Yet despite the shock of Mike's brush with death, Layne was not about to abandon his addiction for anything or anyone.

It's no coincidence that Alice in Chains' second album (unleashed in 1992) bears the name of the substance that stopped Staley's heart and robbed him of his fiancée Demri Parrott. On the midnight streets of Seattle, *Dirt* is not so much a code word for heroin as a synonym. And, heady as a concentrated hit of the substance itself, the band's nightmarish trip on vinyl is cited by Kinney as 'a shining example of just how ugly' things came to be within the Alice camp. More than a match for the muscular grind of Cantrell's doom-laden riffs, Staley's agonised vocals draw listeners ever deeper into a world of darkening addiction – in which hypocritical conceptions of the 'norm' hold little sway and Staley's stoner brethren reign like kings . . . or do they?

Switching from righteous indignation – at the tedious moralists who branded him a 'hopeless fucking junkhead' – to self-loathing so intense it sears, Staley's masterpiece is hardly condemnatory of the junkie lifestyle. But neither did it deserve the tag of straightforward stoner's apology – as Staley himself stated in no uncertain terms back in 1992. 'From song to song,' he explained, 'the album changes from glorifying drugs to being completely miserable and questioning what I thought once worked for me. By the end of the album, it's pretty obvious it didn't work out as well as I thought it would.' Though he had a sincere regard for everyone who truly connected with his music, a poster boy for unbridled hedonism was the last thing Staley aspired to be.

'I wrote about drugs and I didn't think I was being careless or unsafe. Here's how my thinking pattern went,' he revealed in interview with Jon Wiederhorn. 'When I tried drugs, they were fucking great and they worked for me for years; now they're turning against me and I'm walking through hell.

'I didn't want my fans to think that heroin was cool,' he added. 'But then I've had fans come up to me and give me the thumbs up, telling me they're high. That's exactly what I didn't want to happen.'

During this interview, Staley declined to name his own personal poison – preferring it to remain the proverbial elephant in the room. 'If I'm staying busy . . . and I'm doing things I think are great, then I don't have a problem with anything, you know?' the frontman railed in the face of Wiederhorn's unwelcome line of enquiry. 'If I live just on a strictly sugar diet, hey, I like it . . . nobody ever asks Meat Loaf, "What do you eat? Why do you eat so much? Shouldn't you lose some weight?" No, he fucking shouldn't – he's fucking Meat Loaf! He writes songs and he has a great time and none of your fuckin' business. Maybe he eats meatloaf every fuckin' night, you know?'

Foreshadowing Corey Taylor's 2011 defence of the deadly sins by more than a decade, Staley continued, 'People have a right to ask questions and dig deep when you're hurting people and things around you. But when I haven't talked to anyone in years and every article I see is dope this, junkie that, whisky this . . . that ain't my title. Like, "Hi, I'm Layne, nail-biter," you know? My bad habits aren't my title. My strengths and talents are my title.' Layne's lips remained sealed. Yet there was no hiding the tell-tale track marks spreading across the frontman's hands and face. Recorded by Wiederhorn in excruciating detail, these tiny constellations of bruises were damning as any verbal confession. 'At dinner, [Staley's] gloves were gone,' notes the scribe, 'but the sleeves of his white oxford shirt were buttoned between the thumbs and forefingers, revealing his uncut, dirt-encrusted fingernails. When he returned from a trip to the bathroom, his sleeves were unbuttoned, exposing what appear to be red, round puncture marks from the wrist to the knuckles of his left hand. As anyone who knows anything about IV drugs can tell you, the veins in the hand are used only after all the other veins have been tapped out.'

Days later, Staley recognised his own gaunt features on the cover of *Rolling Stone*. 'The Needle & the Damage Done,' read the jaunty yellow headline, printed alongside a close-up of the frontman's furrowed brow and blood-shot eyes. 'Layne wore his soul on the outside,' is backing vocalist Ann Wilson's lasting remembrance of the frontman. And strive as he might to mask the truth for the sake of those who loved him, this much was painfully evident: Staley's battle with heroin was far from over.

𝔉rom cradle to grave: The early life of Nancy Elizabeth Layne is hardly the stuff of fairytales. Pressured into a physical relationship by her very first boyfriend – the less than gracious Phil Staley, almost eleven years her senior – Nancy was barely eighteen when she fell pregnant with her first child. 'I did continue to say no and he got to be pretty obsessed about that,' sighs Nancy in interview with Adriana Rubio. '[He told me] "You give it to me, or I'll get it somewhere else."' Besotted Nancy eventually gave in and before long, 'I did get pregnant and thank God it was Layne.'

The couple were married in March 1967. Yet by the time of Layne's arrival (22 August that same year), Phil's affections were already beginning to wane, leaving Nancy trapped in a 'situation' that was 'out of my control'. 'Here I was,' Nancy continues, 'this eighteen or nineteen-year-old with a new baby and a husband who was never home, closed the bars, slept with the barmaids and was trying to tell me that he sometimes wanted to throw rocks at me! What chance did I have?'

Instead, broken-hearted Nancy invested all her hopes in her baby boy. 'I expected a lot of Layne,' she recalls fondly. 'He was my first child . . .

and I was trying to do everything right. I knew he was a smart little boy and I expected him to be good.' A singularly sensitive child, Layne more than lived up to her expectations. His first ever memory is of gazing up at a musical carousel, hanging high above his crib. At the tender age of five, he charmed his way into a pre-school rhythm band with a rendition of 'Raindrops Keep Falling on My Head' (a veritable Seattle anthem). Despite having his throat bitten by an angry hound outside the grocery store (aged just two, he'd barely learned to walk), Layne grew up to adore all animals – particularly his own pet dog. In *Angry Chair*, Nancy describes the morning when she followed her nose directly to Layne's room and, flicking on the light switch, discovered the source of the unholy odour: Layne's dog was suffering from a nasty case of diarrhoea. Nonetheless, the idea of turning his beloved companion out for the night was unthinkable for young Layne.

> 'My bad habits aren't my title. My strengths and talents are my title.'
> – Layne Staley

But whether Layne was ever literally 'alone' is beside the point. In fact, Staley's childhood memories were tainted by feelings of isolation, abandonment and despair. By Layne's seventh birthday, his parents' marriage was falling apart. In the bitter aftermath, Nancy remembers, 'Phil dropped out of our lives and we never heard from him for fifteen years.'

Evasive as ever, Staley did all he could to downplay the pain of his father's sudden disappearance, reciting the same nonchalant answer time after time. 'No deep, dark secrets there,' he insisted. 'I remember sometimes wondering where my dad was, but most of the time I was too busy running around playing.' It wasn't until 1999, in a one-on-one conversation with Nancy, that Staley was finally able to voice his true sentiments. 'When dad left, my world turned black, everything around me was black.'

And indeed, Layne would remember this dark moment forever – thanks to a malicious lie that was never meant for his ears. 'Phil got into trouble with people from big families,' explains Staley's younger sister, Liz. 'The fact is that Layne got a phone call from SeaTac Airport saying that they found our dad in a body bag dump. It was pretty traumatic for a young boy to hear that. We always knew that Phil lived a lie, but . . . it didn't affect me the way it affected Layne. It was traumatic for him.'

From then on, written off as 'a kid without a future' on the strength of a single failed test at school, Layne had precious little to smile about – when he wasn't sketching Metallica-inspired doodles, penning lines of angst-ridden poetry or attending drum lessons, that is. Yet, all this was to change, with what ranks amongst the most significant discoveries of Staley's adolescence. 'When [Layne] had his first drink,' recalls Nancy, 'he said to himself, "So this is why some people go around with smiles on their faces all of the time; this is how they feel normally."' If 'tristitia' (a state of overwhelming melancholy that matched Layne's vision of the world) were classed as a deadly sin, then Staley would surely be one of the worst offenders in this book (second only to Type O Negative's Pete Steele). Yet to Nancy the solution seemed clear; her son was experiencing a case of textbook teenage angst that would surely fade with time. 'Now I know Layne was suffering from depression,' she laments tearfully, adding that, 'I'm not a professional. I knew what I was seeing was a natural reaction, but I didn't know that Layne wouldn't heal in time, and that he needed help.'

But he'd had already taken the first step into a world of deadly addiction and, despite his best efforts, there was no way back for him.

'Layne had an amazing voice that had such a beautiful, sad, haunting quality about it. He was different because his heaviness was in that voice.'
- Billy Corgan

Moments of madness: Layne was found slumped lifeless on the couch of his condominium on 20 April 2003. 'When we found him,' Nancy recalls, barely able to keep her voice from breaking with grief, 'I walked into the dining area of his home and I sat down with my Layne and I told him I'm so sorry it turned out like this because I always believed 'cause he was smart and he had the money and the time and he knew, he'd been in treatment thirteen times and still it took him out . . .'

Dubbed the 'longest suicide in the world' by his bandmate Sean Kinney, Layne's death – recorded as having occurred on 5 April, in an eerie echo of the loss of Kurt Cobain on the same date years earlier – smacks of the same inevitability as Shakespeare's most excruciating tragedies. In his final years, he removed himself from everyone who'd ever cared for him, claiming that 'they're no friends of mine'; though in truth they'd scarcely have recognised him, haunting the darkest corners of his local bar with neither a smile on his face nor a glass in his hand. So how was it that this 'beautiful man with huge talent' came to 'squander his life and his talents' (in the words of his mother), his remains left to fester in his condo for a full fortnight before anyone (Mike Starr as it happens) thought to call the police?

Of this much Corey Taylor is living proof – cleaning up is a long and painful process, one that's doomed to failure if the heart of the addict is not in it. And perhaps Layne had given up hoping for the future he once dreamt of. After his beloved Demri passed away, Layne seemed to have little left to live for. (In the grip of the same heroin addiction as her boyfriend, her wasted twenty-seven-year-old body was simply too weak to fight off a fatal cardio-respiratory disease.) His sister Liz was witness to the grief that threatened to overwhelm him after the loss of his love. 'I feel so sad for him,' she confided in author Adriana Rubio. 'I know he is still waiting for Demri. A lot of sad things happened to him. He doesn't want anyone to see him the way he is . . . the shame of his own physical being, you know. Demri knew him. The physical illness . . . he just said, "I don't want anyone to touch me again." And that's so sad. I can't imagine . . . I remember him being afraid he would never be with anyone physically again. Demri was his only and true love.' Though forensic science dictates that Staley died of a fatal cocktail of cocaine and heroin (otherwise known as a speedball), there's no way it could begin to fathom the intricacies of Staley's bruised but 'luminous' heart.

'For the past decade,' read Alice's official statement on the eve of their frontman's memorial, 'Layne struggled greatly – we can only hope that he has at last found some peace.'

DEAD (PER YNGVE OHLIN)

16 January 1969 - 8 April 1991

Born: Per Yngve Ohlin

Alter-egos: 'Sometimes I feel I have two personalities,' reads the pseudo-schizoid scrawl of Nikki Sixx's *Heroin Diaries*. Yet for Per Yngve Ohlin – 'Pelle' to his bandmates and associates (for a man who carried the festering corpse of a crow on his person at all times, 'friends' seems entirely the wrong term) – 'Dead' was so much more than just a stage persona, or a crazed alter-ego to be reined in and safely compartmentalised. In fact, Per Yngve's chosen moniker worked upon the man himself like an all-consuming curse – until the grim spring day when it became appropriate in every sense. Whether anything remained of 'Per Yngve' beneath the corpse paint is a question that will remain forever shrouded in mystery.

(Pre) occupations: Lead vocalist with Morbid and Mayhem, Dead is the patron (s)aint who gave black metal its chilling gravitas.

In memoriam: 'Dead didn't see himself as human; he saw himself as a creature from another world . . . he said he had many visions that his blood had frozen in his veins, that he was dead. That is the reason he took that name – he knew he would die.' – Stian 'Occultus' Johansen

Deadly sins: While Dead arguably committed the ultimate sin of taking his own life before his time, it's an act that pales in comparison with the transgressions of his bandmates a matter of hours after his suicide – all of which read like macabre fiction, rather than cold hard fact.

Black metal has come to be considered the most extreme sub-genre in metal history, but with their funereal garb and painted monochrome faces, its devotees would surely have been dismissed as Kiss clones gone mad on tequila-laced holy water had it not been for the suicide of Mayhem's frontman. For, whatever his motives that day, it was undoubtedly Dead's final act of violence which gave the genre its grisly *mise en scène*. Though subsequent random killings – including Faust's callous stabbing of a homosexual pub-goer in August 1992 – coupled with a spate of gratuitous church burnings that same summer, inspired a flurry of semi-hysterical headlines directed at black-metal music and its advocates, none of these acts seemed possessed of quite the same power to shock as Dead's senseless suicide the previous April. Whereas the black-clad legions of Satan had formerly been able to 'walk the streets looking like insane motherfuckers and no one [knew] what the hell was going on', the Norwegian media's chilling exposé into the 'nihilistic rampage of Norway's satanically-minded youth' was enough to ensure no one else poked a mocking finger at the scene's darkest obsession with death.

Needless to say, the extra-curricular activities of this particular section of the nation's youth (setting architectural landmarks alight and slaughtering random strangers) made for less than comfortable reading within this largely secular society. To quote the *Observer*'s Chris Campion, who interviewed Mayhem's longest-serving member, bassist Jørn 'Necrobutcher' Stubberud, in February 2005 during the band's tour of their homeland: 'As far as the Norwegian media were concerned, when it came to black metal, all roads led to Mayhem, whose terrible and bloody history eclipses the debauchery of even the most hardened rock bands.'

𝔉rom cradle to grave: Per Yngve Ohlin was born in the Swedish capital, Stockholm, in January 1969. As a child he suffered from sleep apnoea, a rare and terrifying disorder characterised by irregular pauses in breathing during sleep. As these abnormal pauses can last from anything from a few seconds to several minutes, the sufferer usually requires the aid of a ventilator in order to sleep safely. Owing to his shy, retiring nature, young Pelle was an easy target for school bullies. Inevitably, there came a day when Pelle's tormentors went too far. So brutal was this particular beating that the boy was left haemorrhaging internally – soon to be rushed to hospital with a ruptured spleen. However, rather than risk further punishment by naming the perpetrators, he told his parents that he'd injured himself while ice-skating.

Years later, Pelle would reveal that the loss of blood led to him having what can only be described as a near-death experience: 'I had inner-bleeding and it couldn't be found on x-rays so when it continued to bleed and bleed, I finally fainted and dropped to the floor because I ran out of blood. The heart had no blood left to beat and my veins [and] arteries almost emptied of blood. Technically, I was dead. At that moment when I fell down (into a door, I heard later), I saw a strange blue colour everywhere – it was transparent, so I could for a short moment see everything in blue, till something shining white and hot surrounded me . . .

'It's someone I know, who's had many out-of-body experiences and knows much more than I do about supernatural experience that I asked [about] this, because it was so strange about those colours. She told me that the first "plane" in the astral world has the colour of blue. The earthly plane has the colour of black. Then comes a grey that is near the earthly one and is easy to come to. The next one further is blue, then it gets brighter and brighter till it stops at a shining one that can't be entered by mortals. If any mortal succeeds in entering it, that one is no longer mortal and cannot come back to the earthly planes, nor back to this earth. After the white plane, it goes further with other colours that I don't know of – there only spirits and sorcerers can travel. I was told that the white plane I then entered, without knowing it, was the "dead world" and I had died.'

'I am not a human being. This is just a dream, and soon I will awake. It was too cold and the blood was clotting all the time . . .'

- Dead

Though the surgeons wrenched Pelle back to a world of pain and childhood angst, this tantalising taste of what lay within the white light left an indelible imprint on his fertile young mind, and affected his thought processes ever after. From that moment on death held no fear for him. If anything, he viewed dying as a blessed release from his earthly chains and had no intention of enduring his 'three score and ten' before passing through the white light to the mysteries that lay beyond. And from the moment he adopted his stage name, he literally was a dead man walking.

In 1986, hell-bent on making a name for himself on Sweden's as yet nebulous death-metal scene, Pelle set about searching for like-minded ghouls with whom he could form a horror-themed band. Of course, this proved harder than he'd imagined, and 'Morbid' – the name he'd settled upon for the band – would undergo many transient formations before finally finding a permanent line-up of sorts, with Pelle himself (under the newly-adopted pseudonym of 'Dead') providing the vocals, John 'John Lennart' Hagström and 'TG' on guitars, Jens Näsström on bass and Lars-Göran Petrov on drums. However, the band had barely worked up a set-list when TG found his commitment waning, and it was his replacement,

Ulf Cederlund, who accompanied Morbid into Stockholm's Thunderload Studios to record their debut demo, *December Moon*, in December 1987.

This, however, would prove to be Dead's swansong, for – like Hagström before him – he decided soon after that his future lay outside of Sweden. He established contact with Norwegian black-metal merchants Mayhem, fully prepared to make the move to Oslo.

An established act, Mayhem had been peddling their fearsome brand of 'Total Death Metal' (according to the band's own mission statement) for some two years already. Unlike the vast majority of their Norwegian peers, Jørn 'Necrobutcher' Stubberud, guitarist Øystein 'Euronymous' Aarseth, and drummer Kjetil Manheim tended to avoid religious symbolism in favour of 'death, violence, and having a fucking good time'.

'We just decided immediately that we were going to start a band,' the diminutive Stubberud told the *Guardian*. 'But it was always a cat and dog thing between me and Øystein. We had one similar interest – the band – but everything else was different. While I was out raising hell with all my drug friends, he was home writing letters. He was the quiet type with all the strange friends, listening to Brian Eno and all this "bing, bong, bing bong" music. I didn't have time to fuck around with all of that.'

Mayhem's first studio offering came in the form of a limited-edition demo tape, *Pure Fucking Armageddon*. The band's first proper release, the eight-track EP, *Deathcrush* – featuring the infamous 'Chainsaw Gutsfuck' (whose lyrics were subsequently voted the most gruesome ever by *Blender*) – was released on Euronymous's own Posercorpse label in 1987. Mayhem's reputation as the most extreme band in Norway, coupled with their growing prominence on the underground scene, meant that the initial 1,000 copies of this EP sold out very quickly indeed. Despite this success, the musicians themselves were still living hand-to-mouth. And though money was of little consequence to Necrobutcher and Euronymous, the strain of their situation ultimately proved too much for founding vocalist, Eirik 'Messiah' Nordheim, as well as his successor, 'Maniac'. (And while Manheim was still keeping the blast-beat when Dead joined the line-up, he would soon be replaced by Jan Axel 'Hellhammer' Blomberg.)

Then one day, out of the blue (or perhaps the eerie luminescent white), a mysterious package arrived from a kooky young Swede by the name of Dead. Necrobutcher still remembers emptying out the contents: a demo tape entitled *December Moon*, a letter of introduction and a crucified mouse. Although the bassist tossed the letter and the mouse corpse directly into the bin, he kept hold of the tape and Dead's contact details.

While Dead's choice of introductory gift undoubtedly set him apart from a legion of other young hopefuls, the trio quickly realised that this young pretender had infinitely more to offer. Indeed, his presence gave Mayhem a whole new dynamic, in contrast with the deliberately awkward style of *Deathcrush*. Euronymous and the rest of the band readily adopted Dead's funereal image: black garb, boots, and faces smeared with corpse-paint to mimic the pallor of thirteenth-century plague victims. 'I honestly think Dead is mentally insane,' Euronymous said at the time of Dead's arrival. 'Which other way can you describe a guy who does not eat in order to get starving wounds? Or who has a T-shirt with funeral announcements on it?' And the years haven't altered Necrobutcher's opinion: worn with utter sincerity, Dead's funereal garb was as sacred to him as a habit to a priest. 'It wasn't anything to do with the way Kiss and Alice Cooper used make-up,' he told the *Guardian*. 'Dead actually wanted to look like a corpse. He didn't do it to look cool. He would draw snot dripping out of his nose. That doesn't look cool. He called it corpse-paint.'

A key factor which separated Dead's stage act from the theatrical antics of Kiss et al. is that any blood spilt during performances was his own. Far from a cheap shock tactic, Dead's bloodletting was conducted in the spirit of a gore-drenched social experiment. In contrast with his shock-rocking US peers, Dead was infinitely more interested in *observing* rather than predicting the reaction of his audiences. 'Something I study is how people react when my blood is streaming everywhere,' he explained calmly.

Bård Eithun was also in the audience that night. 'Dead cut himself very badly – intentionally, of course – because he crushed a bottle and took it and cut himself, leaving a big scar,' he said. 'He was supposed to go to the hospital afterwards, but he arrived too late so it was no use to give him stitches. I remember after the gig he was very sick and in pain because he lost a lot of blood. It was in the middle, during the set. He had been talking about it before the set, so expectations were high and he had to do it. It was during a track with almost no vocals, so he had time to do it. He took a bottle and crushed it, took a sharp edge and did it.'

Moments of madness: That Dead and Euro were worlds away from mainstream society – in self-imposed exile from the rest of human race – was blindingly obvious, and 1990 was the year they decided to make the distance literal. Installing themselves outside of Kråkstad, in an abandoned house in the depths of the forest, they commenced work on their tentatively-titled album, *De Mysteriis Dom Sathanas*. The precise meaning of these ancient lines – derived from the (appropriately) dead language of Latin – is as elusive as the lingering Norwegian mist. 'Of Lord Satan Mysteries'; 'Of Lord Satan Secrets'; and 'Of Lord Satan Secret Rites' are all possible translations. Dead, however, did not live to hear the finished album. On 8 April 1991, he shut himself away in his bedroom and slashed his wrists with a blade.

Interestingly, American physician Alex Lickerman views certain suicide attempts as the most desperate kind of 'cry for help'. 'These people don't usually want to die,' he wrote, 'but *do* want to alert those around them that something is seriously wrong.' Yet, when Dead lifted the shotgun – already slick with blood – to his head, he must have known the only possible outcome. Rather than tortured volumes, he left a single hastily-scrawled line: 'Excuse all the blood. Let the party begin.'

> 'Dead actually wanted to look like a corpse.
> He didn't do it to look cool. He would draw snot dripping out of his nose.
> That doesn't look cool. He called it corpse-paint.'
> – Necrobutcher

Though journalist Chris Campion has since speculated that Dead was suffering from Cotard's delusion (a rare condition where the sufferer remains convinced that they're a putrefying corpse, missing blood and/or crucial internal organs) all along, Hellhammer was shocked to learn of his bandmate's violent exit. 'I was at my parents' house when it happened,' he remembered. 'I was planning to go back, but Euronymous called me and said, "You can't go back because the police have closed the house."' Naturally, Hellhammer wanted to know why, but Euronymous's response left him none the wiser. 'Dead has gone home,' Euro stated in strangely deadened tones, leaving the baffled Hellhammer to wonder if Dead had quit the band, returned to Stockholm, or – what? Finally the realisation dawned that 'going home' was a euphemism for something more sinister.

'Euronymous found him,' Hellhammer added. 'We only had one key to the door and it was locked, and he had to go in [through] the window. The only window that was open was in Dead's room, so he climbed in there and found him with half of his head blown away.' Yet, instead of calling the police, Euronymous exited the house, climbed back into his car and drove straight to the nearest store, where he purchased a disposable camera. Not until he'd filled the entire roll of film with photos of Dead's grisly demise did he finally alert the authorities. Yet – macabre as Euronymous's actions may seem (borne of morbid fascination rather than grief) – it's doubtful Dead would have begrudged his bandmate this chance to pore over his shattered remains, if the letters he wrote in his final days are anything to go by.

What I prefer in movies is when they're . . . of the classical HORROR sort – not 'gore' but ESPECIALLY snuff . . . I like to research how one reacts when watching real deaths, or preferably real corpses (not on video). A friend of mine who works in a morgue has told me that those who used to work with preparing autopsies, after a long day's or night's work have to 'return to reality' before they can just walk out from there to go home.

Not content to document the scene for posterity, Euronymous later boasted of how he'd made off with fragments of Dead's shattered skull – and even feasted on parts of Dead's scattered brain, which he claimed to have consumed 'in a stew of ham and vegetables for the pleasure of eating human flesh'. Though there is no tangible evidence to support Euronymous's cannibalistic claims, it has since been confirmed that the guitarist made off with bone fragments, which he and Hellhammer subsequently used as decorative jewellery. If one accepts that Odinism – the pagan religion of the Vikings which predates Christianity in Norway – is the occult philosophy which underpins black metal, then the duo's actions could be construed as a primitive ritual, through which they paid their respects in death as in life: with coldness, feral opportunism, and a denial of any 'sanctity' or 'feelings' toward life – even the life of a friend and collaborator. And Euronymous certainly didn't show any remorse when subsequently asked to defend his actions: 'It is basically [my] hate to humankind,' he shrugged. 'I have no friends, just the guys I'm allied with. If my girlfriend dies I won't cry; I will miss-use the corpse.'

Necrobutcher says he was the last to hear of Dead's suicide. And the account he received was enough to give him serious misgivings as to Euronymous's motives. 'Øystein called me up the next day . . . and says, "Dead has done something really cool! He killed himself." I thought, "Have you lost it? What do you mean cool?" He says, "Relax, I have photos of everything." I was in shock and grief. He was just thinking how to exploit it. So I told him, "Okay – don't even fucking call me before you destroy those pictures."' However, having had twelve years to ponder his opinion he later told the *Guardian*: 'In retrospect, I think Øystein was shocked by Dead's suicide. And taking the photograph was the only way he could cope with it, like, "If I have to see this, then everybody else has to see it too.'"

Despite having promised both Necrobutcher and Hellhammer that he would destroy the photographs, Euronymous kept hold of the prints – one of which somehow made its way onto the cover of Mayhem's 1995 bootleg live album, *Dawn of the Black Hearts*. Yet – as the bandmate who agreed to take the film to be developed – Hellhammer himself is not exactly beyond reproach. 'They were in colour, real sharp photos,' he said of Euronymous's efforts. 'Dead was sitting half-up, with the shotgun [resting] on his knee. His brain had fallen out and was lying on the bed. Euronymous was taking pictures from above, with details of the skull.' The drummer troublingly disclosed that, before Dead's suicide, he'd had every reason to suspect that the band would soon be searching for a replacement frontman: 'I saw [Dead] earlier that day,' the sticksman later revealed, 'and he told me he'd bought a knife. I said, "Okay." Then he told me it was very sharp, and I said, "Yeah, so what?"'

Though subtlety has never been one of Mayhem's watchwords (live onstage in Bergen, the volatile Necrobutcher made up his mind to hurl a severed sheep's head at one unlucky audience member, simply because 'he wasn't watching the band'), Dead could hardly have been more explicit about his plans for that fateful night in the woods.

'But I didn't know then,' stressed Hellhammer. 'The same night he committed suicide, he was talking to a friend near our house, and they were talking very much about it, about suicide in general, and when he left that night he'd seemed very happy.'

Having acknowledged the *Lords of Chaos* authors' suggestion that Dead's suicide reflected his personality – saying their erstwhile frontman was 'depressed, melancholic, dark, and very special' – the drummer went on to reveal one of the many factors contributing to Dead's chronic melancholia. Despite the darkened vision they shared for Mayhem, Euro's behaviour towards his bandmate was perpetually spiteful.

'I didn't care about them [Dead and Euro] fighting because I would just go to Oslo,' he added. 'I was concerned about the band, but not in the same way Dead was. He was far away from Sweden and didn't know anyone because he wasn't the kind of fellow who could get in touch with people very easily. He just sat in his room and became more and more depressed, and there was a lot of fighting. One time Euronymous was playing some synth music that Dead hated, so he just took his pillow outside, to go to sleep in the woods, and after a while the guitarist went out with a shotgun to shoot some birds or something and Dead was upset because he couldn't sleep out in the woods either because Euronymous was there too, making noises . . .'

Dead's tortured soul had barely been laid to rest at the Österhaninge kyrka (Eastern Haninge church) in Stockholm, when rumours began circulating that he hadn't committed suicide at all, but that Aarseth had grown tired of waiting for poisonous jibes to take effect and taken matters into his own hands. Rather than deny his involvement, however, Euronymous did all he could to fan the flames. Bård Eithun stated: 'I know that afterwards Aarseth heard these rumours that he might have killed [Dead]. I remember Aarseth told me, "Dead did it himself, but it is okay to let people believe that I might have done it because that will create more rumours about Mayhem." That's also why he didn't tell people about how he took the brain pieces and made necklaces and ate part of the brain, because he wanted people to make up their own image of what he might have done. He didn't want to say yes or no about this; he was quite an obscure person. But he did use some stuff from the brain to make necklaces.'

In a 1992 interview for Eithun's fanzine *Orcustus*, Euronymous revealed his own unique perspective on Dead's suicide as simply one more element in Mayhem's ongoing war against lesser musical scenes, from which the band was determined to distance itself whatever the cost: 'We have declared WAR,' he raved. 'Dead died because the trend people have destroyed everything from the old black-metal/death-metal scene. Today "death" metal is something normal, accepted and FUNNY (argh) and we HATE it. It used to be spikes, chains, leather and black clothes, and this was the only thing Dead lived for as he hated this world and everything which lives on it.'

Of course, little did Euronymous realise, when he penned this declaration, that his own integrity would soon be tested. For the next victim to be sacrificed at the altar of 'true' black metal – and reunited with Dead in the blinding white light – would be Euronymous himself.

Jimmy 'The Rev' Sullivan

9 February 1981 - 28 December 2009

Born: James Owen Sullivan

Alter-egos: The Reverend Tholomew Plague (abbreviated to the Rev), Rat Head.

(Pre) occupations: Oozing power, grace and charm, Jimmy was black-clad sticksman with Avenged Sevenfold and singer/pianist with Pinkly Smooth.

In memoriam: 'I tore out of my mother's womb as a bloody, screaming mess causing her as much pain as possible. I'd say that was depraved.' – Jimmy 'the Rev' Sullivan

Deadly sins: According to the reminiscences of his A7x brethren, Jimmy's deadly sins were more mischievous pranks – even if some of them resulted in him spending the occasional night in jail. One such instance occurred in 2006 in Amsterdam, where the Avenged Sevenfold boys were opening for Metallica. Though they'd recently picked up MTV's Best New Artist Award, they were finding Metallica audiences a tough nut to crack. Rather than brooding backstage, they decided to venture into the city's red-light district – a true-life 'Bat Country'-style playground – to blow off their pent-up frustrations. Yet for all the distractions on offer, it was a low-flying pigeon that caught Jimmy's eye. In the most random act of avian abuse since Ozzy Osbourne's bat-bothering heyday, Jimmy took a swipe at the bird, smacking it out of the air as though it were a tennis ball. The hapless creature had barely hit the cobbles when the drummer found himself surrounded by cops who – in bandmate M. Shadows's words – proceeded to 'mace the shit out of him'. Jimmy managed to break free by wriggling out of his jacket, but with his eyes still streaming from the macing, the cops had no trouble catching up with him and hauling his ass off to jail.

This would have been disastrous enough had it happened in LA, never mind on foreign soil. And with the Dutch cops taking a dim view of some drunken tattooed rocker playing softball with the city's wildlife, and refusing to give any intimation as to when their drummer might be released, the problem of keeping to the tour itinerary was magnified sevenfold. Some twelve hours would pass with nary a word, before the Rev called to say he was being released – and clearly ready to pick up where the band had left off. Mischievously, he asked the guys to bring him a slice of pizza – with an added topping of 'shrooms (magic, of course).

As with most rockers out on the road, personal hygiene never featured too high on Jimmy's list of priorities, and by the time he descended from his mushroom cloud – with the tour bus wending its way towards the German border – he still hadn't showered.

With the Dutch authorities having drawn a line under the pigeon incident, Jimmy could have been forgiven for thinking he was in the clear as Avenged Sevenfold took to the stage at the Rock am Ring Festival three days later. But, though he'd escaped the Dutch authorities, the mace had lost none of its potency. And karmic retribution struck midway through Avenged Sevenfold's set when the mace-infused sweat running into his eyes forced him into downing sticks.

On a subsequent European (mis)adventure in 2008, Jimmy fell foul of the law once more for settling Shadows's ongoing dispute with an irate native who'd taken issue with the frontman for some reason. Shadows thought he'd put an end to the matter by telling the guy to get out of his face, but the native followed him into the bar and started on his newly-wed wife, Valerie, who'd come along for the ride. Ordinarily as laidback a guy as one could ever wish to meet, Jimmy clearly didn't take kindly to rudeness to women and sent the native sprawling across the carpet with what Shadows described as a 'superman punch'. The manager called the cops, who, having decided that the tattooed rockers were to blame for the altercation, promptly tried to arrest Jimmy. Once again, rather than go along quietly Jimmy wriggled free by slipping out of his jacket and led the cops a merry dance by dodging between the tables until they finally grabbed him.

Despite all his offstage mishaps, however, Shadows insists that – the Rock am Ring aside – Jimmy never missed a beat with the sticks in his hands. Indeed, the only time the others had cause to reel around to remonstrate with their drummer was when he passed out owing to the guy who operated the smoke machine getting a little over zealous.

𝔉rom cradle to grave: Jimmy's parents, Joe and Barbara, would probably use 'zealous' to describe their son's obsession with beating out a rhythm on anything and everything within the Sullivans' Huntington Beach home – from the table edge to his sister's head. Joe would later say that music was 'like a disease' to Jimmy, and that he began his musical exploration around the same time he started learning his ABCs, while Barbara joked that they decided to buy him his first drum kit because it was cheaper than replacing the furniture. It quickly became apparent that Jimmy was possessed of a rare talent, and Joe and Barbara did what any supportive parents would do by introducing him to a local teacher who could help channel his unbridled energy.

'The music I was listening to was metal, so I started transcribing it. [Then] I started tackling more difficult stuff,' Jimmy told *Drum* magazine in November 2007. 'I started getting into faster stuff: first Pantera, then Slayer – classics like that. Then I started getting into prog – Dream Theatre and Rush. Then I started getting into funk, like Dave Weckl and Terry Bozzio. I tried to pick up as many things as I could from all of those influences.'

> 'The type of music we play, we have fans that are "lifers", just like I'm a lifer for my favourite bands. It's always been like an underground pulse. We just want to get to the people that want to be a part of that core audience.'
>
> – Jimmy 'the Rev' Sullivan

His teacher, however, failed to grasp that Jimmy wasn't marching to the sound of any one drum and informed a bemused Joe and Barbara that he no longer wished to tutor their wayward son. In view of this bombshell, they decided it best to let Jimmy continue under his volition – at least until they found someone more on his wavelength. That someone was Jeanette Wrate, a music professor at Harbor College where Jimmy was a student. Jeannette knew instantly how best to nurture Jimmy's talents, and not only did she induct him into her percussion group, the Looney Booms, she also introduced him to playing such unusual 'instruments' as water bottles and brake drums that she'd unearthed in a local junk yard.

'She was very influential to me being a musician in general,' Jimmy said of his teacher in the November 2007 issue of *Drum* magazine. 'She took me into her percussion ensemble, which kind of ended up being a band, and she taught me about music theory as well as drum theory. She's always pumped me up and never failed to point out to me that she thought I had a lot of potential as a drummer. I think a lot of drum instructors don't really influence you to try to write music; they mainly focus on drumming.'

Needless to say, Wrate wasn't the only female at Harbor College to be impressed by Jimmy's talents – especially his seemingly effortless prowess on the bass fiddle. '[The girls] loved it,' he said in the same interview. 'When you're playing double bass and you're in middle school, no one can believe it. I started in sixth or seventh grade. But no one ever taught me, so I didn't really figure out how to build up your endurance and stamina to just do straight sixteenth-notes as fast as you want until much later, until I was about nineteen or so.'

While still at college, Jimmy joined his first band – a local ska outfit called Suburban Legends – but promptly deserted them in favour of forming the risqué-sounding Pinkly Smooth with childhood buddy Brian Haner Jr., soon to rechristen himself Synyster Gates, with whom Jimmy would be reunited in Avenged Sevenfold. Though Jimmy was raised a Catholic, and had regularly attended Catechism classes, it was Matt Sanders – a.k.a. M. Shadows – who suggested the band's doom-laden new

> 'He didn't live in a world where you could be sad or bummed out.
> He didn't let that part of life exist for him.'
>
> – Brandon Saller (Atreyu)

moniker. The book of Genesis 4:24 states that: 'If Cain shall be avenged sevenfold, truly Lamech seventy and sevenfold.' And, with the rest of his bandmates playing around with stage names, Jimmy wasn't about to miss out on the fun; hence, the ordainment of the Reverend Tholomew Plague (or the Rev for short).

Although Avenged Sevenfold's debut album *Sounding the Seventh Trumpet* was recorded on a shoestring, funded by the band themselves doing what Jimmy described as 'lousy day-job kind of stuff', it was enough to get them noticed by Louis Posen, the owner of Hopeless Records. 'That was step one,' Jimmy acknowledged. 'Getting on that indie label and putting out *Waking the Fallen* got [us] noticed by all the major labels.'

As Jimmy says, it was their second studio album, *Waking the Fallen*, which brought Avenged Sevenfold – or 'A7x' as their fans had taken to calling them – to the attention of Warner Bros. With their new paymasters looking for a quick return on their investment, the band elected on a change in musical direction from metalcore to a more classic hard-rock/heavy-metal sound, as Shadows revealed: 'When we started working on this record [*City of Evil*], we said, "You know what? None of our favourite bands are super-extreme; they just write really good melodic songs that are still heavy."'

City of Evil would prove to be the breakthrough both WB and A7x had been working so hard towards. Following its release in June 2005, the album climbed to number 30 on the *Billboard* chart, propelled in part by the top-ten success of the lead single 'Bat Country', and its accompanying promo video being heavily rotated on MTV. And it was this exposure which ultimately helped to land the band the aforementioned Best New Artist Award (though they could hardly be deemed newcomers) at the 2006 MTV Video Music Awards.

In the aftermath of Jimmy's death, many of his friends told his mom that Jimmy had been the life and soul of every party: until the Rev arrived to preside over the festivities, it wasn't even worth getting started. In short, Jimmy's existence was fast becoming one continuous party (echoing Slash's account of the most hazy time in G N 'R history, when Dr. Jack Daniel's provided consultations every morning). As in Slash's narrative, however, there was a sinister flipside. In hindsight, it's hard to credit that no one within the A7x camp recognised the tell-tale signs that maybe Jimmy's drinking was getting out of hand. But at this point in time, the bandmates were currently cresting the wave of *Avenged Sevenfold* slamming onto the *Billboard* chart at number four, on its way to being named 'Album of the Year' at the 2007 *Kerrang!* Awards. Was the hard-working Rev not entitled to share a bottle backstage with his hero, Vinnie Paul Abbott, provided he remained fully focused onstage?

'Some things get blown up about us; there's always hype out there,' Jimmy told *Drum* magazine when asked about the band's reputation for partying. 'We're pretty much relaxed and doing business all day and then we get to unwind after the show at night. At this point, we're mainly focused on our art and going out there and connecting with as many people as possible because that's the truly rewarding thing of it. We've had our wild spells in the past, and they've been publicised and stuff and we do like to have fun whenever we can, but mostly music is the focus these days.'

While touring eventually becomes a chore for most bands, Jimmy thrived out on the road – especially in foreign climes. 'I love it; I live for it,' he enthused. 'I've never been able to stay in one place and I just like the excitement of getting out there and playing live and the whole lifestyle that comes along with it. Being in new countries every week is just awesome when you take in the foreign culture. When we go to other countries, we always make sure we have a couple days in between shows and get to see the places we want to see. It's perfect – you're on vacation and you're working, too. I'm obsessed with seeing as much of the world as possible. The first few shows are always tough – I've been playing balls-out with my hands for sixteen years. But it's better to play, chill out all day and let the muscles rest and then go all-out the next day.

'One of the major aspects of [Avenged Sevenfold] is the spectacle onstage, the pictures that you see of us, the musicianship and everything that goes into the songs and the music that we play. It's all very real and none of it is contrived in any way, shape, or form and I think a lot of our fans can see that and feel it. When I see that in other artists, it's much more attractive to me, and I want to follow it and be a part of it.'

On 16 April 2009, Avenged Sevenfold performed a version of Guns N' Roses' 'It's So Easy' onstage with Slash at the Nokia Theatre in Los Angeles – it was to be the last time Jimmy would ever be glimpsed on a stage anywhere . . .

Moments of madness: Having taken time out from recording the new album to spend Christmas with their respective loved ones, the band reconvened to celebrate the wedding of their close friend, Avenged Sevenfold's long-serving merchandise dealer, Matt Berry. The reception was something of a tame affair by rock'n'roll standards, with only the bride and groom's families and close friends in attendance, but with things getting more raucous as the evening wore on someone suggested continuing the celebrations at Shadows's place – which was apparently the norm. However, Shadows had an early morning golf date, and wanted a clear head for when he hit the fairway. And, somewhat surprisingly given the occasion, when Shadows announced he was calling it a night, the rest of the band decided to follow suit – with the exception of Jimmy. Of course, no one saw anything unusual in Jimmy staying behind; that the drummer partied as hard as he hit the skins was common knowledge. 'Jimmy was having a great time,' Shadows told *Revolver* for the magazine's July 2010 Avenged Sevenfold special. 'He was playing piano, singing, like people are sitting there and just watching him, and he's getting crazy, big beard and just playing with five drinks around him 'cause that's how he rolled. And, like, six hours later he's dead.'

As with every other band who've lost one of their own, those left behind replayed the tragedy over and over in their minds, desperately seeking reason, closure . . . *something* of significance. And from their collective introspections it appears that Jimmy somehow sensed he wouldn't be finishing the ride with the rest of the guys. Shadows's reasoning comes from a comment Jimmy made about having put all he had left into a song called 'Death' (later renamed 'Fiction') while handing over the demo just three days before his own demise. For his part, Zacky recalled how – after he had repeatedly pleaded with Jimmy to cut down on his drinking – Jimmy had purposely abstained from alcohol at a cocktail party to celebrate the guitarist's birthday as a personal gift. An added twist came later that night when Jimmy called to say he'd left his jacket behind. Zacky suggested he return for it; when Jimmy shrugged off the offer, Zacky said he would drop it off at Jimmy's house sometime the next day, but again Jimmy declined. 'It's like he knew, 'cause I always loved that jacket and he knew that I always loved it,' Zacky said. 'And [the] jacket is sitting on my coat rack right now. I haven't touched it.'

Syn's interpretation is eerier still. 'Yeah, he fucking knew he was gonna be gone before 30,' he insisted. 'He told my dad that he was fucking out. Jimmy told him, "I know two things. I'm gonna be in a famous rock band and I'm gonna die before I'm 30." He told my dad that at fifteen.'

> 'When something like that happens, you can't think straight.
> Just really the most absolute definition of devastation.'
> - Zacky Vengeance

Aside from grasping for precognitive straws, they were racked with guilt at having left Jimmy behind that fateful night, none more so than Shadows. 'If the keg[s] had come to my house, Jimmy wouldn't have been elsewhere doing whatever he was doing,' he told *Kerrang!* that same July. 'He'd have been with me and all of our friends and we'd have been able to help him if anything happened. But I was, like "I'm too tired," and then no one wanted to hang out and he went off on his own did his own thing without any of our close friends and then . . . it was just insane!'

Shadows went on to say that he'd been wrapping up his game and contemplating sinking a couple at the nineteenth hole with his golfing buddies when he got the call that hit him like a five-iron.

Over at Jimmy's place, the morning of Monday, 28 December, would have started like any other with Jimmy sleeping off his hangover from the night before, while his girlfriend Leana Silver (it's rumoured the couple had tied the knot owing to their matching tattoos of each other's names on their ring fingers) fed Mr. Bungle, their beloved Bearded Dragon lizard, and got herself ready for the day. It was only when Jimmy had failed to stir by lunchtime that she knew something was wrong.

The initial autopsy results proved inconclusive, and it would be another six months before toxicology reports established that Jimmy's death was due to 'acute polydrug intoxication due to the combined effects of Oxycodone, Oxymorphone, Diazepam/Nordiazepam and ethanol'. Orange County Deputy Coroner Mitchell Sigal told *Rolling Stone* that Jimmy had also suffered from had cardiomegaly (an enlarged heart), which was marked in the coroner's report as a 'significant condition' that may have played a role in his death.

Unable to face the media, Shadows and the rest of the band issued the following statement to the press: 'It is with great sadness and heavy hearts that we tell you of the passing today of Jimmy "the Rev" Sullivan. Jimmy was not only one of the world's best drummers, but more importantly he was our best friend and brother. Our thoughts and prayers go out to Jimmy's family and we hope that you will respect their privacy during this difficult time. Jimmy you are forever in our hearts. We love you.'

When speaking to *Rolling Stone*, the band's equally-distraught manager, Larry Jacobson said: 'To all of us who loved Jimmy, the only thing relevant about 28 December is that is the night we lost, too soon, a son, brother, friend and one of the most talented artists in the world. Every day, his parents and sisters, and his brothers in Avenged Sevenfold smile at the many memories they have of Jimmy and his fans around the world revel in the musical legacy he left them.'

While learning the official cause of death gave some closure, at the time all anyone could think of was that Jimmy was gone. And such was the bond between the bandmates that Shadows, Zacky, Syn and Johnny were left grief-stricken. Because, as they said in their press release: they hadn't just lost their drummer.

'I grabbed my shit and just headed over to his [Shadows's] house and that was the first day of all of us coming together and crying on each other's shoulders,' Johnny told *Revolver*. 'For two, maybe three straight weeks, it was just very surreal. We didn't want to leave the house and we didn't want to leave each other. We were inconsolable.'

'For fucking days we camped out in each other's houses,' Syn added. 'We basically gutted the living rooms and camped out, literally brought mattresses down and just camped out with, like, twenty or 30 people. Some people who weren't staying the night came in the morning and hung out for the afternoon. Jimmy's family came over and shit.'

Though no one could see it at the time, it was this coming together to share their grief that started the healing process. 'Somebody . . . I don't remember who . . . we were sitting around a table, and somebody had the balls to tell a Jimmy story,' Johnny revealed. 'One of the thousands upon thousands. We all kind of laughed a little bit.'

'After his death, nobody told the same story twice and nobody stopped telling funny stories of this guy for days. The fucking stories just never ended,' Syn added. 'The healing process was just so expedited because everybody just fucking laughed the whole time. We would never want to ever show anybody that time, because when we were together we were just guiltily laughing the whole time, celebrating his life.'

On New Year's Eve, while the rest of the world celebrated the dawning of a new year and a new decade, Shadows, Zacky, Syn, and Johnny went out for a stroll to contemplate a future without Jimmy. 'So we go outside and it's the first blue moon we had in ten years,' Shadows told *Revolver*. 'It looked like an eye looking down on us and I was like, "Fuck man, dude. We need to finish the record for Jimmy," and everyone's like, "Dude, we don't want to talk about it." And I was like, "Dude we have to finish the record. Come on. We have to."'

'We just talked and were like, "Do you want to finish this record?"' Syn added. 'We had been hanging out with Jimmy's family and they were like, "Please you just have to put this out." We were getting all of this feedback from everybody and putting it into perspective. If it was one of us would we want the others to carry on? And the answer was, "Fuck, yes." Jimmy completed the most amazing music, and he left so many amazing lyrics saying goodbye to the world.'

On announcing they were going to carry on and dedicate the album to Jimmy's memory, Jimmy's sister Katie suggested they invite all of her brother's favourite drummers to play on the album. However, just because Jimmy liked a certain drummer's style, didn't necessarily mean that the guy in question would be able to copy his style and technique. And seeing as replicating Jimmy's trademark style was the primary concern, there was only one name in the frame – Dream Theater's Mike Portnoy, whom Jimmy had admired since first picking up the sticks. 'I think having his idol play in his stead . . . I mean, hopefully, [Jimmy's] up there seeing Mike Portnoy's approach to his music,' Syn said following the announcement. 'I think that would just be an incredible gift for him.'

Amen to that.

LEMMY KILMISTER COREY TAYLOR

OZZY OSBOURNE VARG VIKERNE

NIKKI SIXX MARILYN MANSC

DAVE MUSTAINE SLASH

AXL ROSE TRENT REZNOR

TRENT REZNOR AXL ROS

SLASH DAVE MUSTAIN

NIKKI SIXX

MARILYN MANSON

VARG VIKERNES OZZY OSBOUR

COREY TAYLOR LEMMY KILMISTE

Survivors

Lemmy Kilmister

Ozzy Osbourne

Nikki Sixx

Dave Mustaine

Axl Rose

Trent Reznor

Slash

Marilyn Manson

Varg Vikernes

Corey Taylor

Lemmy Kilmister

24 December 1945

Born: Ian Fraser Kilmister

Alter-egos: Lemmy.

(Pre) occupations: Bassist and frontman with Motörhead. 'Until [meeting Lemmy] I'd never met what I'd call a real rock'n'roll hero before. Fuck Elvis and Keith Richards – Lemmy's the king of rock'n'roll. [He's] a living, breathing, drinking and snorting fucking legend! No one else comes close.' – Dave Grohl

Live by this: 'In my life so far, I have discovered there are really only two kinds of people: those who are for you, and those who are against you. Learn to recognise them, for they are often and easily mistaken for each other.' – Lemmy

'Don't try to be famous all your life and then fuckin' bitch when you are. I can never be anonymous – especially when I take so much trouble not to be anonymous, right? It means it's working. I mean, if you're a rock star, you should bloody well be a rock star and stop fuckin' around.' – Lemmy

'I hung out a lot with Lemmy on the [Blizzard of Oz] tour. He's a close friend of the family now. I love that guy. Wherever there's a beer tent in the world, there's Lemmy. But I've never seen that man fall down drunk – even with twenty or 30 pints. I don't know how he does it. I wouldn't be surprised if he outlived me and Keith Richards.' – Ozzy Osbourne

Deadly sins: While Lemmy has attained iconic status – and not only within the metal community – for having the constitution of an ox, which still allows him to knock back a bottle of Jack Daniel's each and every day without collapsing in a puddle, by his own admission he's never been one for engaging in the stereotypical on-the-road madcap behaviour that constitutes deadly sins. 'I never really trashed hotels, 'cause I knew Jimmy Page and he told me how much it cost them the first time they trashed one. Even they were shocked by the bill they got,' he told the *motorhead.ru* website in June 2001. 'I figure it's a waste of fucking money [because] whoever's room it is, is going to get the bill. So, I always go to parties in other people's rooms. We destroyed a room in fucking New Zealand once, but we didn't hurt the room. We just took all the furniture out of it and put it outside in the corridor. And we tipped all these fucking flowerpots over. Pete [Gill], our drummer, then woke up and there was nothing in his room. Nothing, except him on the bed, That was it. No telephone, no lamps, no table.'

It also seemed that casual sex had quickly lost its allure: 'Being in a gang-bang is no longer fun. It was when I was sixteen, and lasted about six months,' Lemmy explained. 'After that I started liking girls properly, and that's a different thing. Then all that orgy stuff didn't really occur to me 'cause I didn't think it was fun anymore because you always felt guilty for somebody.

'Whatever ideas [people have], I've probably seen 'em twice,' he shrugged. 'It isn't a question of the grossest thing; it's the whole thing and then the circus rolling down the road. It's like running away to join the army, it's that era, or running away to join the circus. Then you get in a band, and you get the crew and you get two buses and a truck and it's like this idiot fucking circus. It makes no sense at all logistically. We're all fucking crackers. By the time we've been in it two years, you're gone. After that it's just improvements.'

Of course, this doesn't mean to say that Lemmy has led a chaste life, as we shall see . . .

On a highway to hell? By his own admission, prior to embarking on his personal highway to hell (or to having one hell of a good time, depending on one's perspective), Lemmy – who spent much of his spare time working at a riding school in Anglesey, North Wales, following his mother's remarriage – was contemplating becoming a horse-breeder: an ambition which lasted until he heard Little Richard's 'A-wop-bop-a-loo-lop, a-lop-bam-boom' call to arms blasting out of the radio as an impressionable twelve-year-old in 1957. 'Everybody has his own memories, but I remember when there wasn't any rock'n'roll,' Lemmy said. 'There was nothing, and then there was Elvis and Little Richard and all them people, and that to me was the most exciting thing because you had nothing before it. You had fucking

Frank Sinatra and then a wop-bop a bop it was fucking just wonderful. And you were really part of a secret society then because only about ten people in every city liked it at the beginning . . . and then it got bigger.'

His resolve to abandon the farm for a life spent making equally raucous rock'n'roll was strengthened by the spectacle of his heroes playing live – albeit in grainy black-and-white, through a distant glass screen. 'I watched this TV programme, and there was Eddie Cochran, and Gene Vincent and Cliff Richard. And they were surrounded by screaming women. And I thought: that's the job for me,' he told the *Daily Telegraph* in 2004, before revealing his personal manifesto. 'I don't really admire musicianship per se – as is obvious from my own playing. I don't want to watch four guys

'Don't try to be famous all your life and then fuckin' bitch when you are. I can never be anonymous - especially when I take so much trouble not to be anonymous, right? It means it's working. I mean, if you're a rock star, you should bloody well be a rock star and stop fuckin' around.'

– Lemmy

playing their instruments and looking at their shoes, but I do admire a good act. I want to see people from another planet – know what I mean? I want to see people come down and speak to me for an hour and a half and [then] go away again – in the magic spacecraft. I went to see Gene Vincent, and he was definitely from another planet. And that's as it should be.'

Lemmy himself was born in the decidedly terrestrial setting of Burslem, Stoke-on-Trent, on 24 December 1945 – the first Christmas in six years when the phrase 'peace on earth and goodwill to all men' didn't echo with a hollow ring. His father, however – a former RAF chaplain – didn't view his arrival as much of a gift and had abandoned both Ian and his mother by the time Easter rolled round. 'I met him [my father] when I was 25 [at a pizza place on Earl's Court Road],' he revealed during the same interview with the *Daily Telegraph*. 'Nasty little weasel. He was a concert pianist as well, apparently, but he gave it up because it was too precarious an existence. I'm not like him.

'I suppose it was awkward for him – having walked out on someone for whom you were supposed to be the breadwinner and then not a word for 25 years . . . awkward, sure. But it had been bloody awkward for my mum, bringing me up on her own and providing for my gran as well!' Lemmy said, detailing the meeting in his 2002 autobiography, *White Line Fever*. 'He said, "I'd like to help you in your career, to try and make up for not being a proper father to you." I said, "Look, I'll make it easy for you. I'm in a rock'n'roll band and I need some equipment. So if you can buy me an amplifier and a couple of cabinets we'll call it quits, okay?"'

Kilmister senior appeared unenthused by his estranged son's chosen career, and offered a measured opinion about the music business being 'awfully precarious', before suggesting that Lemmy take lessons. The lessons he had in mind, however, were not musical, but rather driving and sales technique, so that he might become a sales rep. In response, Lemmy almost choked on his invective: 'I said, "Bugger off!" and rose up from the table. He was pretty lucky the reunion pizza hadn't arrived, or it would have become his new hat!' And without so much as a backward glance, Lemmy 'strode back into the fatherless street'.

Though Eddie Cochran and Buddy Holly both undoubtedly played their part, it was seeing girls' reactions when a classmate brought his guitar into school that finally inspired Lemmy to pick up a guitar. 'When I was fifteen, we went on a school trip to Paris and I'd learned "Rock Around the Clock". So I played that for three hours one night, even though I'd nearly cut my forefinger off with a flick-knife that refused to do what it was told. I bled on my guitar, and the chicks thought that was absolutely cool. You know – sort of the equivalent of a Sioux warrior going out into the tall grass and killing a bear with his own hands, I suppose.'

Yet not long after the Paris excursion, Master Kilmister was expelled from school for hitting the headmaster with his own cane after being caught playing truant. Having already chosen anarchy over academia, Lemmy wasn't too despondent at being shown the door. 'I had problems with school right from the start,' he admitted in *White Line Fever*. 'The teachers and I didn't see eye to eye: they wanted me to learn, and I didn't want to. I was always like a fuckin' black hole when it came to maths. You might as well have spoken Swahili to me as try to teach me algebra, so I gave up on it early. I figured I wasn't going to be a mathematician, so I might as well fuck off. I played truant constantly, and that was it from day one, really.'

When he wasn't playing truant or eyeing up the girls at the riding school, Lemmy continued learning the rudiments of guitar – allegedly from repeatedly listening to the Beatles' debut album, *Please Please Me*. He subsequently played in a succession of hopeful bands before jumping several rungs up the ladder with the Blackpool-based Rockin' Vickers, who – after ditching the questionable spelling of 'Rockin' Vicars', and abandoning their mock ecclesiastical stage costumes – managed to secure a recording contract with Decca Records. By the time of Lemmy's arrival midway through 1965, however, they had signed to CBS. By Lemmy's own admission, while the Vickers were huge on the circuit in the north, they failed to build a congregation anywhere south of Birmingham. Despite this, however, they were one of the first British bands to play in the former Yugoslavia, which at the time was sealed off from the West behind the Iron Curtain.

However, though the Vickers released two singles during Lemmy's tenure, rather than persevere with the Blackpool-based outfit, he headed for London, where – while sharing a flat with Noel Redding and Neville Chesters (Jimi Hendrix's bass player and manager, respectively) – he took a job as a roadie with the Jimi Hendrix Experience. And what a mind-altering experience living in the capital at the end of the pseudo-mythical Swinging Sixties proved to be. 'It seemed like all of London was out of their heads back then,' he reflected in *White Line Fever*. 'We used to get high [on acid] and go down to the park and talk to the trees – sometimes the trees would win the argument. We were told that acid didn't work on two consecutive days, but we found that if you double the dose, it does!

'Everybody was taking pills too; uppers, like Blues, Black Beauties and Dexedrine,' he continued. 'It was all pills – I never took powder for years and years. Really, if you're in a band, or especially if you're a roadie, you need to take them things because otherwise you can't keep up with the pace. I don't give a fuck what they say – keep fit, eat your greens, drink juice – fuck off! It's not true! I don't care if you eat two hundred artichokes, you still won't last through a three-month tour, doing a gig a day.'

In 1971, Lemmy got his biggest break to date, joining acid-rockers Hawkwind as a replacement for their departing bassist, Dave Anderson, despite having no previous experience whatsoever with the instrument. He'd gone along to one of their gigs – an open-air show in Notting Hill – hoping that he might be able to get the vacant lead guitar slot after Huw Lloyd-Langton took an unscripted five-year sabbatical from the human race. As they had Anderson's bass and no one to play it, the call went out for a stand-in and Lemmy's mate thought it'd be fun to put him forward. Lemmy could, of course, have pleaded ignorance, but his adventures thus far had taught him to never look a proverbial gift-horse in the mouth, and he simply adapted his rhythm-guitar technique by playing chords on the bass, rather than single notes as was the norm, and as a result he inadvertently stumbled upon what would become his trademark style. By this juncture, Hawkwind had released two studio albums, the second of which, 1971's *In Search of Space*, reached a very respectable number 18 on the UK chart. However, it was their June 1972 single 'Silver Machine' that propelled Hawkwind into the national consciousness, thanks to heavy rotation on daytime radio, coupled with appearances on BBC's flagship music programme *Top of the Pops*.

They didn't enter the spotlight willingly, however, because while it's usually the Sex Pistols and the Clash who are credited with being the first bands to refuse to appear on *Top of the Pops*, Hawkwind – as every right-minded musician should have done – also refused to pander to the BBC's stringent rules, whereby they were expected to mime to a pre-recorded backing track. Their argument wasn't without foundation, because while the BBC insisted that artists mime on *Top of the Pops*, those bands invited to appear on *The Old Grey Whistle Test* – another BBC show – could perform live in the studio. However, with their record label pressing them to appear on the programme, a compromise of sorts was reached: a clip of the band performing the song live on stage at the Dunstable Civic Hall was screened, with the single dubbed over it.

It was during this period that Lemmy 'really came out of any shell I may have been in, stage-wise', and on any given night he'd take to the stage with a mixed bag of uppers and downers rattling around his insides. The most memorable occasion, perhaps, was the night Hawkwind played at the Roundhouse in Chalk Farm on 13 February 1972, when – having been up for three days straight speeding his nuts off – he 'whacked down' a near-lethal concoction of Dexedrine, Mandrax, LSD, and Black Bombers just before the show, and had to have the roadies hook his boot-heels onto the back of the stage and strap his bass to his rigid frame. Yet, despite his inability to move anything other than his hands, Lemmy says it was one of the best shows Hawkwind ever played.

Lemmy's predisposition for consuming pills and potions, coupled with his hitherto unrealised talent for songwriting, began to ruffle more than a few feathers in the Hawkwind nest, and the rest of the band waited patiently for an opportunity to oust the usurper in their midst. Such an opportunity came during a US tour in May 1975, when Lemmy was arrested at the Canadian border, caught in possession of what the customs authorities believed to be cocaine. (What Lemmy didn't find out until it was too late was that in order to avoid being hassled by Canadian border patrols it was best to go over the bridge rather than under the tunnel, where the mole-like Mounties were at their most officious. However, with his lesson learnt, and his fingers burnt, he never repeated his mistake.)

'We had just played Detroit, and we left early the next morning for Toronto,' Lemmy subsequently explained. 'Some chick at the show had given me some pills and I had about a gram of amphetamine sulphate [speed]. 'Cause it was early and I wasn't thinking, I stuffed my contraband down my pants. Not a good idea – they searched us to the skin, and the cops got my stash.' The results of the roadside test carried out on the baggie of white powder found secreted under Lemmy's ball sack came back positive, and Lemmy was duly charged with attempting to smuggle cocaine into Canada and hauled off to jail. However, when the drug was subsequently confirmed to be amphetamine sulphate rather than cocaine, the case was thrown out as a 'wrongful charge'. Though the band paid for his flight to Toronto (where he arrived at the venue with minutes to spare), they had spent the interim sharpening their daggers, preparing to plunge the blades into their bandmate's back once the stage lights had sufficiently dimmed.

'I was fired [for] doing the wrong drugs,' he reasoned in *White Line Fever*. 'If I'd been caught with acid, those guys would have all rallied around me. I think even if I'd been doing heroin, it would have been better for them. All I have to say [about speed] is that at least [it] keeps you functional. Why else did they give it to housewives for all those years? . . . It's the only drug I've found that I can get on with, and I've tried them all – except smack and morphine: I've never fixed anything.'

Unlike the vast majority of his *Cemetery Gates* contemporaries, whose all-consuming dependencies on drink and drugs either derailed their careers, or claimed their lives, Lemmy – rather pragmatically, it has to be said – viewed his drug intake simply as a means to a professional end, in that he experimented with a variety of pills and powders until hitting upon the one that helped him fulfil his day-to-day commitments. However, while he was able to remain the master of his medicines, not everyone close to him was possessed of similar restraint. And as with Layne Staley, whose fiancée Demri Parrott succumbed to 'secondary complications' caused by her drug abuse, Lemmy suffered the heartache of losing his girlfriend, Susan Bennett, to heroin sometime in 1973. Shortly after returning from Beirut, where she'd picked up her habit while working as a dancer, she drowned in the bath after shooting up. She was just nineteen years old. (Lemmy dedicated *White Line Fever* to her, and said that she 'might have been the one'.)

By his own admission – even prior to Sue's untimely death – Lemmy had never been keen on trying heroin, simply because he'd seen first hand what it did to people. 'I'd see people turn into grovelling dogs on it. I wasn't gonna do anything that made you that desperate, especially considering how much it costs, and I was right. The thing with junkies is, they have to want to stop and you can't make them if they don't. Needles are evil. That's an addiction in itself.'

It is, of course, for his 37-year (and counting) tenure fronting Motörhead that Lemmy is best known. He'd originally intended to call his new outfit 'Bastard', but after a rethink instead opted for 'Motorhead' – the title of the last song he wrote with Hawkwind – in order to avoid falling foul of Britain's then draconian censorship laws. (The umlaut over the second 'o' was added later.) The founding line-up included former Pink Fairies

'I hung out a lot with Lemmy on the [Blizzard of Oz] tour. He's a close friend of the family now. I love that guy. Wherever there's a beer tent in the world, there's Lemmy. But I've never seen that man fall down drunk - even with twenty or thirty pints. I don't know how he does it. I wouldn't be surprised if he outlived me and Keith Richards.'
- Ozzy Osbourne

guitarist Larry Wallis, and drummer Lucas Fox. Lemmy formed the band with a single, oft-vocalised aim to 'concentrate on making fast, raucous, speed-freak rock'n'roll, which will be so loud that if we move in next-door to you . . . your lawn will die.'

However, the only thing that appeared to be in any danger of dying was Lemmy's career, because the UK music media's fascination with punk rock meant that Motörhead's efforts were continually ignored by their record label, United Artists. By the long, hot summer of 1976, Wallis and Fox had been replaced by 'Fast' Eddie Clarke and Phil 'Philthy Animal' Taylor, and – realising that UA weren't about to get their finger out anytime soon – the band's manager Tony Secunda set about testing the water with alternative labels, securing his charges a one-off single deal with the independent Stiff Records. However, on hearing of the Stiff single – a cover of Eddie Holland's 1963 US hit 'Leaving Here', coupled with 'White Line Fever' – UA stepped in and wrapped the single up in so much red tape that Stiff were forced to shelve it. However, thanks to subsequent licensing deals with Skydog (France) and Blitz Records (Sweden), fans were at least able to get hold of the single on import.

'By this point, the morale of the band was getting pretty low; all our efforts were getting us nowhere,' Lemmy reflected. 'We were starving, living in squats and nothing was happening. I was well prepared to keep going, but Phil and Eddie wanted to give it up. It wasn't their band and they didn't have the commitment I did. So finally in April [1977], after much debate, we decided to do a goodbye show at the Marquee in London and call it a day.'

And that one last burn-out at the Marquee might well have been it had Lemmy not invited Ted Carroll – the head of Chiswick Records – to bring along his portable studio and record the show for posterity. It was here that fate stepped in to lend a helping hand, because Carroll was – for one reason or another – unable to get his equipment to the legendary Wardour Street venue, and by way of compensation he offered the band two days in Escape Studios to record a single.

Lemmy, however, was still intent on leaving something of a longer legacy, and the band barrelled their way through thirteen songs – one of which was the highly-appropriate 'White Line Fever'. The resulting eponymously titled album – which opened with aforementioned 'Motorhead' – was released on the Chiswick label in August 1977, but with punk rock now dominating the national consciousness during the Queen's Silver Jubilee year, the disc didn't make much of an indent on the UK charts.

Ongoing problems with Tony Secunda (who would soon be dismissed), coupled with injuries sustained while out supporting the album on the ironically-titled Beyond the Threshold of Pain Tour, meant that Motörhead's engine coughed and spluttered its way into 1978. Once again, the lack of forward motion began to eat away at Eddie and Phil's resolve, and the duo joined forces with ex-Heartbreaker Billy Rath's ad hoc outfit, the Muggers. Again, that might have sounded Motörhead's death knell had it not been for Secunda's predecessor, Doug Smith, returning to tuck the trio under his protective wing and secure them a second one-off single deal with Bronze Records.

Though the resulting single – a souped-up version of 'Louie Louie', which was written and originally recorded by Richard Berry in 1957, but made famous by the Kingsmen six years later – stalled on the UK chart at number 68, it caught the attention of John Peel, who invited Motörhead to record a live session, and also saw them make their *Top of the Pops* debut. This led to Chiswick reissuing the *Motörhead* album through EMI, which in turn led to Bronze extending the contract and sending the band into Roundhouse Studios. The resulting *Overkill* album and its lead single of the same name both cracked the UK charts. Motörhead were finally on their way, and the subsequent Bronze albums, *Bomber*, *Ace of Spades*, *Iron Fist*, and *Another Perfect Day* – all of which were released within a four-year period – brought the band both national and international acclaim.

Now that Lemmy was flush with success, he decided it was high time he flushed the excess from his body by following Keith Richards's example and having his blood changed – the logic being that a full infusion of untainted fresh blood would save his body from the stress of undergoing detoxification. However, on receiving the blood test results, his bemused doctor informed him that pure blood would kill him. Indeed, the level of toxins was so high that he couldn't even give blood should he so desire. 'In other words,' he recently explained, 'what's normal for me is deadly to another human. And what's normal for other humans is deadly to me – which is okay with me. I suppose that means I've made medical history of some sort.'

Lemmy also set a precedent with his admission – made during the Channel Four documentary, *Motörhead: Live Fast, Die Old*, which was first broadcast in August 2005 – that he has drunk a bottle of Jack Daniel's each and every day since he was 30. Despite his swarthy, gnarled countenance, Lemmy apparently stands as a worthy rival to Warren Beatty and Bill Wyman in the Lothario stakes, for in *Motörhead: Live Fast, Die Old* it was also claimed that the bed-hopping bassist had slept with 2,000 women, while *Maxim* magazine placed him at number eight in their top ten of 'Living Sex Legends'. In the documentary, Lemmy modestly shrugged off the statistics before making the aforementioned confession that his introduction to the fairer sex came early, after seeing girls' reactions when a classmate brought a guitar into school. Though Lemmy's mum had owned a guitar for years, he'd never shown any interest in the instrument before that point. And the very next morning he sauntered into class and, in his own words, found himself 'surrounded by chicks'.

Moments of madness: Those who've followed Lemmy's career will each have pondered how it is that – despite the madness and debauchery that's engulfed him over the years – he's still a living, breathing survivor, rather than a decaying *Cemetery Gates* saint. Indeed, in *White Line Fever*, Lemmy himself questions why he never became a drug fatality – especially during his time with Hawkwind, when 'drugs were our common denominator [and] the only way we freaks could tell if somebody was one of us'.

One particularly close curtain call came during the summer of 1971 – which Lemmy says he can't remember but will never forget – when he and the band's driver, 'John the Bog', were stopped by a carload of cops who suspected that the van's two shady-looking occupants were up to no good. This assumption was correct: Lemmy had been in the process of divvying up a hundred Blues ('pills which had speed with downer mixed in them'). Yet the law-enforcers failed to think anything awry when Lemmy and John stood swaying by the roadside, drooling blue gunk after hurriedly stuffing the pills down their throats in order to dispose of the evidence. On returning to the house he shared with the rest of the band, the effect of fifty Blues simultaneously working their mind-altering magic sucked Lemmy down into a deep sleep. So deep in fact, that his friends initially feared they'd be burying their bassist.

Another brush with the law came when he and a colleague called Graham Mitchell (who would later serve as Motörhead's tour manager) were pounced upon by two cops as they came out of the Speakeasy, the legendary mid-seventies London watering hole favoured by musicians. Lemmy had half a gram of speed on him and was about to eat the incriminating evidence when one of the cops grabbed the wrapper from his hand. But once again the boys in blue were slow off the mark and didn't comprehend the reality of the situation – even with a dusting of suspect white powder covering the upper half of their tunics.

By his own admission, drugs will probably feature in Lemmy's life until the day he looks the grim reaper in the eye and offers him a slug of Jack. Because as he sees it, he's more or less still doing what he did when he first started out – and if something works, why try to fix it? He argued that drug use only becomes too much when the drug in question starts to play you, instead of you playing it.

'If you're doing dope and you start to spend all your time looking for more dope then that's wrong. That's a joke then, because your music suffers, your love life suffers, your self-respect suffers. If you want some advice from someone that knows – and believe me I know – there is only one drug that kills people and that's heroin and occasionally downers. But you have to be a real accident-prone case to die on downers. But speed never killed anybody, coke never killed anybody. Nothing's killed anybody except heroin and that kills everybody. So no matter how elegantly wasted you get, or how cool it seems to be . . . it's not. It's like dying from an embolism in a toilet in the middle of the night and getting found that way. It's not very elegant. Fuck it, you know. But don't die ashamed. Don't ever lie on your deathbed and think, "That was shit." Don't do that, because that's the worst . . .'

OZZY OSBOURNE

3 December 1948

Born: John Michael Osbourne

Alter-egos: Ozzy, Prince of Darkness, Godfather of Heavy Metal.

(Pre) occupations: The scourge of winged creatures everywhere, the Ozz man once lamented, 'I don't even know who Ozzy is,' and such confusion is entirely understandable. Once upon a time, he was Black Sabbath's own mad-as-a-March-Hare-on-methadone frontman and lyricist. But in his other eight lives, he's been a slaughterhouse worker, a solo artist, the bemused star of his own reality TV show, a proud father, a syringe-toting, white-coat-wearing agony aunt and a Hollywood actor (if playing himself in Adam Sandler's crazed theological romp, *Little Nicky*, counts as acting).

Live by this: 'I have a saying, "Never judge a book by its cover." I say that because I don't even know who Ozzy is. I wake up a new person every day. But if you've got a fantasy of Ozzy, who am I to say? I mean, if you think I sleep upside-down in the rafters and fly around at night and bite people's throats out, then that's your thing. But I can tell you now, all I ever wanted was for people to come to my concerts and have a good time. I don't want anyone to harm themselves in any way, shape or form and my intentions are good, whether people want to believe it or not. I'm not going to suddenly become a Jesus freak or anything. But I do have my beliefs and my beliefs are certainly not satanic.' – Ozzy Osbourne

'I know exactly how close I've come. The edge is always closer than you think – especially when you don't mean to jump.' – Ozzy Osbourne

Deadly sins: While there are many pretenders, and several worthy contenders, examined within these pages, Ozzy is undoubtedly the one true Demigod of Metal Debauchery. In fact, there's a good argument for a photo of Ozzy to be placed under the word 'depravity' in the Oxford

Dictionary, because he didn't so much walk on the wild side as move in and call it home. And while it be may be a hackneyed rock'n'roll cliché, it truly is a miracle that he's still walking amongst us. For while Lemmy's blood has been deemed too toxic for transfusion, and Nikki Sixx can boast having heard his obituary on the radio, such sagas – though harrowing in their own right – pale into insignificance compared with Ozzy's madcap antics. Hell, he's spilt more booze and coke than most rockers claim to have slurped or snorted. And this is why Nikki went on record in *The Dirt* to acknowledge Ozzy's undisputed divinity in the drug stakes.

The accolade is well deserved, because while any musician who's been out on the road for any length of time will admit to having engaged in *Spinal Tap*-esque behaviour at some point or other, Ozzy saw so much of himself in the 1984 movie's storyline that he thought Spinal Tap were an actual band, and probably tried booking them for the Barking at the Moon Tour. And while he might be justified in having a 'bee up his arse' about Black Sabbath being credited with inventing heavy metal, there's no getting away from the fact that the band set the satanic template for the Scandinavian black and death metal scenes.

The list of Ozzy's anarchic anecdotes is, of course, endless, but the two incidents that have gone down in heavy-metal folklore involved a bat and bird. The bird-biting incident occurred in 1981 at CBS' Century City HQ in Los Angeles. Ozzy's wife and manager, Sharon, had brought along a crate of doves to the meeting, and the intention was for Ozzy to make a good impression by releasing the birds as a gesture of peace between himself and his label bosses, so that he'd be free to get on with his solo career without too much corporate interference. But by his own admission, he'd been drinking for two days straight, and on realising that the CBS suits were more excited about the imminent arrival of Adam Ant, he decided to make an impression no one present was ever likely to forget by grabbing one of the doves from the basket and ripping the hapless creature's head off with his teeth before spitting it out. 'The dove's head landed on the PR chick's lap in a splatter of blood,' Ozzy recalled. 'Then I threw the carcass onto the table and watched it twitch. The bird had shit itself when I bit into its neck, and the stuff had gone everywhere. The PR chick's dress was flecked with this nasty brown and white goo.'

The following year, on 20 January 1982, whilst performing at the Veteran's Memorial Auditorium in Des Moines, Iowa, during the Diary of a Madman Tour, he got up to more decapitation when he bit the head off the aforementioned bat, which a fan had thrown up onto the stage.

Ozzy initially thought it was a toy, and only realised his mistake when his mouth 'was instantly full of this warm, gloopy liquid, with the worst aftertaste you could ever imagine'. *Rolling Stone* magazine – which, in 2004, would rank the bat-eating incident at number two on their 'Rock's Wildest Myths' list – stated that the fan in question had believed the bat to be dead, despite Ozzy claiming otherwise in the booklet that accompanied the 2002 reissue of *Diary of a Madman*: 'I got rabies shots for biting the head off a bat, but that's okay – the bat had to get Ozzy shots.'

On a highway to hell? On the flyleaf of the jacket for his brilliant 2009 autobiography, *I Am Ozzy*, Ozzy gives the reader a taster of the story to come by saying that every day of his life has been an event – be it quaffing lethal booze and drug cocktails, suicidal overdoses, STDs, or surviving a direct hit by a plane. By his own admission, he's 'done some bad things in my time', having been irresistibly drawn to his 'dark side'.

But he's equally quick to point out that he isn't the devil. He's 'just John Osbourne: a working-class kid from Aston, who quit his job in the factory and went looking for a good time' – regardless of where his journey took him. Though Ozzy has been clean for years, he knows the highway to hell like the OZZY tattoo on the knuckles of his left hand. Indeed, he is a death-defying phenomenon. Rock'n'roll's graveyard is littered with the bones of those who imbibed a mere fraction of Ozzy's prodigious 40-year intake. Some have unkindly said that Ozzy is what happens when you don't die a drug-debauched death, but despite having abused his body with a plethora of pharmaceutical substances for four decades, he is in remarkably good health. Indeed, his involuntary shudders have nothing to do with his past lifestyle, but are in fact a symptom of Parkin Syndrome, from which he suffers.

Somewhat surprisingly, given Ozzy's subsequent penchant for the darker side of rock, his first musical passion was the Beatles, after he heard their 1963 single 'She Loves You' while at secondary school. 'When I heard "She Loves You", my world went up like a shooting star,' he later revealed. 'It was a divine experience. The planets changed. I used to fantasise that Paul McCartney would marry my sister.' Aside from raving about the Fab Four, however, school wasn't much fun for Ozzy, as he suffered from dyslexia. Today, kids with dyslexia can expect help at school, whereas back in Ozzy's day little was known about the disability – indeed, many of his teachers would probably have struggled to spell dyslexia, let alone recognise the symptoms – and as a result they treated him as though he was sub-normal.

On leaving school aged fifteen with little in the way of qualifications, Ozzy – his name now tattooed across the knuckles of his left hand – drifted aimlessly in and around his native Aston, moving from one menial, low-paid job to another. He eventually turned to crime as a means of getting some easy money. However, his career as a master criminal didn't really progress very far, as he was collared for burglarising a clothes shop on a neighbouring street and duly fined £40. They say that crime doesn't pay, and Ozzy found out the hard way that it pays even less if one fails to shell out the requisite fine, and as a result he spent six weeks repenting at leisure in Winson Green Prison.

It's generally accepted that the average working-class British youth has two viable escape routes from a life of mundane servitude – sport and rock'n'roll. And as Ozzy wasn't much of an athlete, shortly after his release from prison he headed down to the Bullring – the name given to Birmingham's circular shopping mall – and paid a nominal fee to have his ad placed in the window of Ringway Music.

'It was a fucking awesome ad: "OZZY ZIG NEEDS A GIG", it said in felt-tip capital letters,' he said in *I Am Ozzy*. 'Underneath I'd written, "Experienced frontman, owns own PA system," and then I'd put the address (14 Lodge Street) where I could be reached between six and nine on weeknights.' Having paid good money of his own for the ad – and with John Osbourne Sr. having taken out a £250 loan to buy his son the aforementioned 50 watt Vox PA – Ozzy was obviously hoping and praying for some kind of response, but even he was taken aback when he peered through the curtains after hearing a knock at the door and saw 'a big-nosed bloke with long hair and a moustache standing on the doorstep. He looked like a cross between Guy Fawkes and Jesus of Nazareth . . . wearing velvet trousers.'

'Guy Nazareth' was, of course, future Black Sabbath bassist and lyricist Terry 'Geezer' Butler, whose hippie-trippy outfit, Rare Breed, were in need of a singer, and – despite Ozzy looking like he'd wrestled a lawnmower, having cropped his hair during one of his 'mod phases' – Geezer offered him the gig. But while Geezer was well-known on the 'Brumbeat' scene, and counted a pre-Led Zeppelin Robert Plant as one of his friends, Rare Breed were crap – and both he and Ozzy were painfully aware of the fact. Having shit himself onstage at the Birmingham Fire Station's Christmas Party – the only Rare Breed gig he can remember – Ozzy had decided to abandon his dreams of emulating the Beatles, but when he announced his intention to quit the band, Geezer simply shrugged and told Ozzy that he was thinking the same thing, as he'd been offered a promotion at the accountancy firm where he worked. And that, Ozzy thought, was that.

Several miserable months passed by in 'Self-Pity City' – as Ozzy subsequently described his life at that time – when there came another late-night knock at his front door. As he'd long since informed the owner of Ringway Music to take down his ad, he was stunned to find two unassuming long-haired types standing within the shadow of the streetlamp, there to see Ozzy Zig. Ozzy recognised one of the long-hairs straight away. It was Tony Iommi, who'd been in the year above him at school. Ozzy remembered that Tony had brought his electric guitar into school one day to impress the girls, and had since become something of a legend on the local music scene. Anyone who was anyone on the scene wanted to be in a band with Tony Iommi – even though he'd recently sliced off the tips of his right-hand middle and ring fingers in an accident at work.

'I know exactly how close I've come. The edge is always closer than you think - especially when you don't mean to jump.'
- Ozzy Osbourne

Tony would overcome this career-threatening deficiency by moulding thimble-tip pads for his injured fingers out of a melted-down Fairy Liquid bottle. And having to learn to play again from scratch, with no feeling whatsoever in the two injured fingers, would inadvertently lead to him developing a style that no one has ever been able to copy.

Unfortunately for Ozzy, Tony's schoolyard memories of Ozzy were somewhat less favourable, and – recognising Ozzy Zig's true identity – he turned on his heel ready to leave. Thankfully, however, Tony's drummer colleague, Bill Ward, who hadn't met Ozzy until that night, was savvy enough to recognise that unseen forces were at play, and insisted that they give him a chance. Tony relented – possibly because, unlike the vast majority of wannabe singers, Ozzy had his own PA. Whatever the reason, Ozzy Zig had landed himself another gig, and the trio began planning their next moves. It was Ozzy, of course, who suggested the rhythm guitar-playing Geezer Butler as a possible bassist, and though both Tony and Bill were already aware of Geezer, they left it to Ozzy to tempt him to switch from six strings to four. And having convinced Geezer that playing the bass was infinitely more exciting than accountancy, Ozzy who came up with 'Polka Tulk Blues Band' for a band name, having espied a then well-known brand of talcum powder in his mother's bathroom, which came in tins decorated with black and white polka dots.

Of course, anyone parting with their hard-earned cash to watch the Polka Tulk Blues Band would do so expecting them to play blues music. And so, having decided to play 'dirty, heavy, Deep South blues', they augmented their sound by bringing in a sax player and a guitarist who could play bottleneck. Though they got as far as playing a handful of gigs as a six-piece, the new recruits never really gelled and the group went back to being a quartet, and back to the drawing board – not only regarding their future direction, but also their name. With the obvious exception of Ozzy, the others thought Polka Tulk Blues Band a bit of a mouthful, and after much haggling, they settled on Bill Ward's suggestion of 'Earth'.

> ### 'We must have snorted about six or seven grams each before I heard the tapping noise outside the door.'
> #### - Ozzy Osbourne

Ozzy says that he, Tony, Geezer and Bill were all incredibly single-minded, but it was going to take more than dogged determination to get a break, and they didn't need Geezer's accountancy skills to see that playing two-hour sets for a couple of quid split four ways was financial suicide. It was Tony who hit upon the idea of perusing the *NME*'s gig guide to see which bands were coming to the West Midlands, and then waiting outside the venue in question with their gear loaded in the back of the van on the off-chance that the headliners wouldn't show up, and then offer to take their place. The odds of such an occurrence were remote, but it's said that fortune favours the brave – and so, one evening, Earth found themselves occupying the stage reserved for blues-rockers Jethro Tull, who had recently released their debut album, *This Was*, via Island Records.

Jethro Tull's bug-eyed, flute-playing frontman, Ian Anderson, was already something of a celebrity on the rock'n'roll circuit – if only for his habit of dressing like a court jester and playing while standing on one leg. Though the crowd were naturally miffed when they realised that the band standing onstage didn't resemble the one on the *This Was* album cover, they were soon won over by the music. Even Ian Anderson – who'd hitchhiked to the venue after abandoning Tull's broken-down tour bus somewhere on the M6 – was suitably impressed by their eleventh-hour stand-ins. So impressed, in fact, that when his lead guitarist, Mick

Abrahams, quit the band shortly before Tull were set to play with the Rolling Stones at Wembley, he offered Tony the gig. And though Earth were now spinning on their own axis, it was a gig Tony couldn't refuse.

'In [December] 1968, John Osbourne was an up-and-coming rock'n'roll star,' Ozzy later revealed. 'I would say in this fake movie-announcer voice as I wondered around the house. In 1969, he was an up-and-coming binman.' But of course, Ozzy never did find out how he might've fared ridding Aston of its rubbish, because Tony – despite being part of 'The Rolling Stones Rock'n'Roll Circus' and playing on the same bill as John Lennon – would quit Jethro Tull after just four days. All Tony asked of Ozzy, Geezer and Bill was that they stop fucking around and get serious by writing their own material. All Ozzy asked in return was that if they were going to get serious then they needed to think up a better name . . .

While jamming ideas for songs during rehearsals, Tony had noticed that whenever the local cinema happened to be screening a horror film, the queues would run right around the block, and suggested they write something that 'sounded evil'. Ozzy and Bill duly obliged by penning a set of lyrics about 'a bloke who sees a figure in black coming to take him off to the lake of fire', which Tony then put to an eerie riff based around the tritone – an interval of three whole tones that has always been synonymous with the devil. 'Apparently churches banned it from being used in religious music during the Middle Ages because it scared the crap out of people,' Ozzy subsequently explained. 'The organist would start to play it and everyone would run away 'cause they thought the devil was going to pop up from behind the altar. As for the title of the song, it was Geezer who came up with that. He got it from a Boris Karloff film that had been out for a while. I don't think Geezer had ever seen the film, to be honest with you. I certainly hadn't.'

The film in question was the 1963 Italian horror film *I tre volti della paura* [*The Three Faces of Fear*], directed by Mario Bava and starring Michèle Mercier opposite Karloff. It was renamed *Black Sabbath* for American audiences. Despite Ozzy's objections, at the time they penned the song that was to change their lives, they were still playing as Earth. And it was only after they inadvertently discovered another band with the same name orbiting the c-list gig circuit that Black Sabbath became a living entity.

'The name "Black Sabbath" made a big difference, I think,' Ozzy reflected in his book. 'At the time there was an occult author called Dennis Wheatley whose books were all over the bestseller lists; Hammer Horror films were doing massive business at the cinema, and the

[Charles] Manson murders were all over the telly, so anything with a "dark" edge was in big demand. Don't get me wrong, I'm sure we could've done it on the strength of the music alone. But sometimes, when it comes to getting a [record] deal, all these little things have to come together at the right time.'

As Ozzy openly admits, the band's taste for drugs was fast taking hold – and he still remembers the first time he got up close to a mirror without thought for checking his reflection as though it were yesterday. The day in question came in early 1971, when Sabbath were playing a show in Denver, Colorado, with a blues-rock outfit called Mountain. 'When you come from Aston and you fall in love with cocaine,' Ozzy reflected, 'you *remember* when you started – it's like having your first fuck!' He was soon living the hedonistic life to the max, blithely staggering along the edge of the abyss with scant regard for the fact that there was no safety net. Even his ill-fated first marriage to Thelma Riley, and subsequent fatherhood, failed to slow him down, as within twelve months of developing white line fever he was 'putting so much of the stuff up my nose that I had to smoke a bag of dope every day just to stop my heart from exploding'.

While recording Sabbath's fourth album (which the boys were seriously contemplating calling *Snowblind* in honour of their newfound love for the white stuff), Ozzy's heart came dangerously close to exploding from other causes. Back at the Bel Air mansion Sabbath were using as a base, Ozzy was cutting up his first line of the day when he heard the distant wail of a police siren, growing ominously louder until it finally cut through the dope-induced fug clouding his brain. Despite the urgency of the situation (the band were in possession of enough coke to stage the Winter Olympics), Ozzy was slow to react, and by the time he'd dragged his carcass off the couch, Tony, Geezer and Bill had already bolted for the nearby Hollywood Hills, leaving him and an American roadie called Frank to dispose of the incriminating evidence.

On hearing the cops pound the door, Ozzy and Frank desperately began dumping the dope into the sink and down the toilet, only to cause an overflow in the system. With the cops showing little sign of leaving, Ozzy and Frank dropped to their knees, cracked open a couple of the coke vials, and pressed their noses to the tiles. 'We must have snorted about six or seven grams each before I heard the tapping noise outside the door,' Ozzy recalled. 'Then I heard the front door open and a woman's voice. She was speaking in Spanish. [It was] the maid! The maid was letting in the cops. *Fuck!* I broke open another vial and put my nose to the floor again.' At the mention of the term 'AC', Ozzy's tripped-out heart can only have begun beating faster still – with the Acting Commissioner of the LAPD leading the raid, he'd be lucky to see Birmingham this side of the millennium. Thankfully, however, the 'AC' in question was the mansion's air-conditioning system, the control switch of which was located next to the emergency call button that was linked to the local police station. On hearing the cops depart, Ozzy collapsed to the floor, making a mental note to show everyone how to activate the air conditioning.

Ozzy would, of course, fall foul of the law a decade later for relieving himself against a 'crumbly old wall' while wandering the streets of San Antonio, Texas – where he was due to perform later that evening – wearing one of Sharon's dresses and clutching a bottle of Courvoisier brandy. What Ozzy failed to realise in his inebriated state was that the crumbling wall in question happened to belong to the chapel of the Alamo

> 'I got rabies shots for biting the head off a bat, but that's okay
> - the bat had to get Ozzy shots.'
> - Ozzy Osbourne

mission, which, some 145 years earlier, had been the site of the legendary battle that had proved a pivotal event in Texas gaining independence from Mexico. Needless to say, the cops didn't take kindly to his pissing on the icon of Texan independence, and they proceeded to toss him in jail without further ado. Though he was allowed to play that night's show, he was officially banned from ever entering San Antonio again. The ban would remain in place until 1991, when Ozzy apologised in public and donated $10,000 to the Daughters of the Republic of Texas, who serve as the official caretakers of the Alamo.

Somewhat ironically, given that the pots were in no position to question the kettle, it was Ozzy's drug habit that led to him being sacked from Sabbath in April 1979. Though it was Bill who broke the news during rehearsals in LA, Ozzy knew Tony was behind the decision, as he hadn't forgiven Ozzy for quitting the band the previous year to work on what would become *Blizzard of Oz*. 'Firing me for being fucked up was hypocritical bullshit,' he said in *I Am Ozzy*. 'We were *all* fucked up. If you're stoned and I'm stoned, and you're telling me that I'm fired because I'm stoned – how can that fucking be? Because I'm slightly more stoned than you are?'

Still reeling from the news, Ozzy booked into the Le Parc Hotel in

West Hollywood. Determined to lock himself away from the world, he embarked upon a Lennon-esque lost weekend which stretched to three whole months. By his own admission, he would have killed himself had it not been for Sharon – whose father Don Arden was the manager of Black Sabbath – and her offer of guidance. Indeed, Sharon would be the one to help him launch his subsequent solo career. Of course, Sharon's involvement with Black Sabbath didn't end with her offering to steer Ozzy's rudderless ship, as it was she who suggested Ronnie James Dio as Ozzy's replacement in the band. And though Ozzy has since admitted to feeling betrayed by his former bandmates, he was astute enough to recognise his sacking as a blessing in disguise, or more precisely 'the shove up the arse I needed'.

While Ozzy's suicidal twelve-week binge shows just how deeply the sacking affected him in the short-term, the fact that he threw away his

'I have a saying, "Never judge a book by its cover." I say that because I don't even know who Ozzy is. I wake up a new person every day. But if you've got a fantasy of Ozzy, who am I to say?'

- Ozzy Osbourne

dealer's number and popped the stopper back in the bottle long enough to allow Sharon to coax him back from the precipice goes some way in revealing his self-belief and strength of character. For whereas more morose souls such as Layne Staley, Axl Rose, Trent Reznor, and Pete Steele would have probably run for the hills, Ozzy simply dusted himself off and pondered his options. After all, just because his offstage habits had been deemed excessive by Tony and Geezer, that didn't mean Sabbath's legion of fans had given up on him. And as everyone knows, it doesn't matter how talented the guitarist, drummer, or bassist might be – it's the singer who steals the show.

Moments of madness: On tour with Mötley Crüe in Florida during May 1984 (circa the release of *Bark at the Moon*), Ozzy – sporting nothing but a skimpy summer dress he'd 'borrowed' from an elderly hotel resident – succeeded in grossing out the decidedly un-squeamish Nikki Sixx. Desperate for a line of coke and hearing from Sixx that there was none to be had, Ozzy began seeking other substances to snort. Nearby, a line of ants caught his eye. Brandishing a straw, he marched over and proceeded to hoover up the hapless insects, aardvark-style. Next, he began to urinate by the side of the hotel pool – in full view of the hotel's other bemused guests. Before anyone could react, Ozzy dropped to his knees and lapped up his own urine. Getting to his feet, he ordered young pretender Nikki to follow suit. As Nikki later admitted in *The Dirt*, the peer – or 'pee' – pressure was on and he could hardly refuse. He whipped out his dick and made his own puddle, but just as he was about to get down on all fours, Ozzy pushed him aside and set about clearing up. 'From that moment on,' Nikki wrote, 'we always knew that wherever we were, whatever we were doing, there was someone who was sicker and more disgusting than we were.'

On 19 March 1982, Ozzy's life was thrown into chaos once more – with the name of his Diary of a Madman Tour proving tragically prophetic – when Randy Rhoads (Ozzy's guitarist and 'brother from another mother') and his girlfriend, Rachel Youngblood, were killed in a plane crash. Following a show in Knoxville, Tennessee, Ozzy and company were back on the road. Yet, en route to Orlando, Florida, their driver Andrew Aycock stopped off at a garage depot belonging to his employers to fix the bus's air-conditioning system. Aycock – who held a pilot's licence, but had failed to take his biennial flight review – espied a four-seater 55 Beechcraft Bonanza standing idle on the adjoining airstrip, and subsequently took Ozzy's tour manager, Jake Duncan, and his keyboardist, Don Airey, for a quick spin, before cajoling Randy and Rachel into the aircraft – despite Randy's chronic fear of flying.

It later transpired that Aycock – who was operating on more than just adrenaline – had wanted to give his passengers a white-knuckle ride to remember, but while attempting to 'buzz' the tour bus, the Bonanza's left wing clipped the bus's roof and veered off into the trees before crashing into the garage. What made Randy and Rachel's senseless deaths all the more tragic was that earlier that evening Randy had told Ozzy that he was considering giving up being a rock'n'roller in favour of going to university to try for a degree in classical guitar.

With the possible exception of Metallica's Cliff Burton, who lost his life in an equally senseless accident on the road, Randy is the cleanest-living musician to feature in these pages by a mile. Accidental or nay, the circumstances of his death are such that they've never ceased to haunt his former mentor. 'It took me a very long time to get over his death,' was the Ozz man's lament in 2011. 'I'm on a low dose of anti-depressants even now. Randy gave me a purpose, he gave me hope.'

However, it wasn't only while out on the road that moments of madness overtook Ozzy's rationale. And it's a testament to Sharon's character that she stuck by her drug-addled husband during the most turbulent years of their marriage, when Ozzy was washing his daily drug intake down with up to four bottles of Hennessy cognac. Yet while Sharon usually gave as good as she got during their fights, matters came to a head during the early hours of Sunday, 3 September 1989, when police were called to their marital home and Ozzy was arrested, carted off to Amersham jail, and duly charged with attempted murder by strangulation.

Ozzy had no recollection of the events, but from the information the arresting officers had gleaned from Sharon, it transpired that, having celebrated their daughter Aimee's sixth birthday, he and Sharon had gone out for a meal at a local Chinese restaurant, where he did his utmost to bump Smirnoff's share price by getting shit-faced drunk. (His switch from cognac to vodka stemmed from his recent trip to Russia, where – somewhat ironically, given the circumstances – he'd appeared at the Moscow Music Peace Festival.) In a November 2009 interview with the *Mirror*, shortly after the release of *I Am Ozzy*, Ozzy would cite his attack on Sharon as his most shameful moment. 'Falling in love with Sharon was the best thing that ever happened to me,' he continued. 'She was patient, she stuck by me. Someone asked me, "Imagine if it was the other way around, you were the sober one and she was the one on the floor covered in piss and puke every day. How long do you think you would last?" And I was like, "Fuck, that's a good question." I really don't know the answer. She stuck it out. Her being sober saved me. She's not a big drinker – she has a few glasses of wine and she goes fucking nuts.'

Ozzy was the one in danger of going fucking nuts after being locked up for 36 hours straight with only his muddled thoughts for company. And with the Thames Valley Police determined to make an example of their celebrity inmate, Ozzy arrived at court fearing the worst. Thankfully, however, his solitary confinement was at an end, as the judge granted bail on the strict proviso that he didn't try to make contact with Sharon, stayed away from their home, and entered a certified rehabilitation programme of his choosing.

Ozzy chose Huntercombe Manor in nearby Maidenhead, and it was here that Sharon came to visit him to say she knew the Ozzy she'd fallen in love with would never harm her, and that if 'bad Ozzy' stayed out of sight, then she was willing to drop the charges. This was the long-overdue wake-up call Ozzy needed, not simply to save his marriage, but also his life, because with his drinking spiralling out of control he was a sure-fire cert for the sanatorium or the cemetery. And although the road to recovery was both lengthy and not without its attendant potholes – into which he occasionally stumbled, either on foot or riding his quad bike – Ozzy has completely turned his life around. And according to his doctors – who are just as baffled as the rest of us as to why he's still shuffling around this mortal coil after putting his body through four decades of abuse – the only thing of note on his medical file these days is a slightly raised cholesterol level.

One might have expected Ozzy's newfound sobriety to curtail his moments of madness, yet against his own better judgement, he acquiesced to Sharon's insistence that allowing a film crew to move into their Beverly Hills home to document their every move was a good idea. This came about because of the success of the 1997 documentary *Ozzy Osbourne Uncut*, which picked up the prestigious Rose d'Or Award at that year's Montreux TV Festival. As we all know from seeing her on reality shows such as *The X Factor* and *America's Got Talent*, Sharon positively thrives on being in the public eye, whereas Ozzy was liable to suffer a panic attack. He had the unshakeable – and not wholly unreasonable – belief that the general public's perception of him was that when he wasn't being arrested for public intoxication he might be found hanging upside down in some remote cave drinking snake's blood.

Owing to Ozzy's popularity on both sides of the Atlantic, the documentary was broadcast on the Travel Channel in the States, and on Channel Five in the UK, and the response was such that MTV came calling with an offer for a one-off appearance on their own hit reality show, *Cribs*. And again, though it shouldn't come as too much of a surprise, the show drew a massive audience, and before Ozzy knew what was happening he couldn't scratch his balls without a camera zooming in on him. Though such overt intrusion brought his temper to the boil, he was sagacious enough to recognise that fame is a double-edged sword, as he explained: 'If I walk down the street and I get recognised, I get kind of pissed off, but at the same time if I walk down the street and I don't get recognised, I also get pissed off.'

Nikki Sixx

11 December 1958

Born: Frank Carlton Feranna, Jr.

Alter-egos: These days little Frankie Jr. goes by the name of Nikki Sixx. Yet, as the self-confessed 'shattered rock star' is only too aware: 'Sometimes I feel I have two personalities. One is Nikki . . . and the other is Sikki,' a hell-raising junkie with 'the emotional stability of a Molotov cocktail'. 'Occasionally it occurs to me that I may be the kind of person that the Sikki of '86 would have hated,' muses Nikki in his harrowing record of addiction, *The Heroin Diaries*. 'That's okay 'cause I don't think I'd like to know Sikki in 2006, so we're even.'

(Pre) occupations: Bassist and lyricist with Mötley Crüe, Brides of Destruction and Sixx AM. In the latest of his nine lives, the irrepressible Mr Sixx has turned his talents to writing and photography.

Live by this: 'I think that somehow [the Crüe] is fuelled by dysfunction. We are fuelled by walking on the edge of insanity and collapse. We are fuelled by hand-to-hand combat. We are fuelled by drugs and overdoses. We are fuelled by hearing that something has gone wrong with another member so he's the bad guy. I don't know if other bands are like that.' – Nikki Sixx

Deadly sins: Back in 1986 – when the pages of what would become *The Heroin Diaries* were first stained with blood, ink and tears – Nikki was ruled by an altogether more demanding mistress than current girlfriend, Courtney Bingham. 'Alcohol, acid, cocaine . . . they were just affairs,' he muses darkly. 'When I met heroin it was true love.' With this admission, Nikki launches into his personal compendium of sins, with a single objective in mind. 'I could burn these diaries,' he reflects, 'and nobody would ever be the wiser. So why have I decided to publish them and show the world just what a fucked up, strung out madman I was at the height of my success? Well, it's simple. If one person reads this book and doesn't have to go down the same road as me, it was worth sharing my personal hell with them.'

Despite his weakness for Catholic girls (as documented in *The Heroin Diaries*, Nikki was so moved by one girlfriend's rendition of the Lord's Prayer that he set about bastardising the verses into lyrics for 'Wild Side'); the sinful Mr Sixx has never been particularly religious. Yet, no stranger to lust (just ask Ton Zutaut, the A&R man who foolishly introduced Nikki to his girlfriend – three minutes later the pair were fornicating before his very eyes), gluttony ('Look, I'm Nikki Sixx,' he once raved down the line to a hapless hotel receptionist, 'I need a bottle of JD now and I will give you a thousand bucks for it'), or wrath, sobriety has instilled in Nikki a sentiment utterly alien to his heroin-fuelled former-self: remorse.

On a highway to hell? Like several other *Cemetery Gates* notables – Lemmy, Slash and Varg Vikernes to name but a few – Nikki came from a broken home. Given his deep-rooted antipathy towards his father, Nikki's desire to change his name at the earliest opportunity is entirely understandable. After all, who'd want to stick with a name that served as a constant reminder of the guy who abandoned you without so much as a backward glance? 'I changed my name because of a long road battling a guy who walked away from me named Frank Serafino – who was my father – and me saying, "Fuck you, I'm gonna reinvent myself, you weren't there for me, and I am gonna become a man called Nikki, create my own family and fuck you." At some point you gotta go. I carried that fucking baggage around for a long time.'

What gives Nikki the edge over his *Cemetery Gates* contemporaries, however, is that he's the only artist to have the ignoble honour of getting his mother arrested, simply because she dared to object to his staying out late, dressing like a slob, playing his bass too loud, and not doing his homework (wayward Nikki was fourteen at the time). Of course, there was no way the cops were going to haul Deana off to jail simply because her son had taken umbrage at being grounded. So, after trashing his room and painstakingly smashing each and every window in the house, Nikki dashed across the street, hoping to borrow a knife. Recognising one of their own, the stoners did the neighbourly thing and tossed him a stiletto. Without further ado, Nikki flipped out the blade and set about slicing up his left forearm. When it was open to the bone and looking 'pretty cool', he called the cops saying his mother had attacked him.

Nikki's aim had been to get Deana out of the way so that he could have the house to himself, dress any way he chose, and play his bass at full volume. The cops, realising straight away that the wound was self-inflicted, used a little reverse psychology to burst Nikki's bubble, pointing out that, while they could certainly arrest Deana, he was a minor living in her custody. If he insisted on pressing charges, then they'd have no choice but to place him in care until he was eighteen. This was a sobering thought: going into care could mean no more guitar for four long years. If that were to happen, how was he ever going to make it as a rock star? Because he *was* going to make it . . . at least in his own mind.

Unlike most musicians, Nikki started touring before he ever picked up a bass guitar. With his father already a fading memory, and his mother content to while away her days in the arms of any guy who caught her eye, he grew up in the care of his maternal grandparents, who moved from

'Stay beautiful, keep it ugly.'
- Nikki Sixx

place to place as the mood took them. Though he loved his grandparents dearly, he describes the enforced estrangement from his mother as his 'introduction to abandonment' – the same sentiment that ultimately festered into lifelong 'sores of anger, rebellion and discontent'.

What set Mötley Crüe apart from the other aspiring glam-metal bands on the early eighties scene was that the Crüe were actually prepared to walk it like they talked it (albeit in hookers' heels). Even a cursory flick through the pages of their collective confessions in *The Dirt* is evidence enough that they were the real deal: every parent's worst nightmare and every rebellious teenager's wet dream. Yet though Tommy, Vince and Mick dutifully played their parts, it was Nikki who served as the spokesman for a lost de-generation. 'To me, the other bands like Poison and Faster Pussycat missed the fuckin' point altogether,' Nikki told *Terrorizer* in 2003. 'We didn't care if we lived or died. And they were celebrating, "Yeah, man, rock'n'roll! Girls! Talk dirty to me!" And I was like, "Fuck you, man . . . shout at the fuckin' devil." We were the real deal. It was doom, gloom, destruction, girls, 24 hours a day, the fastest cars, the loudest guitars – it was all the shit that makes *Spinal Tap* wonderful. And it was scary to people on the outside, and frustrating because we wouldn't do what we were told.'

While Nikki had been tearing along his own personal highway to hell from the moment he picked up a bass – with a hypodermic serving as the rev-counter needle since Mötley Crüe came bursting onto the LA metal scene some six years earlier – 1987 was the year that he crashed and burned. 'People over the years have tried to soften the blow by saying maybe [my] being in Mötley Crüe turned me into an addict, but I don't think it did. That stroke of genius was all my own work,' Nikki confesses wryly by way of introduction to *The Heroin Diaries: A Year in the Life of a Shattered Rock Star*. Whatever his sins, he's honest enough to admit that, while Mötley Crüe gave him the financial resources to be an addict, had the band not hit the big time, he would have simply sought alternate means of funding his habit. Being the sociable soul that he is, Nikki was more than happy to share his stash with the rest of the band. And though at one time or another Tommy, Vince and even Mick all accompanied Nikki into what Tommy would subsequently describe as a 'really dark fucking place', they were at least able to claw their way back out into the light. Nikki, on the other hand, simply hunkered down and called it home.

'Anything worth doing . . . is worth overdoing.'
- Nikki Sixx

While the 'really dark fucking place' Tommy alludes to in *The Heroin Diaries* is metaphorical, whenever Nikki's coke-induced psychosis kicked in he would take refuge in his bedroom closet – a safe haven where he kept his stash (secreted within a Dom Pérignon box), and his grandfather's double-barrel shotgun. Safely ensconced within this shadowy womb, he would hide out amidst his drug paraphernalia with the shotgun primed and pointing at the door. He'd then call West Tech – the company that had installed close-circuit security cameras in his home – ranting of imaginary prowlers trying to break in. West Tech would send a team to Valley Vista Boulevard to investigate, Nikki would see them on the monitor, mistake them for cops, or a SWAT team coming to arrest him, and flush his stash down the toilet. Since the only sure-fire way he knew to bring himself out of his deranged state was to shoot up heroin, the next call would be to his dealer, and so the vicious cycle would begin all over again.

In *The Heroin Diaries*, Nikki writes of his first sickening encounter with mistress 'H'. In the aftermath, he lay flat on his back – his head spinning, his body flipping and a single thought repeating in his brain: that heroin was the 'stupidest drug ever', and 'only the dumb[est] of the dumb' would ever think of reliving the experience. That he chose to do so was out of an intense desire to emulate his hedonistic heroes Sid Vicious, Johnny Thunders, and Dee Dee Ramone, all of whom shared a similar devil-may-care attitude towards life that ultimately saw each of them cut down with the grim reaper's scythe. Following in their swaggering footsteps, Nikki discovered it doesn't matter how well you think you know the steps: dance with 'Mr. Brownstone' and he invariably ends up taking the lead.

Like his heroes before him, Nikki enrolled on a methadone programme, reasoning that a daily dose of synthetic morphine would not only wean him off the heroin that had caused him to lose 40lbs in a calendar year, but also keep him from dirty needles. Yet, Nikki was calling his dealer the moment he stepped out of the clinic door. For all his good intentions, a newfound penchant for methadone was all he'd be taking from his stay.

Sometime during the recording of *Shout at the Devil*, Nikki absconded from a late-night Jacuzzi party (thrown by producer Roy Thomas Baker) and drunkenly clambered behind the wheel of his new Porsche – buck-naked as the day he came kicking and screaming into the world. It very nearly turned out to be his last day amongst the living, for whilst trying to escape the attentions of two amorous females who'd been denied entry into the party and were giving chase in their own car, he slammed into a telegraph pole at 90mph. Save for a dislocated shoulder (and a few cuts and grazes to add to the ones he'd amassed scaling the high wall surrounding Baker's fortress of a home) Nikki was miraculously unhurt. Had anyone been in the passenger seat, they'd have been propelled through the windscreen and into the hereafter. Eerily, a similar smash lay in wait for Vince Neil, yet the frontman was not so fortunate as to be flying solo.

Having chalked up the first of his many near-misses (which surely total way more than nine), Nikki's reaction to the smash was shockingly blasé. Indeed, he walked away from the mangled wreck of his ride with scarcely a thought for how close he'd come to putting himself Sixx feet under, and simply shrugged the episode off by saying that the only good thing to came out of the experience was that he 'developed a lifelong love for Percodan'. And while one could dismiss this as bravado, the fact that he stared death in the face on later occasions – and spat in its eye each time – suggests he really didn't give a fuck whether he lived or died.

Even by Mötley Crüe's hedonistic standards, Nikki was rapidly losing control, and during the Japanese leg of the Girls, Girls, Girls Tour, he finally came off the rails completely. Onboard a high-speed bullet train to Tokyo, he struck a Japanese businessman with a Jack Daniel's bottle. The fact that he'd intended to hit the band's much put-upon promoter, Mr. Udo, carried no water (if plenty of liquor): not with the blood-splattered businessman, not with Udo himself – and certainly not with the stern-faced Tokyo cops waiting on the platform when the train pulled into the station. They arrested Nikki the moment he stepped off the train, and when the band's then manager Doc McGhee tried to intercede, he was also wrestled to the ground, clapped in handcuffs and hauled off to jail. 'After a few hours, they brought Doc and me to the sergeant's desk at the station,' Nikki recalled in *The Dirt*. 'I was wearing leather pants, high heels, a torn T-shirt, and make-up. I was sweaty and still completely high.'

By this time, it was dark in the station. Yet when Nikki removed his shades, Doc suggested that he put them straight back on: his eyes were shockingly bloodshot and streaked with make-up. The po-faced sergeant, who had not taken kindly to finding the scuffed heels of Nikki's slingbacks resting on his otherwise spotless desk, was about to get down to business when Nikki suddenly leant forward in his chair and – glancing at the interpreter hired to translate for Nikki and Doc – asked if he might ask the sergeant a question. Without waiting for a response, Nikki matter-of-factly enquired of the sergeant where his dick would be if his balls were nestled on the sergeant's chin? The police are not noted for their sense of humour in any language and, while Mr. Udo had managed to persuade the businessman to drop the charges against them, Nikki might well have faced some serious jail time had the interpreter chosen to translate the enquiry to the letter.

Moments of madness: Crüe member Nikki is no stranger to *The Dirt*. But in all his chequered history of sex, drugs and spandex, Christmas 1987 stands out as a psycho holiday like no other. Still recovering from the Crüe's rampaging tour of Japan, Nikki opted to take some downtime in Hong Kong. Out exploring the province's seedier side, he happened upon a wizened Chinese soothsayer who took one look at Nikki's palm, muttered something in Chinese and then pushed the hand away as if in disgust. Nikki's interpreter, Li, walked away saying that Nikki didn't want to know what the old man had seen, but Nikki being Nikki insisted that she tell him. Li passed on the soothsayer's grim warning: if Nikki didn't change his ways he wouldn't live to see New Year. The stinging caveat was this: that Nikki was someone inherently incapable of changing his ways.

With the rest of the Crüe keeping him at (leper's) arm's length following the infamous bottle-throwing incident, Nikki decided to call on his Guns N' Roses partner-in-crime, Slash. As the Gunners had a five-night residency in Pasadena set to commence on Boxing Day, Slash and G N' R drummer Steven Adler were taking some much-needed R&R at the Franklin Plaza Hotel. Slash's current squeeze, Sally McLaughlin, had recently arrived from her native Scotland. It was her first night in the City of Lights, and one she would never forget.

At some point in the evening, Nikki – with Ratt guitarist, Robbin Crosby, in tow – rolled up at the Franklin in the rented silver limo which had met him at LAX on his return from the Orient, bearing a stylish beaver-skin top hat meant as a Christmas present for Slash. They'd also set out with a gram of high-calibre cocaine, but of course, some presents just aren't meant for sharing. Had the evening not descended into chaos, one cannot help but ponder which Slash would have found the most disconcerting – that Nikki and Crosby kept the coke to themselves, or that Nikki barfed over the top hat whilst alighting from the limo. While the motley ensemble were making a nuisance of themselves in the bars and clubs of Sunset Strip, Nikki suggested scoring some heroin and retiring to the hotel to continue the party with their good friend Mr. Brownstone in Slash's room, inadvertently leaving a less-than-impressed Sally behind at the Cathouse.

'The funniest thing about Mötley Crüe was that they dressed like chicks but lived like animals. It was an education, even for me.'

- Ozzy Osbourne

By Slash's own admission, he was 'screaming drunk, and couldn't find the floor to fall on', but the returning Sally remembers the unfolding events all too well: 'I started yelling at Slash, but he was too drunk to even argue back,' she revealed in *The Heroin Diaries*. 'A few minutes later, there was a knock at the door. It was Nikki, looking dreadful, and he came in and just fell on the floor. I was thinking, "Great, now I've got two drunks to deal with here," but then the dealer came in, took one look at Nikki, yelled, "Nikki's dead!" and ran off.'

What none of them knew, however, was that the Persian heroin Slash's dealer procured for them was near-pure strength, and as Nikki was 'too sloppy fucked up' to get himself off, he'd allowed the dealer to do it for him – regardless of the fact that the only other occasion he'd let a complete stranger shoot him up it had almost cost him his life. Not so much trawling the depths of his psyche as putting the 'id' in idiot . . .

Nikki's previous experience of near-death by heroin occurred on Valentine's Day 1986. Having wowed an adoring crowd at the Hammersmith Odeon, Nikki, with Hanoi Rocks guitarist Andy McCoy, grabbed a taxi to the wrong side of town to score heroin. As Nikki candidly admits in *The Heroin Diaries*, the problem with procuring drugs from an unknown source is that 'you never really know exactly how potent they are from dealer to dealer'. However, Nikki was so impressed that the dealer had clean needles that he let him shoot him up. Nikki duly OD'd, and when the usual methods of revival failed, the dealer attempted to beat the life back into Nikki with a baseball bat. When that failed to achieve the desired effect, the dealer slung Nikki's comatose body over his shoulder, took him outside, and dumped him in a skip.

Flash forward to that night in 1987: Sally was giving Nikki mouth-to-mouth when Slash came staggering into the bathroom. The sight of Nikki lying comatose on the floor was enough to send his fragile mind into shock, as he'd lost another close friend – Todd Crew, Jetboy bassist and occasional G N' R roadie – in similar circumstances the previous year. 'Slash smashed the shower screen and the glass showered over me and

'Wherever they went, they carried around this massive flight case full of every type of booze imaginable. The moment a gig was over, the lid would be thrown open, and the hounds of hell would be let loose.'

- Ozzy Osbourne

Nikki, so I got up and punched [him] and laid him out,' Sally says. 'I was screaming for somebody to call 911 . . . The paramedics ripped Nikki's T-shirt to give him adrenaline, then whisked him off . . . the paramedics later said that I'd kept him going. The weird thing I remember is that when my breath came back out of his mouth, it sounded like he was snoring. I thought, "Fuck, what if he's just asleep, wakes up and thinks I'm snogging him?"'

Slash, unaware that Sally had punched his lights out, came to again and found the trashed bathroom a hive of activity, with Sally freaking out as the paramedics carried his unconscious friend away on a stretcher. 'When I opened my eyes, everything was a blur of light, colour, and motion,' Nikki recalls. 'I was on my back moving through some kind of corridor. Sounds whooshed in and out of my ears, unrecognisable at first, until a voice slowly emerged out of the white noise: "We're losing him, we're losing him."'

As Nikki tells it, on hearing the unfamiliar voice he tried to sit up so that he could figure out what was going on, who it was they were losing. Remembering something of what had gone down at the Franklin, he braced himself for the expectant pain. To his surprise he felt as light

as air. Realising he was having an out-of-body experience, he serenely
hovered close to the ceiling, looking on while his filthy, tattooed corpse
– covered face-to-toe with a sheet on a metal gurney – was ushered into
an ambulance parked out in front of the hotel. But the tranquil vision
was brought to a painful conclusion as he was wrenched back into the
here and now. 'I came to in a hospital bed. There was a cop asking me
questions, so I told him to go fuck himself,' he said. 'I ripped out my tubes
and staggered in just my leather pants [out] into the parking lot, where
two teenage girls were sitting crying around a candle. They had heard on
the radio that I was dead and looked kind of surprised to see me.'

The fans gave Nikki a lift home, and one of them gave him her jacket
– as if to preserve his dignity. In *The Dirt*, Nikki says that he'd felt utterly
alone while out on the Girls, Girls, Girls Tour, as though he had nobody
who cared for him and nobody to care for. In that supposedly epiphanous
moment, he'd realised that he 'was one of the luckiest guys in the world'.
Yet, despite promising the girls that he'd never do drugs again – and
having paused long enough to change his answering machine message to,
'Hey, it's Nikki, I'm not here because I'm dead' – he then went upstairs
into the bathroom, retrieved a lump of heroin from the medicine cabinet,
and promptly shot himself back into oblivion because 'with one sink of
the syringe plunger [I] realised that all the love and concern of those
millions still didn't feel as satisfying as one good shot of heroin . . .'

In the introduction to his second book *This is Gonna Hurt*, Nikki says
that 'when death knocked at my door I was lucky enough to tell him
to come back later'. But this was more like pissing on the paramedics
who'd refused to give up the ghost and saved his life that same night. He
woke up the following afternoon with the needle still dangling from his
arm, his coagulated blood staining the tiled floor. However, within that
same introduction, Nikki also acknowledges that it's never too late to wake
up, never too late for change, before confiding that he too is changing.
He continues to make music, acts as a mentor for up-and-coming bands
like Black Veil Brides, has grown as a person and abandoned his self-
destructive lifestyle. But his personal struggle also continues, and he will
keep digging into his past, poking into all his wounds with an introspective
fingernail until he has discovered and healed every last one. It's sure to be
a slow and painful process.

Dave Mustaine

13 September 1961

Born: David Scott Mustaine

Alter-egos: The Red Devil

(Pre) occupations: Guitarist and frontman with Megadeth. Metallica's most dreaded ex, Mustaine – the self-appointed bête noire (or perhaps *rouge?*) of James Hetfield and Lars Ulrich – was hardly first in line to buy a copy of their ubiquitous 'Black Album'. 'It wasn't enough for Megadeth to do well,' fumed the axeman in his very own *Heavy Metal Memoir*. 'I wanted Metallica to fail.'

Hailed by rock scribe Joel McIver as the greatest metal guitarist in human history, Dave has defied the naysayers – to say nothing of modern medicine – battling deadly addictions, inner-demons and freak injuries galore (please see below for a lesson in why world-class axemen should remain alert in rehab waiting rooms *at any cost*) for a taste of sweet revenge. And despite his oft-voiced predilection for politics (contrary to all evidence, Dave still refuses to believe that President Barrack Obama was born in the States), he's never been tempted to give up shredding in favour of the Senate. 'I don't want to be assassinated,' he stated vehemently in 2009. Indeed, in the aftermath of a certain appearance in County Antrim, this must have seemed a distinct possibility.

Possibly the only artist in history to give a shout out to the murderous IRA live onstage in Northern Ireland, Dave recalls his eye-watering faux-pas with a sheepish shrug. 'I was drinking,' he sighed in interview with *Metal Sludge*, 'and someone said a person was selling bootleg T-shirts out in the audience. The only problem was they were shirts he was selling to raise money for "the cause". I did not know what "the cause" was, and some seemingly decent person told me that this big complicated problem with the Catholics and the Protestants is just prejudiced religion. He said that I should let them sell the shirts. Once onstage, after four or five pints of Guinness, I introduced "Anarchy" and said, "Give Ireland back to the

Irish, this one is for the cause – anarchy in Ireland!" This did not go down as good as it did when Paul McCartney said it, let me tell you . . .'

Live by this: 'It's not how big your pencil is . . . it's how you write your name.' – Dave Mustaine

'Heavy metal is a way of life.' – Dave Mustaine

'I believe . . . it's a type of protection with Dave to divide the people he really wants to be in touch [with] and people that he doesn't like. I think it's honest . . . instead of smiling with everybody. If you don't want to smile, you don't have to.' – Cristina Scabbia (Lacuna Coil)

'I do see a lot of stuff in the press . . . and say to myself, "Hold on. This is the Dave that we kind of wanted to forget about." You know, the big mouth that wants to just go-go-go. But there is an authenticity about him when he speaks. He doesn't think too much before he does. He just goes off the cuff. Plus, it's well-intended.' – James Hetfield (Metallica)

Deadly sins: Contrary to popular belief, Dave Mustaine is one survivor who's learned his limits the hard way. According to the gospel of born-again Dave, the seven deadly sins as cited in 'the Bible and several other self-help or enlightenment books pretty much cover everything that we do that is sinful . . . or fun for that matter.' And despite his recent return to the flock, Dave's not exactly averse to discussing his sinful past. Indeed, he readily admits to having 'bought into every aspect of the rock'n'roll life; drugs and alcohol being merely the most dangerous and debilitating'. When he and Megadeth bassist, Dave Ellefson, were living together, the first thing he'd glimpse each morning 'through blurry, bloodshot eyes' would be Ellefson himself (or 'Junior' as he was known), perched at the bottom of his bed with a bindle of heroin, pre-wrapped and ready for use. 'And that was it. Gone, baby, gone – for two, three days at a time.'

The two Daves would usually bunk up together while out on the road, as on Megadeth's first UK tour in 1987 to promote *Peace Sells . . . But Who's Buying?* 'I was still fairly naive, full of ambition, and ready to conquer the world,' he says in his oft-harrowing, yet hilarious autobiography *Mustaine: A Heavy Metal Memoir*. 'But there were a few things I had yet to learn . . . like how to drink Strongbow Super Cider.'

Not realising that British ales – especially cider – pack a far greater punch than American beer, Dave downed a dozen cans in a hotel bar before staggering up to his room. Realising he was in trouble before his head even hit the pillow, Mustaine goes on to tell how he awoke at some point during the night with his 'bladder screaming for relief'. However, his unfamiliarity with his 'castle-like' room – the romantic floor-to-ceiling drapes therein only adding to his disorientation – coupled with Ellefson's absence (the six-stringer having not yet returned from a Deep Purple show), left him staggering blindly about the room unable to see his hands in front of his face. 'Finally, I found what seemed at the time to be a lid of some sort,' he subsequently revealed. 'Presuming it was a toilet seat, but not really caring one way or the other, I lifted it up, dropped my shorts and began to piss.'

It wasn't until the following morning that, registering the bemused look on Ellefson's face, Mustaine realised his mistake. The lid in question hadn't been a toilet seat at all, but rather his bassist's suitcase.

'You don't shit where you eat, and you don't try to fuck your bandmate's fiancée - especially when your bandmate is your boss.'
- Dave Mustaine

On a highway to hell? Dave was born in La Mesa, California, but – thanks to his father's preference for lifting a bottle rather than holding down a job – he spent his childhood drifting aimlessly around the Golden State. Much of what Dave remembers of John, the shadowy figure who was married to his mother, is mingled with the horrific stories – telling 'of abuse and general insane behaviour perpetrated under the shroud of alcoholism' – passed down by his elder sisters, Michelle and Suzanne, both of whom were targets of and witnesses to the abuse before their mother, Emily, finally mustered up the courage to leave.

By his own admission, Dave was thirteen the first time he 'got high' on marijuana. 'I liked smoking pot, liked the way it made me feel,' he says. However, while getting high on a regular basis certainly made his life more tolerable, he also reveals that it was his 'experimenting' with weed that led to his branching out into alcohol and other drugs. There was, of course, one major drawback to this new lifestyle – Dave's limited cash flow. In order to fund his habit, he borrowed $10 from one of his unsuspecting sisters, bought an ounce of pot and set to work. 'I rolled forty joints and sold them for fifty cents a piece,' he says now. 'In a matter of just a few hours I had doubled my money. Now I was far from an economics wizard, but I knew a good thing when I saw it.' Indeed he did, and by the time he was fifteen he was living alone and supporting himself by dealing drugs. Owing to an agreement with one of his more desperate clients, willing to trade albums – most notably AC/DC and Iron Maiden – in return for his wares, the entrepreneurial master Mustaine discovered heavy metal. The rest, of course, is the stuff of Megadeth legend . . .

Having learned his chops with LA band, Panic, sometime during the summer of 1981, Dave responded to a 'lead axeman wanted' ad placed in the *Recycler* by an aspiring young drummer called Lars Ulrich. Of course, Ulrich's unnamed band was soon to be christened Metallica. To Dave's bemusement, Lars and the other guys in the band – guitarist James Hetfield and bassist Ron McGovney – gave him the gig without even hearing him play. 'I was convinced that I should be in the band and went to rehearsal. I was tuning up when all the other guys in the band went into another room. They weren't talking to me, so I went in and said, "Well? Am I in the band or not?" and they said, "You've got the gig." I couldn't believe how easy it had been and suggested that we get some beer to celebrate.'

Little did his new bandmates suspect just how much Dave liked to party. 'Dave was an incredibly talented guy, but he also had an incredibly large problem with alcohol and drugs,' Brian Slagel, owner of Metal Blade Records, subsequently revealed. 'He'd get wasted and become a real crazy person, a raging maniac, and the other guys just couldn't deal with that after a while. I mean, they all drank of course, but Dave drank more . . . much more. I could see they were beginning to get fed up of seeing Dave drunk out of his mind all the time.'

Indeed, Dave had barely gotten over his initiation hangover when he was fired following an altercation with James and Ron, whose house had been commandeered as a rehearsal space. Lacking a sitter, Dave had brought his pet dog along to rehearsal. Over-excited and out of control, the creature leapt onto the bonnet of McGovney's car and proceeded to scratch the paintwork. When James lashed out at the dog with his boot, Dave – who possesses a temper to match his fiery locks – flew into a rage and threatened to hit James. It was at this point that McGovney – having watched one too many John Wayne movies – stepped in and told Dave that he would have to go through him to get to James. James pushed past McGovney and issued a similar warning. One can only surmise that Dave had neglected to mention that he was as adept at judo as he was on lead guitar . . . and in that moment, with a red mist clouding his rational brain, he simply shrugged his shoulders and told James he'd won before delivering a right hook of which Wayne himself would surely have been proud. The impact sent James sprawling. McGovney then foolishly launched himself at Dave – only to be expertly slammed against the nearest wall. Lars, meanwhile – having sensibly remained a couple of arms' lengths from the action – told Dave to pack up his gear and to take his mutt with him.

Twenty-four hours and one sleepless night later, a penitent Dave went round to McGovney's place, apologised, and asked to be given another chance. When the equally repentant James and McGovney acquiesced, Dave scurried merrily off to the nearest liquor store so that they might celebrate. Didn't anyone see a pattern forming here?

Though Dave's shredding was perfectly suited to the hyper-charged thrash of Metallica's earliest endeavours, his behaviour offstage was becoming increasingly erratic. Dousing McGovney's bass in beer, for instance, was nothing but an amusing jape to Dave. Yet when McGovney plugged in his instrument, the electrical current was enough to 'blow him across the room and [shock] the hell out of him'. Indeed, this would prove the last straw for the (relatively) sedate six-stringer. Soon after, McGovney announced his imminent departure from the band soon to be known as 'Alcoholica'.

By April 1983, having signed with Megaforce Records and relocated to New Jersey, James and Lars had decided they no longer wanted to make music with Dave. Without further ado, they loaded his gear into their van and dropped him off at the New York Port Authority Bus Terminal with a one-way ticket for Los Angeles.

Inordinately vexed by his dismissal, Mustaine spent the entirety of the gruelling ride home scribbling lyrics on muffin wrappers and vehemently swearing on all he held dear that the band he would put together on his return – which he'd tentatively decided to call Fallen Angels – would be bigger and better than Metallica. 'After getting fired from Metallica, all I remember is that I wanted blood. Theirs! I wanted to be faster and heavier than them,' he later seethed in *Mustaine: A Heavy Metal Memoir*. 'I let that swim around in my aching head for a few minutes – "the arsenal of megadeath . . . the arsenal of megadeath" – and then, for some reason I can't quite explain, I began to write. Using a borrowed pencil and a cupcake wrapper, I wrote the first lyrics of my post-Metallica life. This song was called "Megadeth" (I dropped the second "a"), and though it would never find its way onto an album, it did serve as the basis for the song "Set the World Afire". It hadn't occurred to me then that Megadeth – as used by Senator Cranston, megadeath referred to the loss of one million lives as a result of nuclear holocaust – might be a perfectly awesome name for a thrash-metal band.'

Another bone of contention – on which Dave has been gnawing for the past few decades like a rabid dog – is the songwriting recognition he feels he is owed from his time with Metallica. Though he was given a co-writing credit for several tracks featured on *Kill 'Em All* and *Ride the Lightning*, he still insists that he contributed heavily to 'Leper Messiah' from *Master of Puppets*. 'The writing credits were altered to reflect changes made in the songs during the recording process and, I can only speculate, to minimise my contribution,' he says. 'These songs were primarily mine, and yet James or Lars, or both, took a share of the credit, [and] on each my name was placed last.'

> 'Yeah, I was sorry . . . sorry I got caught.'
> – Dave Mustaine

In the same acrimonious spirit, he began publicly mocking his replacement, Kirk Hammett, claiming that the majority of solos on Metallica's debut, *Kill 'Em All*, were written by him and emulated note for note by Hammett.

With the fledgling Fallen Angels still struggling to unfurl their wings, Dave's avenging avowal must have seemed a mere crack-pipe dream. Yet he remained undaunted and simply began scouting for like-minded recruits: namely bassist Dave 'Junior' Ellefson, guitarist Greg Handevidt and drummer Dijon Carruthers (courtesy of the *Recycler*). In the absence of any satisfactory vocalist, Dave was cajoled by Ellefson into taking on the role himself. He also decided that Fallen Angels was hardly representative of his vision: Megadeth was the ferocious new name for him.

In late 1984 (by which time Handevidt had long-since departed and Megadeth had undergone several rounds of musical drum stools until successfully poaching Gar Samuelson from a jazz-fusion outfit called the New Yorkers), the band signed with New York-based Combat Records. And, before heading into the studio to begin work on their debut Combat album, they augmented the line-up with Samuelson's erstwhile New Yorkers bandmate, guitarist Chris Poland.

Needless to say, Dave celebrated signing to Combat Records the only way he knew how – and with Ellefson and the new recruits all proving willing accomplices, they'd soon blown a sizeable hole in the album's $8,000 budget and were forced to ask for another $4,000 from the label. Their reduced funds meant they had to part company with their producer and oversee the mixing themselves – with Dave taking on the majority of the work. Yet despite their collective inexperience at the consol, the finished album – *Killing is My Business . . . And Business is Good!* – received largely enthusiastic reviews, putting Megadeth on the metal map once and for all.

The follow-up to *Killing*, 1986's *Peace Sells . . . But Who's Buying?* is now regarded as a thrash-metal classic, and was voted one of the '1001 Albums to Listen to Before You Die' (Robert Dimery's epic reference book). Though initially released on Combat, it was later picked up by Capitol Records and subsequently remixed. With such tracks as album opener 'Wake Up Dead', 'The Conjuring', 'Good Mourning/Black Friday' and 'Bad Omen', certain critics inevitably began to point to the band's occult influences. While Dave did not dispute the subject matter, he was keen to stress that: 'We're aware of the subjects we write about – witchcraft, satanic sacrifices and the like – but we're not condoning them. If anything,' he added carefully in 1987, 'the songs are a warning. The bad guys don't come out ahead in our songs. I've learned from past experience that the good guys, even if they don't wear white hats, are the ones who end up happy at the end of the day.'

A decade on, he reflected: 'There was even a time when we were considered black metal! When people heard "Black Friday" and "Bad Omen", they thought we were satanic. The worst thing is, like, going to a truck stop in Des Moines, Iowa, and having someone go [imitates accent of Southern redneck], "You guys in Megadeth? I heard you are satanic." They expect us to have dead goats and babies in our buses. You couldn't get any further from the truth!'

The title and cover – which features Megadeth's Iron Maiden-esque mascot 'Vic Rattlehead' (a skeletal creature created by Dave to embody the phrase 'see no evil, hear no evil, speak no evil'), eye sockets covered by a riveted-on visor, mouth clamped shut and ears closed up by metal caps – provide a surreal glimpse of the world according to Mustaine. Dave apparently appropriated the title from a *Reader's Digest* article entitled 'Peace would sell, but no one would buy it'.

'As long as people keep stealing, hurting and mistreating people, there's always going to be something that you can pick up on and say: "Look, this is wrong,"' he opined the following year. 'Granted, we sing about it, but we take a negative approach to what we do sing about. "Hey, the devil is there, but he's a moron. That's why he's buried in dirt."'

While the devil may be buried in the dirt, he's also in the detail, and during the recording of the album certain members of the band weren't giving the 100 percent dedication to detail expected of them. In the midst of his own private heroin hell, Dave was originally willing to turn a blind eye to the habits of Chris Poland and Gar Samuelson. Yet as time went on, it was becoming increasingly difficult to ignore the elephant in the room – especially when neither would show up at the studio until they'd been able to restock their respective pharmacies.

While in hindsight it may seem a case of the pothead calling the kettle a shade of (thundercloud-like) grey, Dave's decision to give Chris and Gar their cards the following year wasn't so much due to their chemical indulgences, but rather their increasing inability to function without their daily fix. In Gar's case, the age-old adage that a band is only as good as its drummer came into play. Indeed, such was Dave's concern that Gar might implode at any given moment that he had Gar's eventual replacement, Chuck Behler, waiting in the wings for the final few dates of Megadeth's headlining world tour.

Chris's dismissal was rather more straightforward, as the guitarist was caught selling off the band's equipment in order to feed his habit. Indeed, while out on the road in support of Alice Cooper (on the latter's Constrictor Tour), Alice – who's certainly been around the detox block enough times to know what he's talking about – was so concerned by the Megadeth boys' mega-consumption that he summoned them to his bus one night in order to lecture them on the only inevitable outcome should they fail to change their ways. Rather than rock-star renown, they were destined for an early grave.

Forgiving as ever, Dave's never quite forgotten the day he discovered a thief in the midst of camp Megadeth. 'Chris Poland,' he vented during an interview in 1992. 'You know what? He could die tomorrow and it wouldn't affect me . . . Chris has never made amends to me for stealing all my gear. I had a collector's item Echoplex which just disappeared, all sorts of guitars, which were all stolen to cash in for heroin. I'm willing to forgive and forget, but until he comes and makes amends with me then I'm not willing to give in.'

Chris would, of course, ultimately take Alice's advice. Having overcome his addiction (and appeared in front of the cameras to give his side of the

Megadeth story on VH1's *Behind the Music*), he was finally able to make his peace with Dave – who invited the reformed guitarist back to play several solo spots on Megadeth's 2004 comeback, *The System Has Failed*. Unfortunately, however, the healing wound was torn open once more soon after the album's release when Dave was contacted by Chris's lawyers, claiming their client was due unpaid royalties beyond his session fees.

Unlike his fellow New Yorker, Gar Samuelson's fairytale was to have a grim ending as he succumbed to liver failure at his home in Florida on 14 July 1999. He was just 41. 'He was a true friend,' Chris said following Gar's untimely demise. 'Everything I know about time, rhythm and feel, I learned from Gar, so I'll always hear his voice in my music.' On 25 July 1999, whilst Megadeth were onstage at the Woodstock Festival, Dave would dedicate 'Peace Sells' to Gar's memory.

'I don't know if we ever get over it . . . For someone who has flirted with life and death, and drug abuse and alcoholism, something gets broken and you never really recover from that. I was in Texas when I looked up and saw a cross and said to myself, "What have I got to lose?"'
– Dave Mustaine

Though Megadeth's next studio album, *So Far, So Good . . . So What?*, would eventually be certified platinum, at the time of its release it was widely panned by the critics – if only for the ill-judged inclusion of a cover of the Sex Pistols' clarion call to arms of twelve years earlier, 'Anarchy in the UK'. According to Dave, anarchy reigned in the studio during its recording, 'due to substances and the priorities we had or didn't have at the time'. And things went from bad to worse once the band went out on the road to promote the release because of 'the guy we were waiting for after the show'.

Over the next six years the 'guy' to whom Dave alludes – purveyor of an array of poisonous delights – became a semi-permanent fixture both on the road and in the studio. In all probability, he was also a regular caller at Casa Mustaine. And though Megadeth's output remained prodigious, with a studio album released every twelve months or so, Dave was on a Stygian downward spiral, and for a time it seemed almost inevitable that he would be the next heavy-metal hero to wake up dead. Indeed, when Megadeth were invited to record a cover of Alice Cooper's 'No More Mr. Nice Guy' for Wes Craven's cult flick, *Shocker*, director Penelope Spheeris – who was already familiar with Megadeth owing to their appearance in her

1988 documentary, *The Decline of Western Civilization II: The Metal Years*, and her time spent onset with the boys during the filming of 'Wake Up Dead' and 'Anarchy in the UK' – would later recount in the aforementioned *Behind the Music* special that Dave showed up for the video shoot 'so fried on heroin and other drugs that he could not sing and play guitar at the same time,' leaving her no option but to shoot each action separately.

In April 2002, Dave suffered a compressed radial nerve in his left hand and arm, having inadvertently dozed off while awaiting his turn with the doctor at a detox centre. Finding himself unable to play, he had little option but to put Megadeth into temporary hiatus until he'd made a full recovery. In an interview with the *SuicideGirls* website he explained the reasoning behind his decision: 'I went into retirement because my arm got hurt really bad. I broke up the band which at the time was Al Pitrelli,

'I had to go through that, and deal with it all, and without it, my life would be totally different. My problems got very bad, but it was all a learning curve.'
– Dave Mustaine

Dave Ellefson, Jimmy DeGrasso and myself. I was having problems with Al because he liked to drink and we didn't want to show up at places drunk. Al also got married to a nice woman but he wanted to spend time with her. After a few years most married men are willing to die, so I figured if we got a couple of years into the marriage that might have changed. But the fact was Al wasn't fitting. DeGrasso was really hard to be around because he was so negative all the time with his complaining about money and wanting things. Ellefson was all about, "Play my songs, play my songs." I hated being around these guys so when the arm injury happened it was a welcome relief and an indication that I had to stop.'

Of course, Dave's decision was received less than cordially by the rest of the band – especially his second-in-command David Ellefson, who went so far as to make a thinly veiled accusation via *Metal Sludge* magazine that Dave had faked the injury as an excuse to break up them up. The ensuing war of words ended in a court of law, with Ellefson accusing Dave of having wrongfully taken the lion's share of Megadeth's earnings to date – an estimated sum of more than $200 million. The bassist also accused Dave of having libelled him in an online posting, for which he was seeking $18.5 million in damages.

Dave counterclaimed by alleging that Ellefson had executed a settlement agreement in which he'd willingly given up his twenty percent interest in Megadeth. Though Ellefson insisted that he'd been coerced into signing the agreement, the judge ruled in Dave's favour. However, in 2010 Dave offered an olive branch to his old friend by inviting him to take his rightful place in Megadeth for the Rust in Peace Twentieth Anniversary Tour.

Ellefson's case is far from unique. Almost every musician who's played and/or toured with Megadeth over the years has found himself the object of Dave's nuclear fits of temper at some point. In 1994, Pantera were the ones in line for a verbal lashing. Bemoaning the fact that his music was being 'ripped off' by a younger generation of metal bands still rising through the ranks, Dave told MTV's cowering reporter that 'I'm not gonna name anybody 'cause I'm not gonna promote them. Okay, we'll say "panther" in Spanish and Portuguese – you're welcome, guys. We might as well be cooking their dinner for them or pushing their little wheelbarrow to the bank for them.'

Harboured by Dave for more than two years already, this particular grudge stems from the bands' Countdown to Extinction Tour – on which Pantera were billed as Megadeth's support. Possibly because of Dave's attempt to poach the talents of Dimebag Darrell for his own, Pantera frontman Phil Anselmo (an equally temperate personality) had shouted out, 'Fuck Megadeth' and 'Fuck Dave' live onstage.

However, fast-forward to Dave's appearance as compere on a special 2004 memorial episode of *Headbanger's Ball* (in honour of the late Dimebag) and the reactionary redhead made every effort to play down his previous comments, dismissing them as an 'off-camera, off-record' event. Actually, he claimed he'd felt 'flattered' by Pantera adopting a similar style.

Moments of madness: While Dave's past is chequered with dozens of incidents that he'd undoubtedly rather forget, being arrested for 'impaired driving' in 1989 surely takes pole position on his starting grid of shame. Indeed, by his own admission, he was so wasted on a cocktail of heroin, cocaine, Valium, chloral hydrate (a.k.a. 'knock-out drops', a hypnotic drug that has been used to sedate Victorian ladies and anaesthetise pets) and weed – all of which were found in varying quantities in his four-wheeled 'rolling pharmacy' – that somewhere within his purple haze Dave mistook the arresting officers for attentive valets, offering to drive both him and his car safely home. 'I thought that was very nice of them,' he reveals in *Mustaine: A Heavy Metal Memoir.* 'The next thing I knew, there were dozens of flashing lights coming at me from all directions.' Only at this point did the happy delusion start to lift and it slowly dawned on Dave that: 'Uh-oh . . . somebody must be in trouble . . .'

Indeed, *somebody* was. However, rather then consign his sorry ass to the slammer, the court sentenced Dave to ten tedious meetings of Alcoholics Anonymous, as well as an eighteen-month programme to teach him alcohol diversion. Of course, Dave had been in and out of rehab so often that (much like *Cemetery Gates* contemporaries Nikki Sixx, Slash and Ozzy Osbourne) he viewed his stays there as little more than an annoying occupational hazard. Determined to pick up where he left off as soon as he was out the door, Dave arguably shared Nikki, Slash, Ozzy et al.'s belief that they were bullet-proof and above the law. And while he was naive enough to sign in under his own name rather than an alias, he simply got up and walked out midway through the first AA meeting. 'The truth is I didn't think I had a problem,' he mused, before admitting in the same breath that actually, he knew he had a problem, but believed that it was no more than he could deal with on his own. And as for the reckless, self-destructive behaviour which had landed him in his current predicament? 'Yeah, I was sorry . . . sorry I got caught.'

Concerned that his failure to honour his commitments would surely get back to the courts, he bribed Dave Ellefson (though he was hardly without his own problems) into attending meetings in his stead. Dave duly went to the first meeting, and another, and another . . . and though Dave was still paying his agreed stipend, the bassist was no longer holding out his hand. 'Something changed,' Dave realised. 'He [Ellefson] stopped drinking, stopped doing drugs. And one night I found myself looking at him, clean and sober, and I said, "Holy fuck! I accidentally twelve-stepped Junior!"'

Witnessing this profound change in the life of his friend was a revelation for Dave, leaving the frontman in a strangely divided state of mind. While he knew he lacked the moral fortitude to complete a rehab programme of his own, he was struck by the equal certainty that he couldn't carry on as before. As he explains in *Dave Mustaine: Reborn*: 'I sat there that evening, staring at the flames, thinking about my life . . . about the choices I'd made and the consequences of those choices, both positive and negative. Something was missing. I can't do this anymore. This has to be the end of it.'

Ultimately, his Damascene conversion came courtesy of neither Alcoholics Anonymous nor rehab, but from a higher plane. Though he'd been baptised a Lutheran, and raised a Jehovah's Witness, there's no denying Dave had strayed from his religious roots like the proverbial black sheep. Yet when the time came, his hell-raising past certainly didn't stop him from wandering into a nearby chapel. Pouring out his heart to a (presumably bewildered) chaplain, he was able to reconnect with God.

Today, Dave professes to have no regrets and insists that his struggle with addiction has made him a better person. 'I had to go through all that stuff. Sure, I went through some really hard times, I hurt a lot of people during those times and I hurt myself a lot too, which I feel bad about. But I had to go through that, and deal with it all, and without it, my life would be totally different. My problems got very bad, but it was all a learning curve.'

It would prove a 'learning curve' which required constant revision – as Mustaine revealed in a November 2010 interview with the *New York Post*. 'I don't know if we ever get over it . . . For someone who has flirted with life and death and flirted with drug abuse and alcoholism, something gets broken and you never really recover from that. I was in Texas when I looked up and saw a cross and said to myself, "What have I got to lose?" Those six little words were magic, and they changed me. My whole life has changed,' he went on. 'It's been hard, but I wouldn't change it for anything. I'd rather . . . go my whole life believing that there is a God and find out there isn't than live my whole life thinking there isn't a God and then find out, when I die, that there is.'

The devil might still have all the best tunes, but when it comes time for Dave to pass through the cemetery gates, God will certainly have a few cracking solos to call upon . . .

W. Axl Rose

6 February 1962

Born: William Bruce Rose, Jr.

Alter-egos: W. Axl Rose, a.k.a. the 'red-headed one' in G N' R, according to their one-time manager, Alan Niven (possibly the only personality in Axl's entourage who dared to refer to the flame-haired singer as such).

(Pre)-occupations: Frontman and songwriter with Guns N' Roses.

Live by this: 'Well, as you can see, being a fucking psycho basket-case has its advantages . . .' – W. Axl Rose

'The fans don't like when I let them know they don't own me. Sometimes I don't even own myself.' – W. Axl Rose

'Axl is just another version of the Ayatollah.' – Slash

Deadly sins: With his initials spelling out the acronym WAR, it was perhaps inevitable that W. Axl Rose would set himself at odds with the world. Given his insanely mistrustful nature, it's unsurprising that he has kept his friends close, and his enemies closer.

While personal and musical differences have been responsible for many a famous feud within the annals of rock'n'roll, Axl has the dubious honour of being the only frontman who has wilfully brought about a situation in which he is the singer in his own tribute band. Having selected drummer Steven Adler, whom he'd never liked, as a sacrificial scapegoat to serve as a warning to guitarists Slash and Izzy over their own dalliances with 'Mr. Brownstone', Axl bided his time until Guns N' Roses were at the top of their game before – at least according to Tom Zutaut, the man responsible for signing Guns N' Roses to Geffen Records in March 1986 – issuing an ultimatum to Slash, Duff and Izzy: he refused to go out on tour in support of the *Use Your Illusion* albums unless they signed over the rights to the band's name. Of course, what's even more astonishing is that Slash, Duff, and Izzy agreed to Axl's demand.

Perhaps unsurprisingly, seeing as he'd never truly wanted Guns N' Roses to get above playing the club circuit, it was Izzy who first accepted that they'd reached an impossible impasse, and announced his departure following the band's appearance at Wembley Stadium at the end of August 1991. And though Slash and Duff – together with new drummer Matt Sorum and guitarist Gilby Clarke, who was brought in to take over Izzy's rhythmic responsibilities – ploughed on regardless, from that point on, Guns N' Roses were a band in name only. Izzy eventually rekindled his friendship with Axl and occasionally joins Guns N' Roses onstage, and even Duff has let bygones be bygones. Slash, however, whose creative partnership with Axl was akin to that of Mick Jagger and Keith Richards, or Steven Tyler and Joe Perry, insists that he hasn't spoken with Axl since the day he quit the band in 1996, and doesn't foresee the hatchet being laid to rest any time soon.

Of course, it wasn't only his faltering relationships with the guys in Guns N' Roses that provided the media with excellent copy, as Axl's entanglements with the two loves of his life, Erin Everly and Stephanie Seymour, were equally ill-fated. The daughter of Don Everly – who, together with his brother Phil, enjoyed mainstream success on both sides of the Atlantic in the early sixties – Erin was the inspiration behind the Gunners' 1987 US number one 'Sweet Child o' Mine'. However, despite Axl's belief that he and Erin had been together in a previous life – and her long, flowing tresses, which reminded him of a 'warm safe place where as a child I'd hide' – she still suffered regular beatings as a result of his violent mood-swings.

'I always believed things would get better. I thought I could make his early childhood suffering all better,' she told a reporter, sometime after their unhappy union of less than nine months was annulled in January 1991. The warring couple had tied the knot in Las Vegas the previous April, after Axl arrived at her door unannounced in the middle of the night brandishing a pistol and threatening to shoot himself unless she agreed to marry him. However, after falling foul of Axl's temper for having dared to clean his CD collection some six months later, Erin realised the futility of living in permanent fear: 'I didn't think I could survive mentally any longer. I was dying inside,' she told the same reporter. 'At the door, I stopped and turned around and told him, "I want you to take a good look at me because you're never going to see me again . . ." And he never has.'

Stephanie, who like Erin was a model at the time she hooked up with Axl, appeared in the promo videos for the Guns N' Roses singles 'Don't Cry' and 'November Rain', the latter of which sees the couple posing as bride and groom. Though Axl claimed he'd hired a genuine minister to appear in the video, their real-life engagement lasted just three weeks. Axl's fondness for punctuating his sentences with his fists led to Stephanie packing her bags and returning to the arms of legendary Hollywood Lothario, Warren Beatty, whom she'd been seeing prior to getting involved with the singer. According to Stephanie, Axl flew into a rage and smashed up their Mediterranean-style Malibu home before attacking her simply because she'd pressed ahead with a party he'd wanted to cancel.

'Axl is just another version of the Ayatollah.'

- Slash

Aside from the autocratic antics that ruined one of the greatest – and indeed, most dangerous – bands ever to take to a stage, and the physical and mental abuse he inflicted on the women in his life, Axl wasn't above cutting the few friends he had to the quick: the obvious example being respected English rock journalist Mick Wall, who subsequently penned both *Guns N' Roses: The Most Dangerous Band in the World*, and *W. Axl. Rose: The Unauthorized Biography*. Having supposedly acquiesced to Mick's request for an interview, Axl summoned Mick to his West Hollywood lair one night in January 1990, and spent the duration of the interview crowing about how Mötley Crüe's frontman, Vince Neil, was in sore need of 'a good ass-whippin', and that he was just the guy to do it – only to accuse Mick of fabricating the story days later. Not only was this unfair – given that Mick had been openly championing Guns N' Roses ever since reviewing their UK debut at the Manchester Apollo back in October 1987 – it was also blatantly untrue.

'There's always a vendetta going on somewhere with Axl,' Mick recounted for *Wired.com* in November 2008. 'I got there at like 1:00am, and I left at like 5:00am, and we did an extraordinarily long interview all about how he wanted to duke it out with Vince, and he was going to kill that motherfucker, and all the rest of it.'

'I hate to give Vince Neil or Mötley Crüe any credit like this, you know,' he ranted. 'But he's goin' around saying a bunch of crap and it's like, I just want to call him out on it. It's like, he's a liar and he's a wimp. And it's like, if he wants to do somethin' – any time, you know? At wherever. Name a place. Bring who you want. I don't care . . .'

Mick returned to London fully aware of the powder keg in his possession, and before sending the article over to his sub-editor at *Kerrang!*, he'd called Axl to see if he was willing to stand by his comments about Vince. 'A few weeks later, as I'm writing the story, I realise how heavy this looks, so I call him on the phone,' says Mick, continuing with his tale. 'I taped that conversation also, and I said to him, "Let me read you this, because to me this sounds heavy, and I just want to make sure this is how you still feel, and you still want to do this." I read it to him, he laughed, and then he said, "I stand by every single word, motherfucker, go ahead and print it." So I did. And literally within a week or two of the story appearing, as far as he was concerned, I'd made the whole thing up. I was a dirty rotten limey journalist who can't be trusted, and had lied about what went on, and misquoted him. This isn't like, "Ozzy Osborne is crazy," or "Alice Cooper, he's crazy." I don't think it's like that. I think the guy genuinely has personal issues, which, on a completely human level, I totally wish him really all the best with and hope that pain goes away for him one day.'

> 'Me and my friends were always in trouble.
> It finally reached a point where I realised I was gonna end up
> in jail 'cause I kept fucking with the system.'
>
> – Axl Rose

To his even greater detriment, Axl appeared to have little or no respect for the fans that had put him on his lofty pedestal. For anyone attending a Guns N' Roses concert post-*Appetite for Destruction*, it wasn't so much a question of whether it would be a good show, but rather a case of whether Axl would even show. And while Axl tried to excuse his tardiness in an April 1992 interview, claiming that 'I pretty much follow my own internal clock', before making an apology of sorts by explaining that it drove him nuts 'to make people sit around and wait' while he worked himself up to go out onstage. But just because he felt that he performed better later at night, it didn't give him the right to piss on everyone else's schedule. In the same interview, Axl said that his fans 'don't like it when I let them know they don't own me', and according to *Metal Hammer*, a classic example of this mindset came when – sick of receiving batch after batch of demo tapes from aspiring musicians hoping to grab just a fraction of his success – he piled the offending items on the driveway outside his Malibu mansion, clambered into his monster truck and proceeded to crush them into dust, in full view of the hapless senders.

On a highway to hell? If it can be said that we are all products of our environment – our decisions and our character indelibly shaped by however we've been brought up – then William Bruce Rose, Jr. was on a hiding to nothing from the day he was born: namely, 6 February 1962 in the small college town of Lafayette, Indiana.

For unbeknown to 'Bill' (as his mother always called him) his biological father, William Rose, Sr. (whose rabblerousing, barroom-brawling antics provided more than a hint of what was to come once his strawberry-blond namesake reached maturity), had abandoned the family when his son was just two years of age. Needless to say, Bill himself was far too young to remember anything about this schism. Neither did he retain any memories of his mother's second marriage two years later. Sharon Rose's new husband, a Pentecostal preacher named L. Stephen Bailey, already had a son (Stuart) and adopted William, Jr. as his own. Endowed with Bailey's name, Axl grew up believing that the not-so-benevolent reverend was his father. And it was only by happenstance that Axl discovered this not to be the case, as he revealed in April 1992. 'I wasn't told I had a real father until I was seventeen. My real father was my stepdad, as far as I knew, but I found some insurance papers and then I found my mom's diploma with the last name "Rose". I was never born Bill Bailey. I was born William Rose. I am W. Rose because William was an asshole.'

According to Axl, the bible-thumping Bailey was wont to preach to his new family – augmented by the arrival of Axl's younger half-sister, Amy – of the holy commandments as though he'd visited with the Lord himself on Mount Sinai. Yet the stringent Pastor's propensity for lashing out first and asking where it hurt afterwards, coupled with his credo of 'do as I say, not as I do', meant Axl's childhood memories were the stuff of nightmares. For while Nikki, Corey Taylor, Marilyn Manson et al. merely sang of the hypocrisy ingrained within the Christian faith, Axl actually lived the cliché on a daily basis. Indeed, he would later claim – after undergoing past-life regression therapy that allegedly unlocked many buried memories from his formative years – that Bailey assaulted him and his siblings in every sense: physically, mentally, and sexually. And though his mother suffered similar abuse, she stoically refused to leave Bailey – a decision that's perhaps clouded Axl's view of holy matrimony for life.

Axl claims to have been arrested and thrown in jail on more than twenty occasions, on charges ranging from bunking off of school to public drunkenness and brawling in the street. Most of these petty offences warranted nothing more severe than a slap on the wrist – or at worst, a night in the drunk tank. However, his rep as a regular offender led to stiffer sentences, culminating in a three-month custodial sentence in a young offenders' prison following his failure to pay the fine for a previous offence. According to the records of Tippecanoe County Court, in the 26-month period from July 1980 to September 1982, Axl spent a further ten days cooling his heels in adult jail for varying misdemeanours.

'Me and my friends were always in trouble,' Axl reminisced during an interview with Rolling Stone in August 1989. 'We got in trouble for fun. It finally reached a point where I realised I was gonna end up in jail 'cause I kept fucking with the system. This guy and I got into a fight. We became friends afterwards, and he dropped charges against me, but the state kept on pressing charges. Those charges didn't work, so they tried other ones. I spent three months in jail and finally got out.'

By the summer of 1980, the sole point of interest within Lafayette as far as Axl was concerned was the Interstate 65, which stretched all the way to LA where his old pal from Jefferson High, Jeffrey Dean Isbell (otherwise known as 'Izzy Stradlin') had recently moved to further his own rock'n'roll aspirations. Indeed, Axl's striking out west to hook up with Izzy was deemed so integral to the Gunners' history that the scene was recreated in the opening sequence of the 'Welcome to the Jungle' video, showing a doe-eyed Axl looking suitably 'cornpone' for the camera in his back-to-front baseball cap, chewing on a straw and alighting from a Greyhound bus to be met by a plethora of dope-dealers, pimps and other undesirable elements of LA's seedy underbelly.

However, after two years of fruitless to-ing and fro-ing between Lafayette and LA, Axl eventually decided to make his next stay in the 'City of Angels' rather more permanent: on 19 December 1982 – accompanied by on-off girlfriend, Gina Siler – he bid a final and not-so-fond farewell to the Hoosier State. He'd come get a band together, or else join one that was already happening, and the time-honoured way to make this happen was via a well-placed ad in the 'musicians wanted' section of magazines like the *Recycler* and *RIP* magazine.

It wasn't long before Axl's ability to hit (and hold) notes that would have left most of his contemporaries gasping for breath came to mark him out from a crowd of young pretenders. Within a couple of months he was fronting a low-rent West Hollywood outfit called Rapidfire, who – despite his best efforts – continued firing blanks. Izzy was too busy getting his own band off the ground to be of much assistance. Eventually, however, he suggested Axl hook up with a guitarist friend of his called Chris Weber who, at the time, was dangling at an equally loose end. Axl and Weber pooled their resources to form the band Rose, which subsequently evolved into Hollywood Rose – including Izzy in the line-up – and eventually into Guns N' Roses.

Having gone on record to emphasise how he 'didn't know shit about doing drugs, so [he] learned what's safe and what's not, how to get it, how to do it properly and everything else that's involved,' Axl subsequently expanded on the subject of drugs in an interview with *Rolling Stone*: 'I'm not and never have been a junkie. The last interview in *RIP* magazine got taken out of context about me talking openly about my drug use,' he told the magazine. 'That was over two years ago and was only for a few weeks when there was nothing to do. I was also very safe about it. That doesn't mean that at some point I won't get really sick of life and choose to OD.

'I'm not and never have been a junkie. That doesn't mean that at some point I won't get really sick of life and choose to OD.'
- W. Axl Rose

Then people will go, "He was always a junkie." That's not the case, but you can believe what you want: I don't give a fuck. No one's really gonna believe anything I say anyway as far as what I do or don't do with drugs, 'cause it's such a taboo subject.'

Having revealed that he was happy unwinding with a bottle of champagne and a few beer chasers, he then delivered a thinly-veiled attack on his fellow Gunners – most notably Slash, Izzy and Steven – over their respective habits. 'I don't want to see drugs tear up this band. I'm against when it goes too far. Right now, for me, a line of coke is too far,' he declared in the same interview. 'A line of coke puts my voice out of commission for a week. I don't know why. Maybe it's because I did a lot of stuff before. Maybe it's guilt and it's relocated in my throat. All I know is it's not healthy for me right now. And if somebody goes, "Oh, man, he's not a party-er anymore" – hey, fuck you! Do you want a record or not?'

However seriously you choose to take his view of death by overdose as a form of rock'n'roll euthanasia, Axl's apparently throwaway comment about displaced guilt seems altogether more telling. Despite having divested himself of his stepfather's surname, the frontman was still struggling to shake off the same suffocating sense of guilt that blighted his childhood. In stark contrast with Corey Taylor's cocksure conviction that the seven deadly sins are a 'bullshit' control mechanism for the powers that be, the fiery sermons of the good Pastor still rage inside the tortured mind of Axl Rose.

Moments of madness: Every Rose has its thorn – and for the past three decades, the line between creativity and lunacy has been marked by the crazed, drunk-dancing footsteps of W. Axl Rose. Epic feuds and domestic disputes aside, the copper-haired firebrand has gotten himself embroiled in many an unsavoury situation over the years. Aside from standard dust-ups with press, promoters, and record-label personnel, he's been accused of casual racism and homophobia (thanks to the subject matter of 'One in a Million', a track that's peppered with bigoted references to 'faggots' and 'niggers'), and – in keeping with the title of his master opus – an insatiable appetite for random acts of destruction, including shoving a $38,000 piano through the side of the house he shared with Erin Everly.

However, at this tumultuous time in the annals of Axl, his rage was not limited to inanimate objects. 'Neighbour says Axl Rose hit her with a wine bottle; he says she's got a corkscrew loose,' *People* magazine reported in the aftermath of the rocker's epic spat with fellow condominium-dweller Gabriella Kantor in 1990. Axl was duly arrested and charged with assault, yet despite the specifics of Kantor's testimony ('it was a Chardonnay, a really good bottle,' the lady recalled, even after the alleged blow to the head), Rose remained indignant, denying his guilt to the last. 'Frankly,' he sneered, 'if I was going to hit her with a wine bottle, she wouldn't have gotten up. I would have become a criminal at that point, wondering what I was going to do next to not get busted over the quivering body in my hallway.' Whichever the true version of events, the debacle did at least provide Axl with the inspiration for 'Right Next Door to Hell', the opening sonic salvo to *Use Your Illusion I*.

And by the following May, Axl's professional life was fast descending into a similar tragicomedy. Following manager Alan Niven's dismissal in May 1991 – a move orchestrated by Axl himself – no one within the Gunners' infrastructure appeared willing or able to tackle Axl's flash-fire temper tantrums. And the consequences of his bandmates' collective refusal to acknowledge the elephant in the room came during the opening leg of their mammoth, eight-legged 192-date Use Your Illusion World Tour at the recently-opened Riverport Performing Arts Center in Maryland Heights, Missouri, on Tuesday, 2 July 1991. By this juncture the tour was well under way, but while the band's seventh single to date: 'You Could

Be Mine' (the high-octane theme for James Cameron's blockbusting *Terminator 2: Judgement Day*), was riding high on the *Billboard* chart, the parent album(s) had yet to be released. Axl was said to be spitting feathers over the ongoing delay – despite the delay being of his own making (in fact, Axl flat-out refused to put down vocals for either album until Geffen sanctioned the removal of the New Zealand-born Niven in favour of his assistant, the infinitely more Axl-friendly Doug Goldstein). Yet despite Geffen and everyone else connected with the tour now genuflecting at Axl's altar, the mood in camp remained ugly, and it was only a matter of time before some unfortunate soul reaped the whirlwind.

The first hint that the evening wasn't to end well came when the venue's security failed to respond to Axl's request to deal with a biker-type who'd been making a nuisance of himself from the moment the band came out

'All of sudden I'm diagnosed a manic-depressive . . .
"Let's put Axl on medication". Well, the medication doesn't help me deal with the stress, the only thing it does is keep people off my back.'
– W. Axl Rose

onstage. What Axl didn't know, of course, was that the biker in question was Stump, leader of a local gang called the Saddle Tramps. And while Guns N' Roses would be hauling their asses out of town the following day, the hapless security guards in the arena's employ all lived locally and were naturally reluctant to see their names added to Stump's shit-list.

As fans were supposed to have been searched for cameras and recording equipment on entry – owing to the band's intention of documenting the tour for a possible future release – Axl's patience was tested further when Stump gleefully produced a camera from his jacket and proceeded to snap away in plain view of the security guards. It was on seeing the guards turn yet another blind eye that Axl took matters into his own hands by leaping down into the crowd to confront Stump. This unexpected diversion from the evening's scripted itinerary was enough galvanise the security team into action, but only to bodily restore an irate Axl to the stage.

'Thanks to the lame-ass security, I'm going home,' he yelled before stomping off the stage. If he'd only thought to inform the jeering crowd that he was actually going backstage to find a new contact lens to replace the one he'd inadvertently lost during the fracas, then disaster might still have been averted, but the crowd took Axl at his word . . . Storming the stage, they caused an estimated $200,000-worth of damage to both the venue and the Gunners' equipment before order was restored by armed cops sporting full riot gear. 'We were backstage, watching cops on stretchers all bloody and shit, and it was like, "Fuck! How could this be happening?"' Slash later recalled. 'I was so scared that somebody was going to die. It was completely out of hand. The kids had a field day. I lost all my amps, my guitar tech [Adam Day] got a bottle in the head, somebody got knifed, our stage and video equipment and Axl's piano were trashed. I don't know. It was a fluke. It shouldn't have happened . . . but it did.'

In Izzy's eyes, however, there was no doubt as to who was responsible for the carnage that night: 'It took me right back to [Castle] Donington,' he sighed, alluding to the band's disastrous set at the 1988 Monsters of Rock festival, during which two fans – twenty-year-old Landon Siggers and eighteen-year-old Alan Dick – were trampled to death. 'Like, what if someone had died again? Because the singer doesn't *like* something? Like, what are we getting at here?'

> 'Axl's unpredictable mood swings electrified him - a sense of impending danger hung in the air around him. I loved that trait in him. Because his fire could not be controlled.'
>
> - Duff McKagan

Due to the loss of the aforementioned gear, the band were forced to postpone ensuing shows in Kansas and Chicago, while the show's promoters, Contemporary Promotions, in conjunction with the venue's owners, filed lawsuits against Guns N' Roses. But worse was to follow for Axl, as three days later a warrant was issued for his arrest on five separate charges – four counts of assault and one of damage to property – each of which carried a maximum sentence of one year in jail.

Fortunately for Axl, the warrant couldn't be issued outside of Missouri. By the time Axl did give himself up to the authorities some twelve months later, his lawyers had had more than enough time to entangle the charges in reel after reel of expensive red tape and Axl was able to get away with paying a fine.

While fans will undoubtedly argue that this particular moment of madness came with his failure to grasp that the sum of the G N' R whole was infinitely greater than its individual parts, Axl's crowning moment of insanity surely came with the decision to release *Chinese Democracy* under the Guns N' Roses' banner rather than as a solo album – after all, by

November 2008 he was the last Gunner standing from the classic line-up who'd headed into the studio in 1994 to start work on the follow-up to the band's woefully cobbled-together covers album, *The Spaghetti Incident?*, some fifteen years and $13 million earlier. Indeed, by this juncture Axl had become something of a laughing stock as, to all intents and purposes, he was the lead singer in his own tribute band.

In a January 2000 interview with *Rolling Stone* – his first for six years – Axl insisted that *Chinese Democracy* wasn't an Axl Rose album, even if he'd wanted it to be: 'Everybody is putting everything they've got into singing and building. Maybe I'm helping steer it to what it should be built like,' he mused, to the consternation of all concerned.

At the time the *Rolling Stone* interview went to press, G N R's long-serving (and equally long-suffering) manager, Doug Goldstein, was telling anyone who would listen that the album was near completion and that fans could expect a summer 2000 release. Indeed, *Chinese Democracy* had been built up to titanic proportions, but unfortunately for Doug Goldstein, Geffen Records, and anyone else with a vested interest in the project, Axl was by now both captain and iceberg.

Indeed, Geffen's senior decision makers had already tried coercing him into stepping proceedings up a gear with the offer of an immediate payment of $1 million – coupled with a further $1 million should he deliver the finished album before 1 March 1999. Though Axl happily banked the initial seven-figure incentive, Geffen's bribe failed to motivate him beyond moving his hired hands into Rumbo Studios where Guns N' Roses had recorded much of their debut, *Appetite for Destruction*.

One could argue that in releasing the dust-encrusted white elephant that was *Chinese Democracy*, Axl had developed an appetite for self-destruction, but having already sunk so much time and money into endless – and seemingly pointless – remixes of the album, he was always going to find himself wedged between the proverbial rock and a hard place. The cold, unpalatable truth was that *Chinese Democracy* was never going to recoup the eight-figure layout, nor live up to its billing – as was subsequently proved when it peaked at a relatively disappointing number three on the US *Billboard* chart.

†rent Reznor

17 May 1965

Born: Michael Trent Reznor

Alter-egos: Trent Reznor, the raven-haired, black-clad mastermind who dubbed himself 'Mr. Self-Destruct' and lived to regret it. A self-confessed band geek, Trent was a profoundly 'shy, uncomfortable' student, who'd cultivated a unique ability to 'slip' through high school, unnoticed by his self-absorbed peers. 'I hated school . . . fucking hated it,' confirmed Reznor years later in an interview with *Spin* magazine, which recently proclaimed Trent the 'most vital artist in music'. 'The fact that it revolved around something you didn't have access to. If you weren't on the football team, if you were in the band, you were a leper. When people say those were the best years of our lives, I want to scream.'

(Pre) occupations: Multi-instrumentalist frontman with industrial rockers Nine Inch Nails, record producer and composer with How to Destroy Angels and Tapeworm.

Live by this: 'I don't know or care, really, what people think about me. I'll read interviews where I'm portrayed as something that I know I don't think I am, if I know who I am anymore, but I don't care.' – Trent Reznor

'This isn't meant to last . . . This is for right now.' – Trent Reznor

Deadly sins: In *The Birth of Tragedy from the Spirit of Music* (first published in 1872), German philosopher Friedrich Nietzsche opines that it is only through the spirit of music in tragedy that we can experience joy in the annihilation of the individual. The idea being that music carries us beyond individual concerns. The tragic hero, whose annihilation we witness, is a phenomenon of the world-will and his death signifies only the death of the phenomenon, not of the will itself. Man may not comprehend this truth logically, yet he can feel it in the music. It is a treatise which several

Cemetery Gates saints and survivors have taken to heart, but nowhere is its resonance felt more than in Nine Inch Nails' doom-laden canon.

Trent has said that he wished he'd have been able to conduct press interviews in the guise of some outlandish alter ego (Slipknot-style), so that he might be able to keep some small part of his true self for himself, especially when called upon to explain the origin of the vitriol that drives such songs as 'Terrible Lie' from Nine Inch Nails' debut long-player, *Pretty Hate Machine* (1989). 'I believe in God. I was brought up going to Sunday school and church, but it didn't really mean anything,' he told *Spin*. 'Things upset me a lot. It was just a theme I kept coming back to – religion, guilt and doubting,' he added. 'I believe there is a God, I'm just not sure of his relevance.'

While touring with Nine Inch Nails in July 2000, Trent came uncomfortably close to discovering God's relevance first-hand after OD'ing on heroin in a London hotel room. Indeed, it was only thanks to his quick-thinking aides, who managed to sneak him out of the hotel via the laundry room, that his near crash and burn didn't make the front pages. Long regarded as a symbol of darkness and alienation by his fans, his stage persona had crossed over into his personal life some six years earlier during the Self-Destruct Tour in support of Nine Inch Nails' second album proper, *The Downward Spiral*. Shortly before Christmas 1994, while performing in Columbus, Ohio, where Dimebag Darrell would be gunned down a decade later, Trent's beloved golden retriever, Maise, was fatally injured after falling from a third-floor balcony. Trent was inconsolable, and having cancelled the following night's show, flew to Miami where, by his own admission, he wilfully pressed his own self-destruct button.

'I fell deeper into a depression that consumed my entire being. I became lazy, I became irritable, [and] I was a giant fucking asshole to everyone who had been close to me. I made shitty decisions. I was a mess. It was the worst time of my life,' he candidly revealed to the *Los Angeles Times*. 'I got so bad that I couldn't even write down songs that were caught in my head. And then I would feel depressed, so I would go and get more messed up. I finally pulled out of it. Then it was great to discover that I hadn't killed myself and my liver still worked, and eventually my brain started functioning again. And then [I] was enjoying the process again.'

Following a stint in rehab, Trent returned to New Orleans and began work on the songs that would ultimately make up *The Fragile*. Though still in a somewhat delicate state himself, his newfound sobriety allowed him to fully immerse himself in the new project. And while the lyrics were more abstract than specific, the music was revelatory in that it felt like a personalised cry for help. As he told the *LA Times*: 'It was a record of complete fear, as if I had tapped into my insides and captured exactly how terrified I felt. I listened to it the other day for the first time in a long time, and I was amazed how frightened I sounded.'

At the time, however, he was so elated at finishing the album that – by his own admission – he did 'a very foolish thing'. He celebrated with a drink – his first since leaving rehab. Had this been his only relapse he might have pulled away from the brink, but the following day he reached for the bottle again and had a couple more, and each day after that he doubled the measure until he was right back where he started. Like all recovering addicts, he told himself that he was in control. But each time he opened the bottle it wasn't the contents he was ingesting, but rather his anxieties and insecurities. When Nine Inch Nails subsequently headed out on the road to promote *The Fragile*, Trent found his old drug demons

'I don't know or care, really, what people think about me. I'll read interviews where I'm portrayed as something that I know I don't think I am, if I know who I am anymore, but I don't care.'

- Trent Reznor

were riding shotgun. And whereas most musicians relish days off between dates, he would dip his head under the covers in his darkened hotel room, wanting nothing more than to be back in the sanctuary of his own bed, gripped with fear that he'd be ruined financially if he stopped the tour, yet equally terrified continuing would be the death of him. In a previous interview with the same paper he explained that he'd 'hated everyone and everything' – including himself. 'I was certainly depressed and I was in the thralls of withdrawal for about a year after the Fragile Tour. Through my actions, I was certainly behaving in an irresponsible enough way that I was, in a cowardly way, trying to end it.'

Even once the tour was complete his maudlin state of mind was such that he believed his career was over. 'I hated making music,' he admitted. 'From a commercial standpoint, *The Fragile* was a failure. The record company seemed to abandon us. My manager and I weren't getting along. I didn't feel like I could write anymore, and I couldn't even stop drinking.'

Ironically, it was the death of a close friend – in an apparently random shooting – which gave Trent the resolve to check himself back into rehab. It was, he readily admits, a cold-turkey experience that still makes him shudder. 'There was a persona that had run its course. I needed to get my priorities straight, my head screwed on,' he said in an interview with *Kerrang!*. 'Instead of always working, I took a couple of years off, just to figure out who I was and working out if I wanted to keep doing this or not. I had become a terrible addict; I needed to get my shit together, figure out what had happened.'

On a highway to hell? Everyone's got a theory about what's eating Michael Trent, including the man himself. During an interview with *Rolling Stone*, Trent said that Nine Inch Nails was 'big enough and mainstream enough to gently lead people into the back room and maybe show them some things it might have taken them a little longer to stumble into on their own'. The 'back room' in question, of course, is the human psyche and is here used by Reznor as a metaphor to 'represent anything that an individual might consider taboo yet intriguing, anything we're conditioned to abhor'.

What Trent came to abhor most as he passed through adolescence to manhood was the sterile banality of his own existence: 'Maybe my obsessive desire to find extremes has to do with growing up where nothing ever happened,' he mused in later years.

Michael Trent Reznor was born on 17 May 1965, in Mercer, Pennsylvania, a small, nondescript farming town located within the Keystone State's north-western corner. Yet, as with many of his *Cemetery Gates* contemporaries, whose parents' separations put them on the first curve of their respective downward spirals, Trent also had to contend with an enforced estrangement from his baby sister, Tera, who remained with his mother while he was farmed out to her parents, which meant his childhood wasn't as cookie-cutter dull as he perhaps makes out. 'My grandparents are good people and good parents, but I feel like anybody does whose parents split up – kind of ripped off,' he told *Alternative Press* in 1990. 'Subconsciously, it may have some kind of effect, but it didn't seem to be that bad. You just realise you're not on *Happy Days*.'

Of course, having an idyllic childhood comparable to that of the fictional Cunningham family's children – as seen in the long-running American sitcom which made a household name of Henry 'Fonzie' Winkler – doesn't necessarily make for contentment in later life, as Pete Steele, who was raised in a loving household, yet spent his adulthood mired in depression and substance abuse, tragically proves.

Trent would have us believe that the only thing which manifested itself in his formative mind was a burning desire to escape the stagnant constraints of Nowheresville USA. 'Growing up, I so wanted to get the fuck out of where I was, away from the mediocrity and mundaneness of rural life,' he told *Spin* magazine. 'I was intrigued with the limit, the movie that scared the shit out of me, the book – I had a huge collection of scary comic books when I was a kid.'

Upon graduating from Mercer High in 1983, eighteen-year-old Trent – his hair cropped and dyed fire-engine red – enrolled at Allegheny College, a private liberal-arts school located in neighbouring Meadville, to study computer engineering. At first glance, his newfound passion for rock music and his choice of subject appear as mutually exclusive as night and day, but with machine-generated music coming into mainstream prominence with bands such as Depeche Mode, the Eurythmics, and the Human League, who'd scored a number one hit on both sides of the Atlantic with 'Don't You Want Me' the previous summer, Trent had found his *raison d'être*. (Two other electronic pioneers who'd laid the foundations for Trent's sonic blueprint for Nine Inch Nails were David Bowie and Gary Numan – both of whom would share a stage with NIN in later years.)

'I was a giant fucking asshole to everyone who had been close to me. I made shitty decisions. I was a mess. It was the worst time of my life.'
– Trent Reznor

'It was really exciting,' he subsequently enthused. 'Sequencers were just coming out. I was going to college for computer engineering and I thought, "I love music, I love keyboard instruments – maybe I can get into synthesiser design." The excitement of hearing a Human League track and thinking, that's all machines, there's no drummer. That was my calling.' However, at the end of his first year – during which time he'd let his studies slide – he dropped out of college and, in his own words, 'whored myself out for $300 a week playing keyboards in cover bands' before relocating to Cleveland, Ohio. 'Cleveland wasn't that bad,' he reflected years later. 'It's lacking in some things, but it provided a good place for me to get my shit together.'

Trent eventually signed on as an assistant engineer at a Cleveland studio – Right Track Studios – where he was happy to perform the most menial of tasks in return for furthering his engineering education. Right Track's owner, Bart Koster, was so impressed by Trent's enthusiasm that he allowed him to work on his own material during off-hours. And it was the majority of these demos which subsequently made up the track-listing on Nine Inch Nails' debut album, *Pretty Hate Machine*.

When subsequently asked to sum up this transitional period in his life during an interview with *Select* magazine in April 1994, Trent said: 'We [Chris and I] lived in the shittiest apartment; all we ate were peanut butter sandwiches. We were poverty brothers; we got our bills down so low so we could do music instead of getting shitty jobs. I worked in a music shop, which was hellish. The last thing you feel like doing is coming home and playing an instrument. And I cleaned toilets in a rehearsal studio. I wiped many a musician's pubic hair off the toilet seat. It sucked.'

Legend has it that Nine Inch Nails or 'NIN' as they inevitably became known – was in reference to the 'nine-inch nails' used to crucify Christ, but Trent was quick to repudiate this when speaking with *Axcess* magazine in 1994. 'I don't know if you've ever tried to think of band names, but usually you think you have a great one and you look at it the next day and it's stupid,' he reflected. 'I had about two hundred of those. "Nine Inch Nails" lasted the two-week test, looked great in print and could be abbreviated easily. It really doesn't have any literal meaning. It seemed kind of frightening. It's a curse trying to come up with band names.'

'I finally pulled out of it. Then it was great to discover that I hadn't killed myself and my liver still worked, and eventually my brain started functioning again. And then I was enjoying the process again.'

– Trent Reznor

It's hard to imagine now, but back when Trent set NIN's wheels in motion, his sole ambition was to test the water. The plan was simple: he'd put a twelve-inch single out on some obscure European label and then wait around for a couple of years gauging the ripples before approaching a bigger label. But of course, the demos were deemed way too good to be wasted in such a manner and within the year Nine Inch Nails had been signed by the New York-based label TVT Records, which had made its name releasing albums made up of TV theme tunes, but had recently entered the alternative-rock market. TVT's founder and CEO, Steve Gottlieb, was a hard-nosed attorney who'd already garnered a reputation for treating his acts as he did those he was prosecuting in court.

Despite TVT believing *Pretty Hate Machine* to be 'a piece of shit', the album reached a very respectable 75 on the *Billboard* chart, and thanks to MTV's heavy rotation of the lead single 'Down in It', Nine Inch Nails, or more accurately, Trent, was able to build up a loyal and dedicated following of angst-ridden teenagers who were attuned to NIN's sonic howl of despair. The next logical step for a band with a debut album in the shops is to go out on tour to promote the album and hopefully improve its chart placing. But at this juncture Nine Inch Nails was a one-man project akin to Varg Vikernes's Burzum in that, aside from Chris Vrenna's assistance in the studio, Trent had played all the instruments.

With Chris signed on to provide the beat, Trent recruited the other musicians required to take the Nine Inch Nails show out on the road from the Cleveland scene. 'I'm not in a position to offer somebody a thousand dollars a week to rehearse, so I took some young guys who were malleable, who would basically do what I want them to do but expand on it,' Trent said when asked to explain his strategy. 'The only context I've worked with them in so far is, "Here are the songs, here are your parts, learn them." When I start to do the next record, it'll be up in the air as to what happens. I don't see it becoming a democracy, ever.'

While there's no tangible proof that it was Trent's dictatorial edict that brought Nine Inch Nails to the attentions of the equally dogmatic W. Axl Rose, the Gunners' mercurial frontman booked NIN as the opening act on the initial European leg of their mammoth Use Your Illusion Tour. 'He [Axl] was a fan, and wanted to help out,' Trent subsequently revealed. 'We were going to Europe to do a tour, and we figured out what better way to confuse people than to open for Guns N' Roses? So we did, and the audience hated us. 'We were terrified to start with, and then we're walking onstage in front of 65,000 people in Germany [the Maimarktgelände in Mannheim]. The first song goes okay. Second song people realise we're not Skid Row, who came on after us. Third song they'd confirmed the fact that they've heard a synthesiser and it's time to attack.'

I was fortunate enough to be in the Wembley crowd on Saturday, 31 August 1991, to witness Nine Inch Nails' UK debut, and while the opening acts at such events are usually quickly consigned to the mental recycle bin, the wild-eyed, raven-haired Trent – covered in cornstarch, clad in leather (despite the heat), and wearing black lipstick and eyeliner – certainly made an impression. And not simply because he mischievously chose to prop his guitar in front of his amp at the end of their set so that the droning feedback was still reverberating around Wembley's Twin Towers long after he'd left the stage. Though *Pretty Hate Machine* and its singles – coupled with Trent's burgeoning reputation for trashing his guitars and amps, as he had in Phoenix during the opening date of the inaugural Lollapalooza festival several weeks earlier – had helped establish NIN in the US, they hadn't thus far pinged on my sonar. History tells me that the majority of the songs making up their half-hour set were from the debut album, but of course at the time titles such as 'Head Like a Hole', 'Down In It', 'Sin', and 'Sanctified' meant little in the grand scheme of things – not when I was about to witness Guns N' Roses in their consummate glory. However, I do remember them being infinitely more entertaining than Skid Row, and I was at least able to sing along to one of their songs as they did a blinding cover of Adam and the Ants' 'Physical (You're So)' which would feature on NIN's 1992 EP, *Broken*.

While *The Downward Spiral* was enthusiastically received by fans and critics alike, it wasn't until some time later that Trent revealed the 'life-sucking' toll it had exacted on him. 'The idea for this record came about [towards] the end of '91, when we finished the first Lollapalooza, and we went to Europe,' he explained on *MuchMusic* (Canada's answer to MTV). 'I was sitting in the hotel room and I was kind of seeing the energy that Nine Inch Nails was drawing upon. It was a definite negative vibe . . . So this record was focusing on those certain things that were bothering me that I felt needed exploring.

'Thematically I wanted to explore the idea of somebody who systematically throws or uncovers every layer of what he's surrounded with, comfort-wise, from personal relationships to religion to questioning the whole situation,' Trent explained of the thought processes that went into the album. 'Someone dissecting his own ability to relate to other people or to have anything to believe in . . . With *The Downward Spiral* I tried to make a record that had full range, rather than a real guitar-based record or a real synth-based record. I tried to make it something that opened the palette for Nine Inch Nails, so we don't get pigeon-holed. It was a conscious effort to focus more on texture and space, rather than bludgeoning you over the head for an hour with a guitar.'

Moments of madness: Trent had intended to record the new album in New Orleans, but owing to financial considerations he opted to relocate to Los Angeles, where he took an eighteen-month lease at 10050 Cielo Drive: the Bel Air house in which the actress Sharon Tate and several of her high-society friends had been callously slain by members of Charles Manson's so-called 'Family' in August 1969; his macabre sense of humour leading to him christening the studio he'd constructed in the house 'Le Pig', after the message one of the killers had daubed on the front door with the heavily-pregnant Tate's blood. Speaking with *Kerrang!* in April 2005, Trent claimed to have had no designs on that particular house as a base of operations; he had simply chosen it because it offered the best location.

'The house is nothing special, but the front-yard looks right out on the ocean, you've got mountains to the left and Beverly Hills behind you. It's all green and quiet; it was a country-living kind of place. When the facts came out we just thought, well, that's an interesting piece of weird Americana we just inhabited.' He also says that he'd never imagined that he'd still be called on to explain his motives ten years on. But of course, one has to view this comment with a certain amount of scepticism, if only in light of Trent's decision to have the aforementioned front door shipped to his New Orleans studio when the owner finally got around to demolishing the property. That Nothing Studios once served as a funeral home only added to the tale. 'It makes for the dream press-pack, I know,' Trent said with a wry grin. 'But that was never our conscious intention.'

Trent's continued presence on Cielo Drive struck something of a dissonant raw nerve with Sharon Tate's surviving relatives. 'While I was working on *Downward Spiral*, I met her [Sharon's] sister [Patti Tate],' he told *Rolling Stone* in 1997. 'It was a random thing, just a brief encounter. And she said, "Are you exploiting my sister's death by living in her

> '*I had become a terrible addict; I needed to get my shit together, figure out what had happened.*'
> *- Trent Reznor*

house?" For the first time, the whole thing kind of slapped me in the face. I said, "No, it's just sort of my own interest in American folklore. I'm in this place where a weird part of history occurred." I guess it never really struck me before, but it did then. She lost her sister from a senseless, ignorant situation that I don't want to support. When she was talking to me, I realised for the first time, "What if it was my sister?" I thought, "Fuck Charlie Manson." I went home and cried that night. It made me see there's another side to things, you know?'

Speaking with *Kerrang!* in March 2005, some four years after successfully completing rehab, Trent reflected on his self-destructive past: 'There was a persona that had run its course. I needed to get my priorities straight, my head screwed on. Instead of always working, I took a couple of years off, just to figure out who I was and working out if I wanted to keep doing this or not. I had become a terrible addict; I needed to get my shit together, figure out what had happened.

'I didn't realise at the time, but that was the beginning of a pretty intense struggle; it was impacting upon my life. I was drinking – put a few drinks in me and if someone suggested getting some cocaine it would seem like a fantastic idea. It still seemed like a great idea 24 hours later, picking through the grains of the carpet looking for more. After a while I realised I wasn't in control. The price wasn't just feeling bad the next day; I was starting to hate myself. That led to a path of fucking around with it, procrastinating, until I decided there was a decision to be made, which was either to get better or to die.'

While explaining the lyrics to some of his best-known songs to *Kerrang!* in July 2005, Trent admitted that 'Starfuckers, Inc', which appears on *The Fragile*, 'came from bits of lyrics I'd written over a long period' and was aimed at his former friend and one-time protégé Marilyn Manson.

Though Trent produced Marilyn Manson's debut, *Portrait of an American Family*, their relationship took something of a downturn during the recording sessions for Manson's follow-up EP, *Smells Like Children*, in summer 1995, because of a dispute over guitar parts on the demos.

> 'I was drinking - put a few drinks in me and if someone suggested getting some cocaine it would seem like a fantastic idea. It still seemed like a great idea 24 hours later, picking through the grains of the carpet looking for more. I decided there was a decision to be made, which was either to get better or to die.'
>
> – Trent Reznor

And though he scored a co-production credit on *Antichrist Superstar* the following year, which at least suggests a professional relationship, there was to be no thaw as far as their friendship was concerned. Indeed, the ice was still capable of holing a liner as late as 2009, as was all too evident in Trent's interview with *Mojo* magazine that same year. 'During the Spiral tour we propped them [Marilyn Manson] up to get our audience turned on to them,' he explained. 'At that time a lot of the people in my circle were pretty far down the road as alcoholics. Not Manson. His drive for success and self-preservation was so high; he pretended to be fucked up a lot when he wasn't. Things got shitty between us and I'm not blameless. The majority of it though was coming from a resentment guy who finally got out from under the master's umbrella and was able to stab him in the back. He is a malicious guy and will step on anybody's face to succeed and cross any line of decency. Seeing him now, drugs and alcohol now rule his life and he's become a dopey clown. He used to be the smartest guy in the room. And as a fan of his talents, I hope he gets his shit together.'

In October 2009, the man who believed his dedication to his work meant sacrificing 'a sense of normality, a community of friends and a successful relationship,' tied the knot with his Filipino fiancée, Mariqueen Maandig, in a private ceremony at his LA home. Their son, Lazarus Echo, was born the following October, and at the time of writing the couple are expecting another child.

The question on the lips of every Nails fan was whether marriage and fatherhood had mellowed Trent or caused him to re-evaluate his views on God. 'I still don't know who the fuck I am. I know what I don't believe in. I know what I've rejected, but I'm not sure yet what I do believe in,' he said in a recent interview. 'Generally, I've always aspired to be part of something. But it hasn't really happened. It's odd, because I have my big club now, and I'm president. It's not like I'm part of it though. When I went to college, I thought all I wanted to do was just disappear and see what it's like to have friends, be in a group. Two months later, I was like, "Fuck this. I'm not like you." I don't want to lose my identity, my independence, by being around a bunch of people who are also scared . . . hiding behind something printed on T-shirt that gives you a sense of who you are.

'I don't know what I want and I feel crushed because I have this shitty education. There's a lot of things I wish I knew about like Eastern religions . . . I know what I don't believe in. I don't have my own life together really. I don't wake up in the morning feeling spiritually whole, or great about nature or God, or the universe. And I've been on a quest instead of finding a way to start a life.'

Having put Nine Inch Nails into semi-permanent hiatus in February 2009, Trent was free to collaborate with Mariqueen on How to Destroy Angels, a post-industrial combo which also features one-time Tapeworm associate Atticus Ross in the line-up. A six-song EP was released as a free download via the band's website in June 2010, while the retail CD was released the following month.

Trent has also made a name for himself in the movie-soundtrack world. In 2009, he composed 'Theme for Tetsuo' for *Tetsuo: The Bullet Man*, the third and final instalment of Shinya Tsukamoto's cyberpunk trilogy. He followed this up by composing – together with Atticus Ross – the score for David Fincher's 2010 film *The Social Network*, for which they picked up a Golden Globe and an Oscar for Best Original Score. The dynamic duo have also been nominated for a 2012 Golden Globe Award for their score for the American adaptation of *The Girl with the Dragon Tattoo*.

SLASH

23 July 1965

Born: Saul Hudson

Alter-egos: Slash.

(Pre) occupations: Positively oozing cool, Slash (rarely glimpsed without his trademark jacket, hat and shades combo) is the axe-wielding virtuoso who helped Guns N' Roses conquer the world. Though his association with Axl may be over, Slash's prolific musical career is anything but. Post-G N'R, Velvet Revolver, Slash's Snakepit and Slash's Blues Ball have provided a staggering showcase for his unmistakeably epic solo style.

Live by this: 'If drinking doesn't get me, AIDS will.' – Slash

'In a world he did not create, he will go through it as if it were of his own making; half-man, half-beast. I don't know what it is, but it's weird and it's pissed off, and it calls itself Slash.' – W. Axl Rose

'I just like to play guitar. It wasn't about business, or trying to be cool on Sunset Strip, or getting on the cover of fuckin' *Rolling Stone*, or any of that. It was about just getting together with a bunch of guys that could cause something – even if we weren't all on the exact same page as far as [musical] direction goes. Somehow we managed to make a band that was a mixture of everything – of attitude. At the time, the five of us were the only people who could have made up Guns N' Roses, and that I'm proud of.' – Slash

'If there is one thing I am, it's the eternal teenager.' – Slash

Deadly sins: Derived from the Latin for altruistic love, 'charity' is the greatest heavenly virtue of them all. Yet Slash displayed a marked lack thereof when – reeling from the death of his beloved grandma and having 'borrowed' $200 from an unsuspecting friend to score some dope – he turned up at Izzy Stradlin's place in the dead of the night, completely off his gourd, and ready to use his bandmate's apartment as a makeshift opium den. Despite having an early morning appointment with his probation officer, Izzy made sure Slash was comfortably ensconced on the couch before turning in for what remained of the night. By the time Slash woke, Izzy had already left for his appointment, but rather than head home and clean up in time for his grandmother's wake, he decided to make use of Izzy's bathroom instead.

'After my shower I tried to do my fix, still high from the night before but believing it was entirely necessary,' he explained. 'I couldn't find a vein; I got blood all over the bathroom, the towels, the walls, the sink – you name it. I kept at it until I hit an artery. Then I hid my works in Izzy's living-room closet and headed out to my grandmother's wake, leaving Izzy's apartment in a bloodstained shambles.'

Having made a spectacle of himself at the wake, he returned home later in the afternoon to find a message from an irate Izzy on his answering machine. It seemed Izzy, who, being on probation, could expect an impromptu search by his parole officer at any given time, had found the not-so-well-hidden blood-encrusted syringes and spoon in his closet and was not best pleased. 'He [Slash] got pulled over for drunk-driving, and this was when he was using heroin a lot,' sighed a disgruntled Izzy in 1991, shortly after he left Guns N' Roses. 'I was staying at a hotel in Venice [Beach] and he showed up at four in the morning, fucked out of his mind. How he managed to drive there will always be a mystery to me! So I let him spend the night [and] the next morning I find two rigs [syringes] hidden in the closet. I told him, "Listen fucker, I got problems and I just can't have this shit around," 'cause I was on probation at the time.'

On a highway to hell? In contrast with many of the oppressed, repressed personalities featured within these pages, the Hudsons' approach to parenting was relaxed to say the least. 'I was given a lot of freedom as a kid,' Slash stated candidly. 'I grew up in a kind of rebellious hippy household. I started saying the word "fuck" when I was, like, seven or eight years old, telling my parents to "fuck off" all the time. They were always very attentive and I don't have any problems with my family, nothing at all compared to a lot of musicians who complain about getting kicked out of the house because they grew their hair, or were told to "fuck off and get a job". I never had that. There was music in my house all my life.

'We moved to Laurel Canyon in '77 when I was twelve and that was the beginning of my slippery slope. The public school system in the US really sucks. There was nothing to hold my attention so I just fucked off. And then I started playing guitar . . . that was the beginning of the end.'

The guitar in question – a battered old flamenco which had seen better days – supposedly only had one string, yet was still enough to divert Slash's attention from his beloved BMX bike, which until that juncture had been his sole *raison d'être*. Indeed, such was Slash's dexterity on the bike that his racing rivals were wary of entering the same competitions, while his friends expected him to turn professional. But, of course, the BMX world's loss was to be music's gain.

Though Slash's younger brother, Albion, was born shortly after the Hudson family's relocation from the seemingly unending brown-brick row houses of Stoke-on-Trent, England, to the sunnier climes of Los Angeles

'In a world he did not create, he will go through it as if it were of his own making; half-man, half-beast. I don't know what it is, but it's weird and it's pissed off, and it calls itself Slash.'

- W. Axl Rose

around 1970, his parents' marriage was already in slow decline and would ultimately end in divorce. According to Slash, his softly-spoken English father, Tony, and his rather more outgoing African-American mother, Ola, had met in Paris some six or seven years earlier. Tony, an aspiring artist, had abandoned his hometown and caught the boat to Paris where, while finding himself, he'd also encountered the fun-loving seventeen-year-old Ola, who nurtured dreams of becoming a costume designer and had left her native LA to see the world and hopefully make connections in the fashion world. While connecting with a struggling twenty-year-old painter hadn't featured in her tour itinerary, she readily accepted Tony's proposal of marriage and accompanied him on his prodigal return to Stoke, where they were subsequently married.

Soon after Slash was born – in leafy Hampstead, north London – Ola returned to Los Angeles to make use of the connections she'd made on her travels, while Tony and their toddler son moved in with his parents. Needless to say, the placid Potteries held little interest for a bohemian soul like Tony, and as soon as Slash was old enough he began taking his son to London to experience the hippy-shaking sights and smells of the capital's swinging scene. 'We'd crash on couches and not come back for days. There were lava lamps and black lights, and the electric excitement of the open booths and artists along Portobello Road,' Slash recalled in his eponymous 2007 autobiography. 'My dad never considered himself a Beat [Beatnik], but he had absorbed that kind of lifestyle through osmosis. It was as if he'd handpicked the highlights of that type of life: a love of adventure, hitting the road with nothing but the clothes on your back. My parents taught me a lot, but I learned their greatest lesson early – nothing else is quite like life on the road.'

By the time Slash was reunited with his mother towards the end of the decade, Ola's career had truly taken off and she was designing clothes for John Lennon, Ringo Starr, Helen Reddy, Linda Ronstadt and James Taylor among others. Tony, of course, had long since accepted that he was never going to set the art world alight, but thanks to Ola's connections within the thriving LA music scene, he was able to channel his artistic bent by designing album covers – most notably the cover for Joni Mitchell's hit 1974 album *Court and Spark*. Owing to the carefree, creative spirit of both, it was perhaps only natural that Tony and Ola would set up home amongst their own. In the late sixties and early seventies, Laurel Canyon Boulevard was a cosy enclave of artists and musicians including Joni Mitchell, Jim Morrison and Frank Zappa. And having already had a taste of the countercultural scene from regular father-son sorties to London, Slash took to his new surroundings like a native.

Despite having lived with Tony before the move to America, when his parents broke the news that they would be going their separate ways Slash elected to live with Ola. Because of the nature of her work, this meant that he and his little brother would more often than not be left in the care of his grandmother, also named Ola. With Tony and Ola remaining friends following their separation, Slash could have been forgiven for hoping his parents might get back together at a later date, but if so, these illusions were shattered when his mother introduced him to the new man in her life – David Bowie.

'[Bowie was] the first guy to replace my dad when my mom and dad separated,' Slash reflected. 'I can remember him tucking me up in bed.' Ola had first encountered the self-styled 'Space Oddity' when she was invited to design costumes for Bowie while he was recording his 1975 album *Young Americans*, as well as the outfits worn by the pop chameleon for his cinematic debut in Nicolas Roeg's sci-fi flick, *The Man Who Fell to Earth*. Though Bowie was married at the time – and often brought his wife, Angie, and son, Zowie, round to Ola's new home in West Hollywood – the relationship inevitably extended beyond the professional. 'The seventies were unique [as] it seemed entirely natural for Bowie to bring his wife and son to the home of his lover so that we might all hang out,' Slash reflected. 'At the time, my mother practised the same form of transcendental meditation that David did. They chanted before the shrine she maintained in the bedroom.'

Despite the strange noises emanating from his mother's bedroom at all hours of the day, Slash says he came to accept having a living legend around the house. Indeed, he found that knowing Bowie offstage enriched his appreciation for seeing him onstage, as he subsequently explained: 'His entire concert was the essence of performance. I saw the familiar elements of a man I'd gotten to know exaggerated to the extreme. He had reduced rock stardom to its roots: being a rock star is the intersection of who you are and who you want to be.' Bowie's chameleonic career has, of course, served as a blueprint for many other *Cemetery Gates* inductees, such as Marilyn Manson, Per 'Dead' Ohlin, Corey Taylor, Paul Gray, and Erik Danielsson – all of whom adopted stage personas to mask their true selves. And while the teenage Slash was as yet unsure of who he was (let alone who he wanted to be), being surrounded by such weird and wonderful personalities during his formative years meant he too was destined for a life less ordinary.

Slash says that discovering the guitar was like discovering a side of himself that he hadn't previously known existed. It not only defined him, it also gave him a purpose – not to mention a creative outlet through which to express himself. 'Finding my voice through guitar at fifteen was, to me, revolutionary,' he revealed. 'It was a leap in my evolution; I can't think of anything that made more of a difference in my life. The only moment that came close had occurred two years before when I first experienced the mystery of the opposite sex.'

Though his mom and dad were undoubtedly both aware of their son's newfound fascination, it was actually his grandmother who purchased him his first 'real' guitar – a Gibson Explorer copy – which in Slash's own words was 'cheap and nasty, and virtually impossible to keep in tune'. 'I didn't really know how to start,' he later recalled. 'I was looking at a book playing scales and didn't know where I was going, 'cause that didn't sound anything like "Cat Scratch Fever" [the opening track of Ted Nugent's 1977 album of the same name]. But my grandmother used to play piano. She was very patient and supportive because she'd come from a rich black family where, at the time, soul music was considered in bad taste and she wasn't even allowed to listen to it. So when I'd crank up "Black Dog" she'd get really upset. And of course, being the punk that I was, I'd crank it up even higher.'

Slash – having by this time received his enduring nickname from the father of a school friend on account of his always being in a hurry, zipping from one thing to another – devoted much of his spare time to practising, and developed his trademark style playing along to his grandmother's sizeable record collection. It soon became obvious to all who heard him play that he was a natural on the guitar, but Slash says that at the time he had no thought of making a career out of music. However, his rock'n'roll epiphany came courtesy of Joe Perry's licks on Aerosmith's multi-platinum 1976 album, *Rocks*, at a moment when Slash's mind was on other matters. 'I'd been trying to get into this older girl's pants for a while, and she finally let me come over to her house. We hung out, smoked some pot and listened to Aerosmith's *Rocks*,' he later recalled for *Rolling Stone*. 'It hit me like a fucking ton of bricks. I sat there listening to it over and over, and totally blew off the girl. I remember riding my bike back to my grandma's house knowing that my life had changed forever. Now I identified with something.'

Of course, the connection was more than purely musical (Perry could almost be counted amongst the ranks of hell-raising survivors featured within this tome), and as Guns N' Roses' star steadily rose, so did the guitarist's own appetite for destruction.

Like other wayward teens before him, Stash experimented with both pot and acid, and while there's no definitive proof that taking supposedly 'soft' drugs leads users onto stronger alternatives, when he was subsequently introduced to freebasing coke by his mom's photographer boyfriend, it surely dissolved any taboos surrounding heroin.

His initial dalliance with 'Mr. Brownstone' didn't come until 1984, by which time he and his future G N' R cohorts were all orbiting the same world and feeling each other out in short-lived outfits such as Road Crew, Black Sheep, and Hollywood Rose before finally coming together. Indeed, it was Slash observing how cool Izzy made smoking heroin look while they were jamming together that finally pushed him over the line – even if, by Slash's own admission, 'chasing the dragon' left him 'feeling queasy and not very high at all'. However, the queasiness didn't completely eradicate his curiosity, and on 'mainlining' a few months later, heroin crept into his life 'like ivy up a wall'.

As the song goes, he started with a little, but the little got more and more.

And because heroin was readily available to those who knew where to look for it, to his mind smack was 'strictly recreational [and not] supposed to be the centre of the universe'. Indeed, he didn't even realise the extent of his dependency until he found himself unexpectedly cut off from his supply. Having been cuffed and taken in for questioning by the cops when the friend he happened to be with was found in possession of a hypodermic needle (the two had been driving around West Hollywood in the early hours looking to score), Slash had no choice but to go cold turkey. His friend was charged over the needle, given a court date, and sent on his way, whereas Slash was left to sweat it out in one of the holding cells. He couldn't understand why he was still being detained, because while it was no secret that he and the rest of Guns N' Roses (who were by this juncture the hottest ticket in town) liked to party, they'd taken all the necessary precautions to ensure they didn't draw any untoward attention from the cops.

'If there is one thing I am, it's the eternal teenager.'
- Slash

'I had no idea what was coming next. My high had started to wear off; I was a few hours away from complete withdrawal,' Slash revealed, before going on to explain how he and the other prisoners were loaded onto a bus with gated windows, shackled at the ankles and wrists, and chained to the guy in front. 'I still had no idea why I was there, but I realised that I was going to county jail, so I immediately started chewing off my black nail polish. There was no way in hell that I was going to county with fingernail polish on.'

It turned out that Slash had been hauled off to jail because of an outstanding warrant over an unpaid ticket for jaywalking six years earlier (circa 1979). After being released, he arrived back at the Gunners' communal apartment/rehearsal space – having stopped off en route to replenish his medicinal supplies – with quite a tale to tell, and no one seemingly interested in hearing it. It wasn't until later that he discovered it had been Axl who'd scraped together the money to make his bail. However, rather than view his narrow escape as a wake-up call, Slash chose to pretend he was still in control. He even convinced himself that heroin served as his muse – a crucial source of inspiration for any songwriter. Izzy and Steven were also injecting on a daily basis at this juncture, and with Duff desperately trying to drown his own demons at the bottom of a bottle, the word on Sunset Strip was that it was only a question of time before someone within the

Guns N' Roses camp ended up on a mortuary slab with a tag on his toe. And alas, this chilling prophecy would come to pass when Slash's good friend, and occasional G N' R roadie, Todd Crew, OD'd in late 1986.

'There I was with my best friend in my arms in the bathtub,' Slash subsequently recalled. 'I was freaking out; I'd OD'd before, but I'd never dealt with anyone else OD'ing on me. I did everything I could to keep him conscious.' Slash's ad hoc administrations initially appeared to do the trick, and having dried Todd off he put him to bed. But while he was on the phone speaking to a girl named Shelley, who was the only person he knew in New York well enough to confide in, Todd suddenly stopped breathing.

'I dropped the phone and shook him, and slapped him,' Slash says continuing his harrowing tale. 'I beat on his chest but he wouldn't come around. I called 911, [and] then threw water on him, but nothing worked. I couldn't save him. Todd, all of 21 years old, died in my arms.'

> 'I may have realised how crippling addiction
> was whenever I got clean, but after I was clean a while,
> I'd reminisce about how much I loved to get high.'
>
> – Slash

Slash, of course, isn't the only one on the *Cemetery Gates* roll call to lose a friend or loved one to heroin, as Lemmy and Layne Staley both suffered the anguish of watching the women they loved throw their lives away, with Layne blithely following his fiancée into brown sugar's bittersweet embrace. But whereas Lemmy's loss only served to strengthen his resolve to avoid temptation, Slash simply opted to switch poisons. 'I was naive enough to think that I was so tough that I'd gotten myself all clean and had no problem with addiction whatsoever – the truth was I hadn't changed anything,' he later reflected. 'I'd only substituted the substance. I transitioned my addiction from illegal to legal because alcohol was acceptable to everyone. It was an expected facet of everyday life in rock'n'roll, so if I was drinking heavily but not shooting up, those in my circle were fine with that. What did they know?'

While Slash has a point about society's double standards where alcohol and substance abuse are concerned, seeing a close friend suffering from a hangover is infinitely preferable to watching them undergo the personal hell that is heroin withdrawal. Yet, as Ernest Hemingway wrote in *For Whom the Bell Tolls*, 'Of all men, the drunkard is the foulest.' For while the thief is no different from his neighbour when he isn't on the prowl, the extortioner doesn't practise in the home, and the murderer will wash the blood from his hands on reaching the sanctuary of his lair, the drunkard 'stinks and vomits in his own bed and dissolves his organs in alcohol'. Hemingway could well have been describing a heroin addict with these same lines, for like the drunkard, he or she is content to wallow in their own filth as long as they have their fix.

Slash himself may have seen booze as the lesser of two evils, but whereas he could carry out his duties as G N 'R axeman well enough while his mind was in a heroin fug, his booze intake became such that he needed a slug of Jack Daniel's on waking just to stop his hands from trembling. Not so much a case of the 'hair of the dog that bit you' cure-all, but more a question of keeping the salivating, bacchanalian beast at bay for long enough to function – as Slash readily admitted: 'The only problem was that during this period, the parties never seemed to stop, and so I began a cycle. I woke up with a hangover every day, so I started every day with a fresh drink, and then drank through to the next party that night. In no time, the parties blurred: I was drinking all night into the next day and into the next night, into the night after that. There really wasn't a day when I took time off from drinking because there was generally a party to get to every day; it was all part of my daily routine.'

While Slash hadn't officially renounced heroin and all its inherent evils, with Izzy working hard at keeping his bloodstream clean following his arrest for urinating on a commercial flight while the plane was still in midair, one might have expected him to stick to his guns. But as long as he was happy dancing to Mr. Brownstone's tune, it was perhaps inevitable that he would succumb to temptation. For despite having a friend die in his arms, Slash says he still viewed taking heroin as an adventure – a means of retreating to a 'private hideaway in my own body and mind'. While this is certainly an interesting perspective, it's undoubtedly viewed through hindsight's rose-tinted lens. And, of course, as Layne Staley's prolonged suicide shows, one person's private hideaway is another's prison.

'After I'd been through withdrawal and gotten clean more than once, the inescapable discomfort never discouraged me,' Slash reflected in his autobiography. 'I may have realised how crippling addiction was whenever I got clean, but after I was clean a while, I'd reminisce about how much I loved to get high.' Though the axeman professed not to see the writing on the wall, those closest to him could see his obituary was all but set in stone unless he sought help. His mother suggested he speak to David Bowie, but while the self-styled 'Thin White Duke' was certainly qualified to give advice on the dangers of particular potions and powders, Slash says he couldn't take the conversation seriously given that some sixteen years and a river of Jack Daniel's had passed under the bridge since the two had last spoken.

One singer who had been close enough to monitor Slash's slide down into oblivion, however, was Axl – and the Gunners' mercurial frontman wasn't known for keeping a lid on his emotions. Matters came to a head on Wednesday, 18 October 1989, on the opening night of Guns N' Roses' four-show stint opening for the Rolling Stones at the Los Angeles Coliseum. The rock cognoscenti were split between viewing the Coliseum dates as either a symbolic passing of the torch, or a direct challenge from the young colts to the old masters, but they and the rest of the 83,000-strong crowd were stunned into silence when Axl – who was certainly no saint himself – brought proceedings to a halt with an impromptu announcement: 'Unless certain people in this band get their shit together,' warned the pint-sized, flame-haired frontman, 'these will be the last Guns N' Roses shows you'll fucking ever see, 'cause I'm tired of too many people in this organisation dancing with Mr. goddamn Brownstone.'

It was a night that Slash has never forgotten. 'I was so pissed off about that,' he recalled. 'And [Axl] was so pissed at me for being a junkie that I spent the better half of the show facing my amps. Nothing was together that night, the band sounded horrible. In my state of mind I walked offstage, got into my limo, and went to get high in my room.'

The following morning Axl let it be known through intermediaries that he would play the remaining Stones dates – but only if Slash was willing to apologise for being a junkie, onstage that evening, in front of the entire audience. 'That was a pretty hard pill to swallow. In retrospect, I understand why Axl singled me out rather than Steven. I am the stronger of the two of us and Axl relied on me more. My presence was important to him; he felt that I was a link in the band that couldn't afford to be out of control. Still I didn't think a public gesture was necessary.'

As part of his Coliseum contrition act, Slash told the hushed crowd that no one in Guns N' Roses advocated the use of heroin, and that they weren't going to be one of those weak bands that fall apart because of it – and yet even as he spoke, his dealer was waiting in the wings. 'I was certainly going through my problems at the time, and trying to come to terms with the whole situation, which wasn't easy. So that colours my perspective on those gigs with the Stones,' Slash revealed in an interview the following year. 'There were so many people setting us up against the Stones – you know, the bad boys of rock'n'roll come face to face [. . .] that

I wasn't interested in hanging out with Keith Richards and seeing which one of us would end up drinking the most Jack Daniel's.'

In any other walk of life, alcohol and substance abusers are treated like lepers and kept at arm's length, and yet in the music industry – especially within the heavy-metal fraternity – they're not only tolerated, they're positively encouraged to cook up another fix or drain another bottle. Indeed, Slash and the other guys in Guns N' Roses saw it as *de rigueur* to be seen cradling a bottle of their favourite poison, which inevitably led to certain highly impressionable fans following suit. And with the band strutting around in T-shirts bearing the company's logo, Jack Daniel's shares went through the roof.

'I transitioned my addiction from illegal to legal because alcohol was acceptable to everyone. It was an expected facet of everyday life in rock'n'roll, so if I was drinking heavily but not shooting up, those in my circle were fine with that. What did they know?'

– Slash

Moments of madness: Like everyone else in the G N' R camp, Axl feared that Slash was one fix away from a one-way ticket to the funeral home, and living in expectation of the dreaded call. But when the call came – to the Gunners' beleaguered tour manager, Doug Goldstein, who was babysitting a strung-out Steven at the Venetian, an exclusive golfing resort near Phoenix, Arizona, a few weeks after the LA Coliseum dates – it wasn't to say the band's errant lead guitarist had a tag on his toe, but rather that he was very much alive: buck-naked and running amok through the luxury complex.

For reasons known only to himself (though he would later admit that 'this was when I was in my worst drug period'), Slash had followed Doug to the resort. '[Doug was] on the golf course and all of a sudden the fuckin' police came looking for him saying, "We've got a naked guy in handcuffs. He assaulted a maid." I'd smashed up my room, there was glass [everywhere], I was all bloody,' Slash confessed to *Mojo* in February 2005.

Unbeknownst to Doug, Slash had arrived at the resort the previous evening. Holed up in his room, he'd spent the next few hours shooting up until his stash was but a blissful memory. There followed what Slash would describe as a 'trip-out scene' of epic proportions. 'I took off, running naked out of the shower – went through the glass shower windows, ran naked onto the resort, into one of the rooms, ran over this maid and kept running. It was a big scene. I thought these two little guys were after me and they had these huge fucking knives. I ran outside through this resort and I just broke everything. I couldn't believe the damage I'd done when I saw it the next day. And I hurt myself pretty bad too. I was naked when I ran out and I cut my arms, my legs, my face – everywhere. I don't want to go into what I was on at the time – it was a combination. But that really forced me to quit a lot of the weird shit I was doing. You just don't need it.'

Thanks to Doug's ability to smooth things over – both with the resort's unimpressed management, and the local cops – Slash was bundled onto the next available flight to LAX. 'I passed out and woke up to what they call an "intervention". I ended up going for the first and only time to rehab, which lasted for all of about three days. I said, "I'm not that fucked up." I just hired a car and got the fuck out of there. I took myself to Hawaii and dried out. I've never had that serious a problem since. I knew I wasn't fucked up enough to be in rehab, so I just got away from the whole scene for a while. I was lucky to be able to do that, but I don't think I was ever in as bad a shape as some people thought.'

Once again, Slash is guilty of viewing his past through rose-tinted spectacles – he wasn't so much in bad shape as knocked out of anything vaguely resembling one. The Phoenix fiasco might have served as Slash's wake-up call in terms of heroin, yet cocaine and booze remained on the menu – especially as his second wife Perla had similar tastes – and as the years rolled by he moved with the times and developed a taste for ecstasy. He may well see himself as the eternal teenager, but his past inevitably caught up with him. In 2001, while out on the road with his solo project Slash's Snakepit, he was diagnosed with cardiomyopathy, a form of congestive heart failure that occurs when the heart has swollen to the point of rupture. Indeed, his condition was deemed so severe that the doctors who fitted him with a defibrillator to keep his heart from packing up altogether gave him between six days and six weeks to live – but not much more.

Ozzy may be conscious of the proximity of the edge – always closer than you think – but with this diagnosis, Slash suddenly found himself close enough to see his coffin being lowered into the abyss. Confined to a hospital bed at the time, he had little option but to take the news lying down. Nevertheless, he remained determined to prove the doctors wrong. He embarked on a rigorous regime of physical exercise and healthy eating.

However, while he readily gave up the booze that had slowly been sucking the life out of him, he innate inability to just say no saw him get hooked on OxyContin, an analgesic medication that's basically a synthetic heroin. 'That which we call a rose, by any other name would smell as sweet . . .'

And one has to wonder whether Slash would ever have been able to throw the monkey from his back had Perla not discovered she was pregnant, because this, more than any other incentive he'd ever had, was the karmic get-out-of-jail-free card that straightened him out. And though he has suffered the occasional wobble while riding the temperance wagon, he's been clean and sober since 2006.

While it was the impending arrival of new life which led to Slash turning his personal life around, it was the death of a friend which resuscitated his ailing career and brought about a Guns N' Roses reunion of sorts. Randy Castillo, one of the best drummers for hire on the metal circuit (most notably with Ozzy and Mötley Crüe) sadly lost his battle with cancer, and when Matt Sorum (who drummed for G N' R between 1990 and 1997) approached Slash to play a benefit show for Randy's family, he leapt at the chance. Duff was equally eager to be involved, and when Izzy was spotted hanging around the studio, the question on every G N' R fan's lips was whether Axl would join his erstwhile pals onstage. But that was one can of worms no one was keen to open. And though Izzy quickly slinked back into the shadows from which he now preferred to operate, Slash, Duff, and Matt were so invigorated by sharing a stage together again that they took it to the next level and formed Velvet Revolver.

With three one-time Gunners in the line-up, it was a sure-fire cert that Velvet Revolver would be snapped up by one of the major labels, and having signed with RCA they headed into the studio to begin working on songs for their debut album, *Contraband*, which debuted at number one on the *Billboard* chart following its release in June 2004. A second album, *Libertad*, followed in 2007, but the band's long-term plans were thrown into confusion the following year when vocalist Scott Weiland elected to rejoin the reformed Stone Temple Pilots. And though songs have been stockpiled for a third Velvet Revolver album, Slash says the band will remain on temporary hiatus for the foreseeable future, while he, Duff and Matt concentrate on other projects.

Slash's 'other project' was his eponymous solo album, which was released to critical acclaim in April 2010, and featured an impressive array of vocal talent including his *Cemetery Gates* buddies Ozzy and Lemmy. A second solo album, *Apocalyptic Love*, followed in May 2012.

Marilyn Manson

5 January 1969

Born: Brian Hugh Warner

Alter-egos: Marilyn Manson, God of Fuck, Reverend Marilyn Manson, Omega (adopted solely for 1999's Last Tour on Earth Tour), self-styled all-American Antichrist . . . not to be confused with Kevin Arnold's bespectacled sidekick from the *Wonder Years*, of course.

(Pre) occupations: A bona fide hack of all trades, Manson's offstage talents are many and varied. Director, painter, poet and absintheur – a bottle of the (S)aint's very own alchemical creation, Mansinthe, can be purchased via an array of outlets – the God of Fuck is nothing if not versatile.

Live by this: 'I feel like someone I wouldn't let my own daughter fuck, and I feel like someone who, if I was that daughter, I would want to fuck more than anyone else . . .' – Manson's diary entry, Tuesday, 11 March 1997

Deadly sins: To paraphrase the four apostles of Kiss, God may have given rock'n'roll to the world, but there are those who would have you believe that heavy metal was spawned from the rancid loins of the devil himself . . . and none more so than Brian Hugh Warner, the frustrated former journalist who unleashed his alter-ego Marilyn Manson on a largely unsuspecting world. 'Marilyn' was, of course, an homage to the sultry screen goddess Monroe, who died of a suspected overdose in 1962; while Charles Manson – the mesmeric Beach-Boy-gone-bad who incited members of his so-called 'Family' to embark on a spree of shockingly violent killings in the late-sixties – provided Warner's sinister new surname. 'Although she remains a symbol of beauty and glamour, Marilyn Monroe had a dark side, just as Charles Manson has a good, intelligent side,' Manson himself mused at the time. 'The balance between good and evil, and the choices we make between them, are probably the single most important aspects shaping our personalities and humanity.'

Of course, serial killers were certainly in vogue *circa* 1991, thanks to the cinematic release of *The Silence of the Lambs*. Yet, Manson's claim that 'the minute I scribbled [Marilyn Manson] on paper I knew that it was what I wanted to become' hints at a deeper connection with Thomas Harris's novels. In *Red Dragon*, (prequel to *The Silence of the Lambs*), Francis Dolarhyde (a.k.a. the murderous Tooth Fairy) believes only via the act of murdering – or 'changing' – his victims will he ever fully 'become' his alternate personality. In his disturbed mind, Dolarhyde envisions himself emerging as the Great Red Dragon from William Blake's damned-yet-divine painting of the same name. Similarly, Manson was hell-bent on becoming the 'Antichrist Superstar' of the MTV degeneration.

Creating an alter-ego is practically *de rigueur* on Planet Metal. As well as adding an air of mystique, fanciful pseudonyms like Axl Rose, Dimebag Darrell and Nikki Sixx also allow the artists concerned to embark on sprees of wanton debauchery, burning through life obeying no one and nothing beyond their own desires while remaining detached from the consequences of their actions. 'It wasn't me your honour, it was the other guy – the one in the mirror . . . ' Indeed, while reading Manson's harrowing yet hilarious autobiography, *The Long Hard Road Out of Hell*, one cannot help but be reminded of Lestat de Lioncourt, fanged anti-hero of Anne Rice's 1985 novel, *The Vampire Lestat*. For like Lestat, Manson recounts his drug-fuelled (oft-misogynistic) misdeeds calmly – simply because he is what he is and should feel no shame for acting accordingly.

With more relish than repentance, Manson recounts the most sordid escapades of his existence, not least his and Trent Reznor's debasing of a hapless female known only as 'porpoise fish-woman' or 'sea bass'. Her head wrapped in a towel, this nameless girl allowed Reznor and Manson to prod and poke between her legs. What follows is worthy of a place in Baudelaire's *The Flowers of Evil*, or perhaps the Marquis de Sade's *The 120 Days of Sodom*: having set her pubic hair alight, her tormentors proceeded to throw 'sea bass' out with the trash. From born-victim (molested as a child) to *Born Villain*, Manson's tale positively dares the reader to disapprove.

Though Manson was something of a late starter when it came to mastering his Class A, B and Cs, he quickly made up for lost time, developing a taste for under-the-counter pills, powders, and potions of every description. Indeed, by the time he and his band were recording *Antichrist Superstar* at Trent's New Orleans studio, he was in with a serious chance of being named 1996's pharmaceutical fuck-up of the year. After four fruitless months, all Marilyn Manson had to show for their time in the Big Easy was 'five half-finished songs, sore nostrils, and a hospital bill'. However, rather than stand up to Reznor – taking control of the direction of his troubled opus – Manson took to dialling his dealer, retreating deeper into his own personal heart of darkness.

Aside from costing him upwards of $200,000, and playing a significant role in the break-up of his marriage to burlesque beauty Dita Von Teese, Manson's coke habit also put paid to the life of *Empyrean* magazine. According to *The Long Hard Road*, the magazine's owners vetoed a 1995 interview with Manson on the grounds that hapless – and soon-to-be-on welfare – scribe Sarah Fim followed 'unethical procedures in order to extract information' from her genial subject. One can only imagine their thoughts on reading Fim's opening salvo. Lounging nonchalantly in his hotel room – unperturbed by the images of naked boys and rotting corpses flickering across the TV screen – Manson sets about snorting, 'some of the finest cocaine the editors of *Empyrean* could afford'.

'All drugs should be legal,' Manson once told *High Times*. For, seen through the crazed filter of his heterochromian contacts, substance abuse is no social evil. '[With drugs] people who want to kill themselves will have the opportunity to,' he continued. 'You know, a bit of Social Darwinism weeds out the weak. I do drugs just to know that I don't have to. I do it as a test to myself, to challenge my personal strengths.' In another interview with *Esoterra*, Manson unveiled his policy for keeping gun-use under control. 'They should just open up the gates and let everybody do whatever it is they want. Then the people who are strong enough to survive will. People too stupid to live will be crushed under the wheels of progress.'

However, adopting Aleister Crowley's aphorism, 'Do what thou wilt shall be the whole of the law,' was to have repercussions after all. In the wake of the Columbine High School Massacre in 1999, it was Manson who found himself in the firing line. With the perpetrators beyond reproach (at the end of their rampage, crazed seniors Eric Harris and Dylan Klebold opted to turn their guns on themselves), America's media, eager to lay the blame at someone's door, set its jaundiced sights on Manson. 'Devil-Worshipping Maniac Told Kids to Kill,' screamed the lurid headlines.

Not until Michael Moore's 2002 documentary *Bowling for Columbine* would Manson be granted airtime to respond to the charges. Having voiced his belief that American society is based on 'fear and consumption', he responded to Moore's line of questioning with startling insight and empathy: 'I wouldn't say a single word to [the killers]; I would listen to what they have to say, and that's what no one did.'

'I always knew that I never felt guilty or that I did something wrong. I despised people who accused me of doing that,' Manson told the *Orange Playlist* in 2007. 'The whole point of my name was to make a statement about the very same thing I was being blamed for. I almost feel cheated if Columbine is talked about and I'm not mentioned because I went through so much bullshit and torment, emotionally and personally, and so much concentrated effort to destroy me that I feel I'm being left out when I'm not mentioned. No one else can take credit for or take responsibility for what I already got blamed for.'

Ten years on, he was no less bitter. 'Blaming me was ridiculous. It's a lack of responsibility from everyone,' he seethed in *Kerrang!* on the anniversary of the killings. 'If you want to blame something, well, I went to a Christian school. That's why I write what I write. Shall we blame the Christians? I essentially lost everything because of Columbine but, if it happened now, it just wouldn't have the same impact. There has to be that first person who takes the arrows in the back and I guess that was me. If there was a Grammy award for death toll, it would be mine. I don't think anyone has been blamed for as much violence as me.'

Manson, of course, has just cause to resent his treatment. In truth, neither killer was so much as a fan of his. Yet, Manson's blatant worship of a certain Anton Szandor LaVey was all that his decriers needed to know . . . and Manson had been a devotee of the 'Doctor' (as the High Priest of the Church of Satan preferred to be known) long before he was finally granted an audience in 1994. 'I admired and respected him. We had a lot of things in common,' Manson said of LaVey. Fixated upon criminology, serial killers and the writings of Nietzsche, the two men shared a fierce commitment to Satanism: the pragmatic philosophy against repression of the individual that shaped the careers of both. A more exotic claim of Manson's is that both men 'successfully placed curses' on their adversaries. As proof of LaVey's mystic powers, Manson cites the Doctor's guilt over the death of former flame, Jayne Mansfield. LaVey's curse on her new lover supposedly resulted in the crash which claimed Mansfield's life. And even if you see his hexes as hokum, LaVey was certainly gifted with otherworldly powers of persuasion. How else could a guy who resembled Emperor Ming possibly have charmed Mansfield into bed? Perceived as the 'Working Man's Monroe', she was still way above LaVey's pay grade. (The Doctor would also allude to a dalliance with Monroe herself, but as with Mansfield, Marilyn wasn't around to challenge the claim.) Of course, one might argue the same case against Manson when considering his relationships with Dita Von Teese and Evan Rachel Wood – not to mention his trysts with celebrated porn stars Traci Lords and Stoya.

Manson is not the first musician to set himself up as an iconoclast, and nor is he unique in paying homage at LaVey's altar. Varg Vikernes – dubbed the 'Charles Manson of the black metal scene' following his callous slaying of Aarseth 'Euronymous' Øystein – also holds the self-styled Black Pope's philosophies in high regard. However, unlike Varg, who never got to meet LaVey in the flesh, Manson was invited to join the order. Again, the joining of esoteric sects is nothing new in rock'n'roll – the most obvious example being Led Zeppelin guitarist Jimmy Page's supposed induction into the Ordo Templi Orientis (Order of the Oriental Templer), which was at one time headed by another of Manson's major

'All drugs should be legal.'
– Marilyn Manson

influences, the Great Beast 666 himself, Aleister Crowley. But whereas Page and other initiates of the OTO are called upon to take a vow of silence in regard to their order's practices, no such restrictions impede Manson from revealing what occurred during his own ordination. Though he's clearly proud to have been 'passed the torch' by LaVey, anyone hoping for graphic descriptions of nudity, animal sacrifice or ancient incantations was to be left sorely disappointed by Manson's 'revelations'. LaVey merely handed him a crimson calling-card certifying him as a minister – like 'an honorary degree from a university' – rendering the whole thing more sanctioned than sinful.

On a highway to hell? Of all the crazed rumours surrounding the career of MM, there's one that simply refuses to go away. 'Manson was Paul in *The Wonder Years*,' recites the God of Fuck with palpable ennui. Nonetheless, Manson's formative years in Canton, Ohio ran strangely parallel to those of the fictional Paul, in that his goofy appearance made him an easy target for bullies, and he constantly fretted about whether his looks would hold him back in the girl-getting stakes.

Rather than leave his fans to speculate 'the seeds of who I am now', *The Long Hard Road* serves to demystify the anti-hero's childhood once and for all. In the manner of a patient on the therapist's couch, Manson relates an array of scandalous family secrets: molestation by his military cadet neighbour (a pint-sized sadist called Mark, whose hobbies included playing at 'prison' and torturing dumb animals), as well as the day when he and his cousin – having already uncovered a sordid stash of dildos, bestiality porn and women's underwear in his grandfather's basement – were unlucky enough to catch the cross-dressing septuagenarian knocking one out: two storylines which never featured on *The Wonder Years*! To add to the horror, there was the old boy's tracheotomy. To this day, Manson's never forgotten the sound of his wheezing climax – like 'a car engine . . . when someone turns the key in the ignition when it's already on'.

Yet, for all his closet perversions, Grandpa Warner was as outwardly pious as they come. Taking pride of place in his grandparents' kitchen was a 'large hollow, wooden crucifix with a gold Jesus on top, a dead palm leaf wrapped around it and a sliding top that concealed a candle and a vial of holy water' – 'hollow' and 'dead' being the operative adjectives . . .

Religious education served to warp Master Warner's impressionable young mind further still. Years later, Manson told how the formidable Ms. Price (with the aid of handy apocalyptic flash cards) browbeat him and the other sixth-graders into believing that the end of the world was nigh. Rather than twee nursery rhymes, Brian and friends would leave class with Revelation 13 – 'Let him that hath understanding count the number of the beast' – ringing in their ears. Before long, Brian began to suffer terrible nightmares. 'I was thoroughly terrified by the idea of the end of the world and the Antichrist,' he revealed. 'I became obsessed with it, watching movies like *The Exorcist* and *The Omen*.' He devoured doom-laden prophecies like Nostradamus's *Centuries*, George Orwell's *1984*, and *A Thief in the Night*, which – in keeping with Ms. Price's scare-mongering sermons – told of people being decapitated because they hadn't received the fabled 666 tattoos on their forehead.

In the 1972 film adaptation of *A Thief in the Night*, anyone not bearing the 'mark of the beast' (three rows of '0110' on the forehead or the hand) will be banned from using money in any context. 0110 is binary code for six; hence having it repeated three times equates to the fearful number attributed to the end-of-days prophecies outlined in the Bible. One can imagine a deeply traumatised Brian frantically scanning his forehead and hands for the mystical numerical marking that would enable him to survive the imminent Armageddon.

These days, of course, Manson's favourite hobby is collecting kiddies' lunchboxes after happening upon his old Kiss lunchbox in the attic. Pandora-esque, the find unleashed a flood of memories from his days at Heritage Christian School. Ironically, given the damaging teachings of Ms. Price et al., the school actually forbade him from bringing the rock'n'roll lunchbox into school on the grounds that it was 'satanic' with the potential to 'corrupt the other kids'.

Unsurprisingly, Manson hated Christian school with a vengeance. Outside of the weekly fire-and-brimstone tutorials, the majority of his supposedly corruptible classmates were wont to pick on him mercilessly. With Price already eyeing his lunchbox as an instrument of the devil, he thought to end his daily torture by slamming it into the face of one of his tormentors. 'Thinking back, I really wanted to get kicked out but I didn't realise it at the time,' he revealed. 'The final straw was when I got caught stealing money out of girls' purses during prayer. I think it was pretty poetic in a way. I was the punk kid, so I grew up not being accepted too well by the other kids. I found later that I could relate to the kind of mentality that a lot of serial killers fall into. That, "someday I'll show you" attitude. I think that a lot of serial killers want to show the world. They want to be a star. All these things inspired me to write the song, "Lunchbox" . . . metal lunchboxes do come in handy. It's kind of funny, because lunchboxes were outlawed in Florida in 1976. A kid bludgeoned another kid, not to death but into a pulp with a metal lunchbox on the playground. We can only hope that when we make Marilyn Manson lunchboxes that the same thing happens.'

As well as wrath, vengeance and lust ('despite Ms. Price's terrifying seminars, I found something sexy about her . . . I could tell there was something . . . passionate waiting to burst out of that repressed Christian façade. I hated her for giving me nightmares . . . but . . . I hated her more for the wet dreams,' recalls Marilyn), Heritage Christian School also provided Manson's first lesson in drugs, as he revealed in interview with *High Times*: 'The very first time I smoked marijuana was when I was about sixteen . . . I went over to this kid's house . . . and his brother pulled up in a GTO. He got out of the car and instantly started firing off a pistol into the sky . . . He had this special party room that was real dark with lava lamps and all these posters of grim reapers and skulls. He broke out a bong and we started smoking marijuana while listening to Ozzy Osbourne. Then, he talked me into drinking the bong water. I got sick for, like, a week.'

Manson was to get his wish in waving goodbye to his 'cornfield childhood' – middle-finger aimed squarely at Heritage High – when he and his parents relocated to Fort Lauderdale, Florida, in 1988: 'That last night in Canton, I knew that Brian Warner was dying. I was being given a chance to be reborn, for better or worse, somewhere new . . . But what I couldn't figure out was whether high school had corrupted me or enlightened me. Maybe it was both, and corruption and enlightenment were inseparable.'

The one pitfall in leaving behind everything and everyone he knew was that he now had no friends at all. In the absence of potential bandmates, he set about committing his 'most twisted fantasies' to paper in the form of poems, stories and novellas, which he then posted off to various magazines such as *Night Terrors Magazine*, *The Horror Show*, *The American Atheist* and even *Penthouse*, in the hope that at least one of these publications would put his work into print. But all that the postman carried in his sack each morning – at least in his mind's eye – was disappointment, a feeling that 'followed me like a ball and chain that first year in Florida'.

While studying journalism and theatre at Brownard Community College, he took a job as night manager at Spec's Music, where he proceeded to abuse his position by cajoling two female co-workers into stealing tapes of his favourite bands. In return, he turned a blind eye to their penchant for sneaky joints in the store room. One purloined cassette was Jane's Addiction's *Nothing's Shocking*, and his first article for Brownard's college newspaper, the *Observer*, was a review of Jane's Addiction's Miami show in February 1989. Further forays into the literary world came with penning music critiques for a local freebie entertainment guide called *Tonight Today*, which helped him gain a foot in the door at *25th Parallel*, the glossy, South Florida lifestyle magazine, where his ability to lie about having a journalism degree while looking the owners in the eye ('you shall bear false witness,' Ms. Price undoubtedly would have reminded him) secured him the position of senior editor. However, the world of music journalism wasn't nearly as glamorous as he'd imagined. 'The problem wasn't the magazines or my writing,' Manson revealed in *The Long Hard Road*, 'but the musicians themselves. Each successive interview I did, the more disillusioned I became. Nobody had anything to say. I felt like I should be answering the questions instead of asking them. I wanted to be on the other side of the pen.'

Yet – whether the college scribe realised it or not – the day he laid eyes on a certain black-clad frontman 'sulking in the corner during sound-check' was set to change the course of his career irrevocably. 'His dreadlocked tour manager hovered protectively over him,' reminisces Manson. 'Once we started talking, [Trent] thawed and became affable. But I was just another journalist. Talking to me was as good a way as any to kill time before a show in a city where he knew no one. The next time Trent Reznor came to town, I was his opening act.'

To set his meteoric rise in motion, Manson was forced to call upon his devilish powers of persuasion once more, convincing the owner of a local club called Squeeze to start an open-mic night – giving the Antichrist-to-be a crucial platform for his writing. 'Every Monday, I stood awkward and vulnerable behind the microphone,' Manson explained. 'All the bizarre characters who attended told me my poetry sucked, but [that] I had a good voice and should start a band. I told them to fuck off. But inside I knew that no one really likes poetry anyway and that their advice was right – if only because no one else I interviewed or listened to was writing songs with any intelligence. I had always dreamt of making music. . . but until then I never had the confidence or the faith in my abilities to pursue it seriously. All I needed were a few resilient souls to go through hell with me.'

One such soul was Scott Putesky, who had certainly made an impression on the local scene – if only because every musician he'd worked with before had (in Manson's words) 'wanted to kill him because he was very pretentious, and had deluded himself into thinking that he was much more talented than he actually was'. Having decided that the dichotomy of good and evil would make a fascinating backdrop for the music, he set about creating a secret identity so that he could write about his own music in *25th Parallel* without risking the ire of his bosses.

When the invite to open for Nine Inch Nails came, Marilyn Manson and the Spooky Kids had just seven songs, a bass player still learning to play and a keyboardist without a keyboard, but as Manson says: 'it was too good an opportunity to pass up just because we sucked'. On the auspicious night at Miami's Club Nu, he took to stage sporting an orange mini dress – an acid tab under his tongue and a girlfriend trailing behind him on a leash. Thanks to their highly flamboyant stage presence, the Spooky Kids quickly built up a reputation as a 'must-see' act. Yet for all the excitement, the Spooky Kids rarely ventured out trick or treating beyond their own backyard. And having blown whatever money they'd made on travel to New York for a fruitless showcase for Epic Records, the future didn't look particularly promising for Manson's fledgling *cirque du freak*.

But little did Manson realise that serendipity was about to smile upon them all. I conversation with *Empyrean*, he revealed: 'We returned home practically broke, and I went by the record store where I used to work and bought Nine Inch Nails' *Broken*, which had come out that day. I was thinking that I hadn't heard from Trent in a while because every now and then he would call just to say hi and keep in touch. As I was listening to it, I got a call from Trent's manager asking for a copy of our demo tape.'

Having adopted a philosophical outlook whereby everything in life happens for a purpose, Manson wasn't overly surprised when a few days later Trent called from LA where he was renting the same house – 10050 Cielo Drive – that had been the scene of Manson's namesake's most heinous crime. In the throes of shooting, what Trent had to offer was a cameo role in the video for 'Gave Up'. Recording his own version of Charles Manson's 'My Monkey' on the infamous Cielo Drive was one of Manson's life-long ambitions. Of course, he jumped at the chance. And though the video was never officially released, it was during this time that his friendship with Trent was cemented, leading to Marilyn Manson signing to Trent's newly-formed record label, Nothing.

In July 1993, Marilyn Manson hit Criteria Studios, Miami, with producer Roli Mosimann to begin laying down tracks for *Portrait of an American Family*. However, owing to Mosimann's failure to grasp the band's trademark dichotomy, the finished product, *The Manson Family Album*, was a disappointment for all concerned. 'I thought, "This really sucks,"' Manson later revealed. 'So I played it for Trent, and he thought it sucked.'

Indeed, so underwhelmed was the Nine Inch Nails frontman that he insisted on remixing the album personally, spiriting both the masters and the band to his LA lair. Needless to say, it didn't take much to persuade his protégé to return to Cielo Drive. Speaking with *Esoterra*, Manson explained the house's irresistible hold on him. 'My fascination is similar to that of people stopping to look at car accidents or wanting to go to an amusement park and get on a ride that says "ride at your own risk". People love their fear, whether they realise it or not. People are afraid of death but love to get closer to it vicariously through serial killers, horror movies, the O.J. Simpson trial, Lorena Bobbitt, or whatever it may be.'

However, as with the mystery of Tori Amos's disastrous chicken dinner, Manson was to experience similarly inexplicable happenings whilst residing on Murder Drive. 'We were mixing "Wrapped in Plastic",' he told *Empyrean*, 'while we were working on that song the Charles Manson samples from "My Monkey" started appearing in the mix. "Why does a child reach up and kill his mom and dad?" And we couldn't figure out what was going on. We got totally scared and we're like, "We're done for the night." We came back the next day and it was fine. The Manson samples weren't even on the tape anymore. There's no real logical or technological explanation for why they appeared. It was a truly supernatural moment that freaked me out.'

The press was equally perturbed by goings-on down on Cielo Drive. And though it was Trent's name on the tenancy agreement, it was Manson who ended up taking the flak. '[As] Trent was living at the Sharon Tate house, I end up looking like I'm this Marilyn Manson guy that's riding Trent Reznor's wagon, which is kind of funny. But I never got a chip on my shoulder because otherwise I would never have gotten to record there and sleep there, and get freaked out by the ghosts there.'

He did, however, get a chip on his shoulder at having his thunder stolen by a certain W. Axl Rose. 'What happened was that Trent took me to a U2 concert one night and backstage I met Axl Rose,' he told *Empyrean*. On finding himself serving as Axl's shoulder to cry on while the Gunners' frontman – whom he uncharitably called a 'total fucking flake' – bemoaned his psychological problems and split personalities, Manson thought to steer the conversation into calmer waters by telling Axl about how his band were playing an adaptation of 'My Monkey' from Charlie

'If there was a Grammy award for death toll, it would be mine. I don't think anyone has been blamed for as much violence as me.'

– Marilyn Manson

Manson's album, *Lie*. 'He [Axl] was like, "I never heard of that before." I told him, "You should check out the album, it's cool." And lo and behold six months later Guns N' Roses put out *The Spaghetti Incident* and Axl covers "Look at Your Game, Girl" from the *Lie* album.'

Though the *Portrait* remix was taking shape, the studio at Cielo Drive had its limitations and so Trent and the band relocated to the Record Plant on West Third Street where they remained holed up for several weeks until Mosimann's wrongs had been righted. *Portrait of An American Family* was finally released in July 1994 (under the marginally less offensive title suggested by Reznor). The initial response was unenthusiastic at best. But, of course, prodding a sharpened stick at Middle America's sensitive midriff was hardly a concern for Manson – it was a motive. 'The whole point of [*Portrait*] was that I wanted to address the hypocrisy of talk-show America,' proclaimed the God of Fuck (*Empyrean*). 'How morals are worn as a badge to make you look good and how it's so much easier to talk about your beliefs than to live up to them . . . as kids growing up, a lot of the things that we're presented with have deeper meanings than our parents would like us to see, like Willy Wonka and the Brothers Grimm. So what I was trying to point out was that when our parents hide the truth from us, it's more damaging than if they were to expose us to things like Marilyn Manson in the first place.'

'When you were young you didn't pick up on the innuendoes and references that were being made. These ideas were implanted in your head at an early age,' Manson mused in interview with *Esoterra*. 'A character like the Child Catcher from *Chitty Chitty Bang Bang* wouldn't be acceptable by today's standards. It's politically incorrect for somebody to go around stealing little kids . . . Now, they've decided that it was all wrong and they want to take it back. America's gone to great lengths to create Marilyn Manson and now they want to deny that they've done so.'

Manson's fascination with the seamy side of classic fantasy is what inspired his directorial debut, *Phantasmagoria: The Visions of Lewis Carroll*. Loosely based around *Alice's Adventures in Wonderland*, *Phantasmagoria* delves deeper down the rabbit hole, uncovering a sinister world in which creativity and mental illness are impossible to separate. 'I want to take the children's story that we all know, and discover the horrifying roots that grow beneath,' Manson raved. 'The characters may be wrapped in puzzles, but the author himself is the story that I find painfully close to me. Lewis Carroll is far more complex than the world's narrow perception of him as a quiet deacon, a mathematician . . . possibly one of the most divided souls living in his own hell that the world has overlooked.'

And in division, Carroll and Manson are united: 'I felt like there were a lot of things about his personality that were like mine. His creativity thrived mostly at night . . . He was very much a Jekyll and Hyde . . . haunted by his own demons and had a split personality. He couldn't find happiness; he couldn't find a family. He didn't sleep. I think that he was seeing things. You start seeing things differently, stuff that normal people don't see – stuff that I have seen now and again.'

Manson's own dreams, however, have seemingly evaporated into the ether. At the time of writing, the film is no nearer completion than when first mooted back in 2005.

Marilyn Manson's follow-up release, *Smells Like Children*, was recorded at Trent's New Orleans home studio and released in October 1995, the sixteen-track EP (adorned with an image of Manson as a tripped-out Willy Wonka turned Child Catcher), contained a sinister but spellbinding cover of the Eurythmics' hit 'Sweet Dreams (Are Made of This)', warped into something altogether more sinister. 'Midway through the record,' Manson revealed, 'We included one of the taped confessions we had gathered, from a girl who molested her seven-year-old male cousin. It underscored the subplot of the album, about the most common target of abuse: innocence.

I've always liked the Peter Pan idea of being a kid in mind if not in body, and *Smells Like Children* was supposed to be a record for someone who's no longer a child, someone who, like myself, wants their innocence back now that they're corrupted enough to appreciate it. What began as a very disturbing record had become a record that disturbed only me.'

While *Smells Like Children* introduced Marilyn Manson to a wider, weirder audience, it was the success of the second album proper, *Antichrist Superstar*, that would make household names of both the band and its enigmatic frontman. Though Trent took the production helm on *Smells Like Children*, and would go on to co-produce *Antichrist Superstar* with Manson, their friendship began to sour from the moment he and Twiggy presented the rough, four-track demos of the songs which would make up the EP. Trent expressed his concern that Twiggy had put down the guitar parts rather than Scott Putesky who, in Trent's opinion, was 'the backbone behind Marilyn Manson'. Furthermore, he and his manager, John Malm Jr. (with whom he'd set up Nothing Records), were both adamant that the band was known for Putesky's guitar style.

Incensed, Manson could hardly believe what he was hearing. 'In many ways, I was my own worst enemy because I still didn't trust myself. I was so new at this that I looked up to and believed publicists, lawyers and label heads,' he explained. 'I followed their instincts instead of mine, so I forgot about the songs we had written and, for the first but soon to be last time, compromised. Whatever flaws I found in *Portrait* paled in comparison to the disaster that this EP turned out to be. It was like stitching together an elaborate outfit for a party but catching the hem on a nail when leaving the house and watching helplessly as it unravelled and fell apart. The nail in this case, being Time Warner – Interscope/Nothing's parent company.'

While Trent would receive a co-production credit on both *Smells Like Children* and *Antichrist*, their relationship – both professional and personal – had been holed below the waterline. With Marilyn Manson signed to Nothing/Interscope, Manson maintained a dignified silence – at least up until penning *The Long Hard Road*. It's been argued that Trent gained his revenge by launching an attack on Manson in Nine Inch Nails' song 'Starfuckers, Inc.' But if this was the case, why would Manson have agreed to co-direct – as well as make a brief appearance in – the promo video? Many fans took this as proof that the pair had settled their differences, but nothing could have been further from the truth as Trent's vitriolic outburst in the June 2009 issue of *Mojo* revealed. Though he was careful to point out that he wasn't blameless for things getting 'shitty' between them, he claimed Manson was a malicious backstabber who 'finally got out from under the master's umbrella'. Then, having made mention of how drugs and alcohol were now ruling Manson's existence, he delivered the *coup de grace* by branding him a 'dopey clown'.

The gloves were most certainly off and Manson hit back with a few choice barbs of his own in an interview with the *Herald Sun*: 'Since I've known Trent he's always let his jealousy and bitterness for other people get in the way. I'm not talking about me – I sat back and watched him be jealous of Kurt Cobain and Billy Corgan [Smashing Pumpkins] and a lot of other musicians in the past. I just don't find the time to do that. I stopped thinking about him a while back, but I know that every day I have a song played that money will go to him, forever.' And having mentioned that he'd be 'financially attached' to Trent for as long as Marilyn Manson remained signed to Nothing/Interscope, he added: 'In the words of his own song ['The Hand That Feeds'], you shouldn't bite the hand that feeds you – you should take that hand and punch yourself in the face.'

Moments of madness: In the aftermath of the Columbine killings, Manson was subjected to trial by media, but two years prior to this he'd found himself being subpoenaed for real when an unnamed twenty-year-old resident of Oklahoma County hereby swore, affirmed and declared under oath that while attending a Manson show in Dallas, Texas, the previous month, he did witness the accused (Manson) inciting both his band, and the audience – which supposedly contained kids as young as nine or ten years old – into having 'real and simulated sex with each other', while Manson had intercourse with a dog.

And in November of that same year, a Senate panel hearing was convened to discuss the effects of popular music on American youth. The father of a fifteen-year-old who'd committed suicide believed Marilyn Manson had contributed to the death of his son because the boy had been listening to *Antichrist Superstar* on a portable CD player when his body was found. 'Obviously it upset me that someone would think I would encourage that type of behaviour,' Manson retorted via his website. 'I've always said that people who would harm themselves or others over music or film or books, they're just being ignorant . . . It's a wake-up call for parents to teach their kids to be more intelligent, to interpret art with some sort of intelligence. If you want to blame music for someone hurting themselves, then you can just as easily blame Shakespeare for writing *Romeo and Juliet*. I think the key lesson is that parents don't understand their kids. If you take more time to talk to your kids, your kids are going to live happier lives.'

Manson, of course, is one of the few *Cemetery Gates* survivors who can boast of never having fallen under heroin's spell, but this is hardly surprising given that heroin is the ultimate derailer, and he was a man bursting with ideas. As such, it was cocaine which fuelled his creative fire and desire. For someone who had never danced to cocaine's frenetic beat before going out on the road on the Self Destruct Tour, he effortlessly made the transition from neophyte to connoisseur, and from that point on a rolled-up 'Benjamin' ($100 bill) was never out of reach. Indeed, the 'white line fever' which took hold of him would lead to the break-up of his two-year marriage. 'I get the impression he thinks I was unsupportive,' Dita told the *Sunday Telegraph*. 'But the truth is I wasn't supportive of his lifestyle, and someone else came along who was.'

That 'someone', of course, was his teenage *Phantasmagoria* co-star Evan Rachel Wood, whom Dita reportedly caught in her husband's embrace – with Evan clad in skimpy lingerie from Dita's own Von Follies range. In *The Long Hard Road*, having stated categorically that he'd never cheated on his girlfriend because he 'plays by the rules', he then goes on to list said semi-tongue-in-cheek rules. A far cry from the Ten Commandments, even this sinful set of loop-holes fail to include any proviso for being caught in flagrante delicto with a nubile nymph young enough to be one's daughter.

The book also lists the rules of engagement regarding drug use, yet while cocaine abuse is nothing new in the annals of rock'n'roll, Manson can almost certainly lay claim to being the first band to instigate a bone-snorting fest. While recording new material at Trent's home studio, he and Twiggy would fire their respective imaginations with Jack Daniel's and copious amounts of coke, and then go out trawling the city's burial sites, as Manson subsequently revealed in the aforementioned 1995 interview with *High Times*. 'When Twiggy and I were living in New Orleans, we went out one night grave digging because in New Orleans bones stick out of the ground everywhere. So we had a big bag of bones that we carried with us on the road. Telling anyone who asked that they were the remnants of our former drummer, Freddy (Frederick Streithorst Jr. – a.k.a. Sara Lee Lucas), who we had burned alive. About five months ago in LA, we were in a hotel room, and there were all these people there we didn't know. We talked them into chipping off pieces of the bones, putting it in a pipe and smoking it. We smoked it too. It was terrible . . . it smelled like burnt hair, gave you a really bad headache and made your eyes red.'

Varg Vikernes

11 February 1973

Born: Kristian Larsson Vikernes

Alter-egos: 'It is a Norse tradition to give names to people as they suit them, as you view them,' Varg once mused in interview with *AORTA* 'zine. And, fixated upon the elemental ferocity of his country's heritage, Varg is hardly the man to deviate. 'I am a man of many names,' he grins wryly, 'and I like that . . .'

Hence, Vikernes is Kristian by birth; Varg in the eyes of the law . . . and any variation upon Greven/Greifi/Count Grishnackh to the legions who've followed his career since its unholy beginnings. Though murderous Varg may be the crown prince of darkness (derived from the archaic Norse word for 'wolf', his chosen name certainly speaks volumes about Varg's self-image), Count G is certainly not to be confused with Bram Stoker's fictitious fanged aristocrat Dracula. Though newsworthy in itself, the idea of his being the 'evil Count' was simply misinterpreted by the media, because according to Burzum's site, he simply took the title 'Count' due to its root in the Latin 'Comtes', meaning 'companion' – specifically identifying himself as a companion to the Germanic peoples – while Grishnackh, albeit a slight variation of the Orc captain who served Sauron, stems from his having never quite grown out of his adolescent obsession with Tolkien's allegorical fantasy, *The Lord of the Rings*, and the 'veil of hidden mythology' contained therein (as the would-be Orc overlord would have it, at least).

(Pre) occupations: The enigmatic mastermind behind one-man project Burzum – a 'magic weapon' for Varg to bring his own twisted ethos to the masses – the multi-instrumentalist is also the homicidal bassist who ensured that Mayhem's 1993 line-up could never be reunited.

Live by this: 'Killing a person with an 8cm-long blunt knife is a bloody affair . . .' – Varg Vikernes

Deadly sins: 16 May 1994 was not a great day for Varg Vikernes' inner
'Chieftain'. On this date, he found himself condemned to an 'unhappy
life without joy or pleasures beyond the absolute necessities', otherwise
known as a 21-year prison sentence – the maximum under Norwegian law
– for the murder of his mentor and former Mayhem bandmate Øystein
'Euronymous' Aarseth, as well as the wilful arson of four historical stave
churches. The spate of church burnings, which began with a small,
ineffectual fire at Storetveit Church in Bergen in May 1992, and escalated
to the destruction of several stave churches – regarded as Norway's most
notable cultural landmarks – made headlines throughout Norway. Despite
being found guilty on several charges of arson, including the attack on
Storetveit Church, Varg has continually denied complicity.

'They still have no evidence. They don't have one single technical proof,
nothing,' he seethed while giving an interview from his cell for Michael
Moynihan and Didrik Søderland's excellent tome *Lords of Chaos: The
Bloody Rise of the Satanic Metal Underground*. 'The only reason I'm sentenced
is because of those people who might have done it themselves, *saying that I
did it*. That's the only reason I was found guilty. It's all based on testimony
from people who were later found guilty of lying in court! Perjury!'

Nonetheless, the fact that he used a photograph – which many believe
he took – of the still-smouldering, charcoaled ruins of the Fantoft Stave
Church (a charge he was acquitted on) for the cover of the Burzum mini-
album, *Aske* (Norwegian for 'ashes'), was enough to convict him in the
eyes of the public. Nor was his case helped by the circulation of certain
flyers and posters, emblazoned with a map of Norway . . . with desecrated
churches helpfully pinpointed. 'Burzum: coming soon to a church near
you,' read the jaunty caption.

It is often said that 'revenge is a dish best served cold', and on the evening
of 10 August 1993, Varg, together with Euronymous's supposed best
friend, 22-year-old Snorre 'Blackthorn' Ruch – who, like Varg, had also
recently joined Mayhem to help Euronymous complete *De Mysteriis Dom
Sathanas* following Necrobutcher's departure – set off for Euronymous's
apartment in Oslo with an age-old recipe formulating in his murderous
mind. For, to paraphrase another well-worn cliché, Norway's black-metal
scene was no longer big enough for both of them.

As with Trent Reznor and Marilyn Manson, Euronymous had signed
Varg's solo project, Burzum, to his recently-incorporated DSP (Deathlike
Silence Productions) label, as well as inviting him to join Mayhem. But
whereas Trent and Manson's relationship had extended beyond the

professional, Varg and Euronymous's master-pupil relationship was fundamentally flawed because neither one was willing to be subordinate. They came from totally opposite standpoints. Euronymous saw himself as the principle figurehead on the nascent black-metal scene – in the wake of Dead's suicide he'd opened a record store named 'Helvete' (read: 'Hell'), serving as a meeting place for fans and musicians alike – whereas Varg saw himself as a latter-day Vidkun Quisling (the Norwegian politician who founded a collaborationist pro-German government during the Second World War), and was violently opposed to the existence of any scene at all.

Somewhat surprisingly, given that he'd gone to trouble of preparing an alibi by renting a video, Varg still insists that he killed Euronymous in self-defence, upon learning (from Samoth of Emperor), that Euronymous was boasting about how he intended to lure Varg to his lair under the pretext of an unsigned recording contract, only to videotape himself torturing Varg to death. It could have been nothing more than an empty

'Killing a person with an 8cm-long blunt knife is a bloody affair . . .'
- Varg Vikernes

boast, for the benefit of Euro's minions. Yet, Varg took the view that since Euronymous – whose inability to keep his own counsel had gained him quite a rep – wasn't running around telling everybody on the scene (as was his wont), he should take the threat seriously.

Varg also told how he drove to Euronymous's apartment in the early hours of the morning (sometime around 3:00am) to have it out with him. Euronymous – dressed only in his underwear – had panicked. 'And in his panic he attacked me.' Yet, if Varg's crime was self-defence, why have Ruch drive him to a nearby lake to dispose of his blood-soaked clothes before returning to Bergen?

According to Varg's version of events, Euronymous struck the first blow: a kick to the chest which initially stunned him. He then grabbed hold of Euronymous and threw him to the floor. When Euronymous made a dash for the kitchen, he assumed he'd done so to grab a knife. 'I said, "Okay, if he's going to have his knife then I'm going to have a knife," and I pulled my knife.' So far, so acceptable – as grounds for self-defence, or even manslaughter. Yet Varg slashes a gaping hole in his testimony by admitting to having stabbed Euronymous even *after* he'd prevented him from arming himself. This wound was obviously far from fatal as – again, according to Varg – Euronymous made a dash for the bedroom, where Varg believed he kept the shotgun Dead had used to kill himself.

'Perhaps he didn't have it,' Varg shrugged later when asked to justify his actions. 'The point is that at the time I believed he did.' Of course, whether Euronymous was in possession of said shotgun or not, Varg knew for sure that he was the owner of a stun-gun. Euronymous had boasted to Samoth that he intended to use this same weapon to neutralise Varg before torturing him to death. However, instead of running to the bedroom, Euronymous bolted out the front door and past a startled Ruch. Frantically, he began ringing his neighbours' doorbells. And it was this 'cowardice', rather than any threat of torture, that settled his fate in Varg's mind. Convinced that Euronymous would come after him at some point in the future, and may well succeed in killing him, he says he decided to end it there and then. Again, a jury might well have accepted a plea of mitigating circumstances had Varg not then, depending on which article you read, proceeded to inflict anywhere between 23 and 26 stab wounds in Euronymous's head, neck and back.

> 'Euronymous's death means nothing to me.
> I will dance and piss on his grave,'
> – Varg Vikernes

While Dead's suicide had given the black-metal scene its grisly gravitas, musicians going around killing each other sent a ripple of revulsion – if not fear – across the length and breadth of this darkened realm. 'The newspapers wanted it to be some kind of struggle between rivals, but that's just bullshit,' Varg sneered. 'That's how they want it to be, so they can make it seem like a big danger.' Indeed, Burzum's site goes so far as to cite Varg's as the last 'show trial' of the twentieth century – a farce in which the jury was not sequestered. The site also stresses that some of those who testified against Varg were later 'convicted of perjury'.

His ongoing feud with Euronymous was no secret on the scene and Varg knew that his name would feature at the top of the list of potential suspects for the murder. He thereby formulated an alibi by renting a video of a movie both he and Ruch had already seen so they could describe the plotline. The writers of *Lords of Chaos* also claimed that Varg had arranged for another confederate to use his ATM card in Bergen as further evidence that he couldn't possibly have been in Oslo at the time of the murder. There was a hitch, however, since Varg allegedly left the wrong cash card. However, these claims were publicly dismissed by the man himself, who insists that the card – if one ever existed outside of the authors' imaginations – must have belonged to Snorre Ruch. Varg never has and never *will* own a such a card owing to his distrust of the banking system. He also vehemently denies the claim that he left bloodied fingerprints behind. However, seeing as Varg is hoping for a retrial to clear his name of the church burnings once and for all, one cannot rule out that he may have been attempting to undermine the book's evidence in the hope that doing so might help his case.

Should his car be spotted in the neighbourhood where Euronymous lived, Ruch was to say he'd borrowed the car in order to return the aforementioned record contracts, which the guitarist had posted to Varg for him to sign. Another mooted reason for his accompanying Varg to the apartment was to play Euronymous some new riffs that he'd come up with for the upcoming Mayhem album.

Even in the shadowy ground beyond the cemetery gates, however, such speculation counts for naught. Varg was caught and nailed in the most incriminating of circumstances. In the aftermath of his arrest, police were astounded to discover some 150kg of explosives, and 3,000 rounds of ammunition stashed at Varg's home.

On a highway to hell? Whilst all *Cemetery Gates* inductees are guilty of committing at least one of the fabled deadly sins, Varg Vikernes stands alone as a sinner who broke the most sacred commandment of them all. 'Thou shalt not kill,' states the gospel in no uncertain terms. And whether the result of a fleeting moment of passion or hours of premeditation, Varg's act is such that – to the minds of many – he's on a one-way track to the same inferno of which he always dreamt. To the casual observer, he is the 'Charles Manson' of heavy metal. For while Brian Warner merely flirted with Manson's shocking namesake, Varg's claim to the title is authentically scrawled in blood.

Varg was just twenty years old at the time of Euronymous's slaying. Yet, even back in 1993, the mindset of this latter-day Teutonic warrior was formed for life. Aside from advocating Vidkun Quisling's theory of 'Universalism' – which basically attacks Christianity for believing that God created the world while refusing to accept the possibility of other inhabited worlds – Varg also sees himself as a soldier of Odin and adheres to strict Odinism, which again eschews Christianity in favour of Norse traditions dating back to the days of the Vikings. 'We want to create the most possible fear, chaos and agony so that the idiotic and friendly Christian society can break down,' he revealed when asked about his beliefs. 'We are overall not interested in that the truth comes through. When we spread lies we cause confusion and confusion leads to chaos and at last breakdown. People shall be oppressed and we support everything that oppresses man and takes from him his feelings as free individuals.'

Varg's deep-seated resentment of authority figures came courtesy of his relationship with his father – as his mother Helene revealed in *Lords of Chaos*: 'His father very authoritarian. Their relationship started going bad quite early. His father wanted things his way, and Varg had his own ideas about how things should be done. Possibly because he had these problems with his father, I had a very close relationship with him. I often felt that it was appropriate to look after him a bit extra because of all the conflicts between Varg and the school, his father, and so on.'

'I have very little contact with him,' Varg responded brusquely when asked about his father in 1995. In stark contrast with Layne Staley's lament – 'when dad left, my world turned black' – the Norwegian stated simply: '[My parents are] divorced. He left about ten years ago. There wasn't any big impact. I was glad to be rid of him; he was just making trouble for me, always bugging me. He's a hypocrite. He was pissed about all the coloured people he saw in town, but then he worried about me being a Nazi.'

Due to Norway's shameful part in the Nazi's genocidal 'Final Solution' – which saw another of Varg's heroes, Vidkun Quisling, seizing power of the country in a Nazi-backed coup d'état – anything and everything relating to Hitler's Third Reich was considered taboo. So much so that, while growing up, Norwegian children were exposed to vast quantities of American culture – which, of course, didn't sit well with a certain disaffected teenager.

'I responded with hate towards American culture!' he ranted during an interview conducted from his prison cell. 'Like when reading the war comic books, it was always the Americans and British shooting the Germans – like one British soldier shooting a whole platoon of Germans. This is bullshit, of course. We didn't like it. We liked the Germans, because they always had better weapons and they looked better, they had discipline. They were like Vikings. Our hope was to be invaded by Americans so we could shoot them. The hope of war was all we lived for . . .'

To Varg's dismay, however, there was little likelihood of US troops invading Norway anytime soon, and aged seventeen – having played guitar for three years or so by this juncture – he was forced to turn his attention to music, joining his first death-metal band, Old Funeral. Though he would remain with Old Funeral for two years, he never truly felt a sense of belonging with his former bandmates. By Varg's own admission: 'These guys were just interested in eating. They didn't care about my sawed-off shotgun, or my dynamite, or any of these things. They were just interested in hamburgers. Originally, [they played] thrash metal, and then it became death-thrash metal or techno-thrash, and I lost interest. I liked the first demo. It had ridiculous lyrics [. . .] and that was why I joined them. They developed into this Swedish death-metal trend: I didn't like that so I dropped out.'

'Take a walk in the middle of a winter night in a forest all alone, and you will understand what I mean . . . it actually speaks.'
- Varg Vikernes

Having dismissed Old Funeral as unworthy of his time and effort, Varg began focusing on Burzum, a one-man musical project that he'd set up while still with Old Funeral. He'd originally named the project 'Uruk hai', in homage to J. R. R. Tolkien's breed of uber-advanced orcs – as described in *The Lord of the Rings*, another tome that remains close to Varg's obsessive heart.

'There's a lot of Norse mythology in Tolkien,' he said in *Lords of Chaos*. 'We were drawn to Sauron and his lot, and not the hobbits, those stupid little dwarves. I hate dwarves and elves. I sympathise with Sauron – that's partly why I became interested in occultism, because it was a so-called "dark" thing. I was drawn to Sauron, who was supposedly "dark and evil", so I realised there had to be a connection.

'[Burzum] is a fictional word, originally. Tolkien was a professor in Norse mythology and Norse language. When he wrote the fictional language in *The Lord of the Rings* books, it was very much based on Norse. So Burzum – "Burz" means night or dark, and if you take the word in plural it has "um" added, and becomes "Burzum", meaning much night or darkness. Just like democracy claims to be "light" and "good", I reasoned that then we obviously have to be "dark" and "evil".'

Drawing upon all the most thrilling elements of black metal – distorted, tremolo-picked guitar riffs, brutal vocals and the use of double-bass blast-beat drumming techniques – Varg soon established himself as a forced to be reckoned with on Norway's nascent black-metal scene. His growing reputation inevitably brought him to the attention of Øystein Aarseth, who signed Burzum to his label.

During a highly-productive nine-month period between January and September 1992 – the same year he joined Mayhem – Varg would record a full four Burzum albums for DSP. Alas, however, his musical achievements were somewhat overshadowed by his offstage antics. For while he still insists he played no part in the church burnings, and denies the allegations that he incited others to embark on similar church-burning and grave-desecration sprees, his subsequent self-mythologizing history, *Vargsmål* (penned in 1994 while Varg was still in prison) leaves little doubt as to his complicity. 'It's quite simple. [The Christians] desecrated our graves, or burial mounds. So it's revenge. The people who lie in the graves are the ones who built this society, which we are against! We show them the respect they deserve. I have absolutely no respect for the people who built this society. [The desecraters] can just smash their graves, piss on them; dance on them.'

Of course, Varg had already used this soundbite to jaw-dropping effect when interviewed by *Kerrang!* magazine in relation to Aarseth's then-unsolved murder: 'Euronymous's death means nothing to me. I will dance and piss on his grave,' was Varg's irreverent boast. 'Now he is dead, we [the Norwegian Black Metal Circle, also known as the Satanic Terrorists] can get on with more serious work. Now that all the idiots are shit scared and running away because things have got too extreme for them, the hardcore contingent can only get stronger.'

Moments of madness: By October 2003, Varg was serving out the remainder of his sentence at Tønsberg Prison – where inmates are allowed out on short, unsupervised breaks with a view to slowly integrating them back into society. He was one such privileged inmate. However, his first taste of freedom in a decade proved to be insufficient for Varg, and at the time appointed for his return, he failed to materialise.

Given that Varg's prison status had been reduced to a low-risk category, the Norwegians might have been surprised to read in the media that the authorities had mounted a nationwide search. However, the mood would have changed when the errant Varg was picked up in a car – reportedly stolen from his father – fully equipped with an unloaded AG3 automatic rifle, a handgun, a collection of large knives, a gas mask, camouflage clothing, a laptop, a compass, a GPS device, various maps and even a fake passport. Following his capture, the unrepentant Varg was sent to a maximum-security prison in Trondheim, where he spent 23 hours of the day locked in his cell, and a with another thirteen months added to his existing sentence.

At the time of his initial incarceration, any prisoner serving a maximum 21-year sentence was expected to serve a minimum of twelve years before being eligible for parole. However, as the Norwegian Parliament had extended this to fourteen years in 2002, the self-styled 'Count' had to scratch off a further 730 days before going before the parole board. Though the Department of Criminal Justice denied applications for parole in both June 2006 and June 2008, he was moved to a second low-security prison and permitted to leave the prison at weekends to visit his family. With Varg being an intensely private person away from his music, very few people were aware that he had a daughter with his longstanding – and I dare say, long-suffering – girlfriend. 'My daughter is still in elementary school . . . I don't see [her] very often – twice since 1993, to be exact,' he revealed during an August 2004 Q&A session with his fans which appears on the *burzum.org* website. 'In fact I haven't seen anybody in my family since October last year, but that is due to "prison circumstances". After I was transferred to Trondheim prison, last month, I can take a visit every week actually. I have a good relationship to my family, although my daughter doesn't know me very well – obviously.' When asked about his 'wife', Varg responded: 'I don't know what you are talking about. I have never been married to my daughter's mother, nor have I ever been married to anybody else. You could say I'm still waiting for that princess to come falling down from the sky and into my lap . . .'

According to a June 2008 newspaper article, however, Varg had obviously given up on waiting for a Valhallan princess to fall into his lap, as he and his partner now had a son, who was born the previous year, and it was also reported that a third child was on the way. While waiting to see if his fifth parole appeal would prove successful, he said that he was 'ready for society [and] have been for many years. I have learned from my mistakes and become older. Now I just want to be together with my family . . . I have barely seen my son since he came into the world. Even though I hear his voice on the phone almost every day, it is very tough to not be present while he is growing up.'

When Varg was finally released on probation on 24 May 2009 – having served a full fifteen years of his sentence – he took his family to live on a farm in Telemark on Norway's south-eastern coast. And while roaming the Norwegian wilds he has always been so passionate about, true to his word, he resurrected Burzum and to date has released three further albums.

Corey Taylor

18 December 1973

Born: Corey Todd Taylor

Alter-egos: #8, the Great Big Mouth, the Sickness, Ceiling-Fan Guy.

(Pre) occupations: Party-loving Corey Taylor is not just the leader of melodic metal merchants Stone Sour. An incurable schizophonic, he's also the man behind the dead-skin mask of Slipknot's number eight. 'When you put that mask on, you can go places that you would never have imagined,' the gregarious frontman told an audience of undergraduates at the Oxford Union – all of whom had come for a glimpse of the waxen-faced monster responsible for raising a little hell onstage with the 'Knot.

Live by this: 'The thing you have to remember about "nowhere" is it is merely just a combination of "now" and "here". Grammatically I know that is incorrect, but if you have not spent your whole life in the Land of Nowhere you do not know what the fuck you are talking about.' – Corey Taylor, *Seven Deadly Sins*

'The seven deadly sins are bullshit . . . We all struggle to maintain civility in a savage world. But there are times when it is our right as people to let these sins wash over us like a warm Caribbean wave.' – Corey Taylor, *Seven Deadly Sins*

Deadly sins: Up until July 2011, *Seven Deadly Sins* (a tell-all tome published by Ebury Press) was nothing more than a twinkle in the frontman's eye. 'I've been threatening to write a book for a long time,' Corey once drawled, 'but since every Tom, Dick and Harry writes an autobiography, I didn't want to just do that. My approach to writing is the same as my approach to music: I don't want to do what everybody else is doing.' And the finished product certainly didn't disappoint. Masquerading as yet another shock-rocking autobiography, Corey's blistering treatise on the true nature of virtue and vice is as deviant a design for life as you'll find this side of Machiavelli's *The Prince*. And, given Corey's sinful CV, there's none more qualified in all the flaming circles of hell to expound upon this subject. Growing up in Des Moines, Iowa – which he described as a godforsaken 'hole in the ground' – Corey nonetheless found myriad ways to 'entertain' himself. By the ripe old age of fifteen, he'd already overdosed on cocaine. Twice. Fast-forward several years and his only concerns were 'drinking, fucking, lying, raging and exploration . . . I was the only person in the known galaxy and I wanted what the fuck I wanted sooner rather than later. When I speak about sin, I know what I'm talking about.'

Yet – unique among the tortured souls featured within these pages – Taylor has succeeded in turning his darkest demons into his closest allies. In interview with *Explore Music*, he shed further light on the skewed philosophy that helped him rise to the top. '[*Seven Deadly Sins*] is basically me taking the piss out of the whole religion thing,' explained Corey. 'My

> 'The seven deadly sins are bullshit . . . We all struggle to maintain civility in a savage world. But there are times when it is our right as people to let these sins wash over us like a warm Caribbean wave.'
>
> *- Corey Taylor*

interpretation of the seven deadly sins is basically they're not sins at all. They are human characteristics that we all share . . . they're the kind of things that connect us all – we're all horny, hungry, angry motherfuckers, basically. But that does not make it a sin.'

So, how to transform oneself from sinner into winner? In the manner of a debauched daytime chat king, Corey believes he's found the solution. 'You meet people . . . they can't let a lot of stuff go and that's one of the reasons why so many people carry so much with them. You can see it in their eyes. It's like they're carrying three backpacks full of lead and they're just walking through life . . . but, if you're carrying it *that* far, you need to take something from it and leave the rest behind. You can't let your past define you. You can let it guide you, but you can't let it define you, because at the end of the day the present is where you should be. You spend too much time in the past, you miss your life. People have so much guilt these days I think they're afraid to live.'

And, of all the charges you could lay at Corey's door, fear of living is certainly not one of them. By the frontman's own admission, 'I was the kid who saw more on the horizon than what was in front of me.'

Fatherless, drug-addled and dispossessed, Corey's definition of home was pretty much wherever his mom chose to park her car that day. The fact that he even *survived* his deprived Des Moines upbringing speaks volumes about his strength of character. Yet, as the frontman of not one, but two of the most successful metal acts on the planet, Corey's doing so much more than just surviving. In stark contrast to the tragic saints who feature on the flip side of this book, Mr. Taylor is positively thriving, and it's all thanks to his ability to harness his own sinful urges. 'One person's envy is another person's drive. I've always been driven. If you're not striving to be number one . . . for me it's never enough.'

On a highway to hell? More than anyone, Corey Taylor is aware that he's living the best kind of rock'n'roll cliché. Born on 8 December 1973, on a ward of Des Moines' very own 'ghetto hospital' (as the frontman fondly remembers it), the odds were stacked against him from the very beginning. Corey's father was never part of the Taylor family portrait, leaving his mother to raise him and his younger sister single-handedly – with little in the way of money to support them and no fixed address. Thus, *On the Road* is not just the title of Corey's favourite novel; it's also the way he was raised. 'I had more backseats than bedrooms, let's put it that way,' the frontman sighs in interview with *Revolver* magazine. 'By the time I was fifteen, I'd already lived in 25 different states.'

But whichever way you spin it, the family's rootless existence left a lasting impression on the vulnerable young teen. More than a decade later, Corey would pen the bitter lyric for 'Eyeless' – not so much a song as a crushing four-minute assault upon the senses. Tapping an untold reserve of pain and longing for the family life he never had, Corey spits out the story of his faceless father. A phantom presence in his son's life, he's as elusive as empty air. 'I am my father's son,' proclaims the bulbous-headed mutant glimpsed on *Slipknot*'s cover.

Thankfully, aged just nine, Corey hit upon the exceptional gift that helped him escape the 'hole in the ground' that was Des Moines. Inspired by a rather unlikely soundtrack, Corey still remembers his moment of epiphany, witnessed by his cousin and – much to Corey's humiliation – the entire Taylor clan. 'We were listening to Journey, the *Frontiers* album,' explains Corey. 'And I started singing along with "Separate Ways". My cousin freaks out, calls all the family into the living room, stands me in a corner and goes, "Corey's going to sing for everybody!" I was stunned. I must have been crimson, you know? But she dropped the needle on the record, I stood in that corner and I sang every fucking note . . . It was the first song I ever sang to an audience. They hooted and hollered and it left an impression on me.'

After discovering a cache of old Elvis records at his grandma's place, Corey was hooked. 'Teddy Bear', 'In the Ghetto' and 'Suspicious Minds' were the frontman's favourites, providing a soundtrack to some of the best times of his childhood.

Before long, Corey determined to try his hand at baritone and tuba, winning him much kudos with his fellow band geeks – 'I've got five or six blue ribbons for playing tuba.' But before long, the limitations of his classical training became all too evident, as a string of altogether darker influences began to take hold of the young musician. 'By ninth grade I was into drugs,' Corey revealed, 'and I was teaching myself the guitar, because I wanted to write songs and I just could not write the songs I wanted to write on a fucking tuba. It was really hard to teach myself guitar, because I didn't know anything about chords. I would just tune the guitar to an open chord and I'd just one-finger that shit. That's how I started writing songs. And then the drugs got worse and I kind of put that away.'

By this time, Corey's mother had finally settled into the Forest River Trailer Park. Though given the location, the backseat of a car may well have been preferable. Suffice it to say that the park's picturesque name proved misleading in more ways than one. 'It was right next to a dike,' remembers Corey, 'and there was a forest and me and my friends would just go back there and get ripped. At a place like that, there's only two things to do really: you take drugs and you fuck.'

Never one for half measures, Corey partook in both these activities with equal enthusiasm. In interview with *Kerrang!* magazine, the frontman confessed: 'I am so fucking ashamed to say that I lost my virginity when I was eleven years old . . . it was with a very fucked up and very giving babysitter, let's put it that way!' This first encounter was enough to put Corey off sex for the next two years of his kidulthood. 'I don't think I was very good at it that first time,' he mused. 'After that I had a dry spell until I was thirteen. I was a bit better at it all by then, I think – I hope so anyway.'

Underage sex was not Corey's only illegal indulgence. By the frontman's own admission, education about the dangers of drug abuse in the town of Waterloo left much to be desired. 'Crank was just starting,' shrugs Taylor. 'I was a total speed freak and totally into coke [and] I remember waking up one morning in a dumpster. This is all conjecture on my part because I lost a couple of days, but I think I OD'd at a party. And instead of taking me to hospital they took me somewhere and dumped me in a trash can, thinking I was dead.' Corey was just fifteen years old when he woke amongst the rancid waste, missing clothes, friends and bleeding profusely from his head.

'So, I come to,' continues the frontman. 'I've got no shoes on, I've got no T-shirt; I've got blood on my face. I'm twelve miles from my house and I proceeded to walk from there. The whole way home I was like, "I gotta get out of here."' And get out of Waterloo Corey did.

At the end of ninth grade, Taylor moved into his grandmother's place, back in Des Moines. Determined to get clean while school was out, he quit cocaine cold turkey and spent his days picking out new melodies on the guitar, reasoning that, if there was anywhere he could make his resolution last, it'd be under his grandma's roof. 'I've always felt drawn there; I've always felt peace there,' he stated simply.

> 'My job is to give you that voice . . . it's the primal scream;
> it's more healthy than a lot of people would admit, because I'm free.
> I'm a better person because I'm in a band like Slipknot.'
> – Corey Taylor

However, all was not to run smoothly. There's a strong possibility that the Great Big Mouth's fiery temper was inherited from his gran – and before long, the troubled teen found himself back on the streets. 'I remember walking up and down Park Avenue on the south side of Des Moines with a trash bag full of clothes and a twenty-ouncer of Mountain Dew and a cigarette,' Corey sighs. 'Just enough time until I could beg a floor to squat on from a friend. I still tried to go to school on top of that, but because my life was so gnarly, I just couldn't get it together.'

Taylor's dreams of entering the world of academia seemed to be sliding further out of reach. 'When I was at school' – Corey's Des Moines drawl resonates round the lofty halls of the Oxford Union – 'I wanted to be a history teacher. I was passionate about history, learning where we came from. If you don't know your history, you're doomed to repeat it.' Left to ponder his own personal history for decades (Corey's only recently become acquainted with his father), it's all too easy to read into the pregnant pause that follows . . . to not know one's father is to be 'Eyeless' and in danger of walking blindly into the same mistakes.

Then the Great Big Mouth gets back into gear. 'I used to have mock classes for my little sister,' he continues. 'She was about seven. I'd be like, "That was 1887, damn it! What do you mean, you don't know?" As time went on, I came to realise that I wasn't built for the school system. I could learn; I knew all the answers in class, but I wasn't prepared to put in the hours and hours of homework.'

Outside the classroom, however, was a different story, thanks to a chance encounter with guitarist Shawn Economaki. Against all probability – Corey was dating Economaki's ex at the time – the two became firm friends. Under the moniker of Bloodfest, they started jamming together on a strictly casual basis. Yet, to Economaki's mind, this was always more than just a drunken past-time. Fast-forward a year and '[Economaki] and his friend were putting a band together,' Corey explains. 'They had everyone but a singer and Shawn thought of me. If it hadn't been for that . . . man, I don't know how long it would have taken me to get into music . . . Now that I think about it, Shawn was the catalyst for me being where I am today.'

Josh Rand on bass completed the line-up, resulting in Kriminal Mischief – a pop-metal outfit that simply wasn't to last. Though the chemistry between all three players was palpable, it wasn't until they hooked up with Denny Harvey – another Des Moines kid who clearly wasn't alright – that things truly started to fall into place. Drawn to the goofy gothic anthems of *The Rocky Horror Picture Show*, Corey can still recall their first meeting – at a screening of the ultra-camp seventies classic.

'Denny and I sat down and talked forever that night,' Corey reminisces. 'He was jamming with Joel [Ekman, Stone Sour's future drummer] and needed a singer. I sat down . . . and played some of the stuff I'd written and they were just fuckin' blown away. I was like, "Really, you like this?" I started hanging out with that whole crew and felt I finally found a family . . . the misfit of the misfits; the creative fuckers – the people who didn't think in two dimensions. It saved me from feeling like I was insane and I just didn't fit in anywhere.'

Meshing together like the constituents of Corey's favourite cocktail – whisky, orange juice and just a dash of sour – Stone Sour was the name that finally stuck for his crew of misfits. In 1995, they recruited Jim Root as their permanent axeman. Yet two years on, the band was no closer to its ultimate goal: getting the hell out of Des Moines. Indeed, Corey was still working behind the counter of the town's very own Adult Emporium. Even in this less-than-salubrious establishment, Corey's distinctive appearance (at this time he was rocking a head full of putrefying dreadlocks) raised more than a few eyebrows. 'People would look at me like I was a freak,' Corey recalls, 'but they were the ones in the porn shop at four in the morning! Straight-looking people I'd know would come to the register with fourteen-inch dildos and then they'd recognise me sitting there, and I'd be like, "Any lotions or lube with that?"'

Fortunately for them, Taylor was there to serve, not judge. According to the same accepting philosophy that underpins *Seven Deadly Sins*, Corey went on to explain: 'I didn't want anyone to feel dirty in the shop – because people are made to feel dirty every day of their lives, and that's bullshit.' Precisely how much longer Taylor would have remained behind that counter is anyone's guess. Yet matters were taken out of the vocalist's hands the day Shawn 'Clown' Crahan and Paul Gray paid their first visit to Adult Emporium, prepared to make Corey an offer he couldn't refuse: 'Join our band or we'll kick your ass.' And it proved mightily effective. Of course, Taylor was well aware of the band they were referring to.

With horrifying clarity, Slipknot's five-minute epic, 'Left Behind', depicts the ashen skies and dust-choked plains of Taylor's infernal Iowa. Glimpsed through the eyes of the video's semi-cute boy protagonist, America's beloved heartland is as hostile and oppressive a 'land of nowhere' as you could imagine. Populated by pintsized sadists and glassy-eyed authority figures, it's all too easy to see how the place came to mark Corey and his contemporaries as palpably as the Sanskrit tattooed above the frontman's naval. (Unsurprisingly, this ancient scrawl translates as 'darkness'.)

'From all over Iowa,' raves Corey in *Seven Deadly Sins*, 'tribes of misfits packed Billy Joe's [cinema] . . . we were the greatest motherfuckers of our generation and we had nothing to do. So we turned nothing into something [. . .] and we defended it with our blood.' Born of the same stifling community, Slipknot – the formidable nine-strong juggernaut assembled by Paul and Clown – were a strangled voice for Taylor and a legion of other lost boys just like him: forgotten faces who simply didn't fit in around the eerie Pleasantville where they were raised.

Ushered into the 'ancient Slipknot incubator' (the band's dismal basement practice pad, soundproofed with urine-reeking carpet scavenged from the local pet shop) back in May 2001, *Alternative Press* scribe John Pecorelli gained a unique insight into the town where the 'Knot was tied. 'Everyone's so straight-laced about not wanting to let the "bad" element come into effect,' Joey Jordison (a.k.a. Slipknot's number one) revealed, 'because when something like that happens in a city this small – and this is the *capital* of Iowa – then it spreads like a disease. All of us were so used to having the middle finger thrown at us, that when we threw it back, we did so with ten times the venom.'

Moments of madness: Fast-forward to 2003 and things were decidedly less than rosy for Slipknot's new recruit.

On paper, he'd achieved everything he ever dreamed (with the exception of terrorising generations of history students, of course). No longer a covetous 'misfit', he was in the enviable position of doing what he 'was built to do' onstage with Slipknot every night of his life. Sprawling across his skin like entries in a living journal, he'd acquired a clutch of new tatts, including 'Scarlett' – a tribute to the new woman in Corey's life. '[Scarlett] is my wife,' he gushed in interview with *Metal Hammer*. '[She] got my name and I got hers and we used the same needle.' And it seemed the old wounds of his fatherless upbringing were finally beginning to heal.

> *'I would disappear for long periods with no regard for my own safety or anyone else's. I wouldn't even know where I was until the next morning.'*
> *– Corey Taylor*

'Fatherhood [is] great,' the new dad assured *Kerrang*'s Emma Johnston. 'I'm just trying to filter out all my bad stuff and put the good stuff into Griffin [Corey's son]. If I can build a really good foundation for him then at least I've tried to guide him down a road that's better. I never grew up with a dad and I had to try and figure things out for myself. I think that's why I'm really hands-on with my son.'

Nonetheless, *something* was eating the troubled Mr. Taylor. And on the evening of 14 November 2003, in the luxurious confines of LA's Hyatt Hotel, the father-of-two came perilously close to ending his own life. 'I tried to jump off the balcony of the eighth floor of the Hyatt on Sunset Boulevard,' states Corey matter-of-factly. 'Somehow [Scarlett] stopped me. It wasn't the first time I tried to kill myself either . . . '

So, how is it that Des Moines' finest – a hard-living, fast-talking 'drifter with no leash, no money and no cares' – found himself hanging off the balcony that night, staring death in the face? Opening with his most riotous drunken misadventure to date, chapter one of Corey's *Seven Deadly Sins* proves that the Great Big Mouth has lost none of his ability to spin one hell of a yarn.

Far from the 'skeletal wreck of a man' glimpsed on the Hyatt balcony, Corey was once 'the coolest dude' at the party, and the instigator of a series of debauched events known only as 'The Night'. On this fateful evening back in 1995, Corey's band of 'motherfuckers' invaded one of Des Moines' most innocuous 'three-bed, two-bathroom cookie-cutter' houses with mischief in mind. Without further ado, Corey commenced necking copious amounts of Jägermeister, along with any other variety of 'shitty booze' he could lay his hands on. Corey's memories of the first few hours – spent pouncing on moving cars and vomiting back the aforementioned Jäger – are hazy to say the least. Yet as he muses, 'It is always the nights you can't remember that eventually become the stories you don't forget. 'During a lull in the roar of the insanity, I made myself scarce to catch my breath.' In the cool of the garage, Corey encountered 'two comely vixens' with a 'proposition' for him. What they wanted was a ménage à trois. 'Things could not look better, right?' writes Corey, adding ominously, 'Well, as I have been shown time and time again, fate hates us all.' Yet, tripping happily up the stairs, this was surely the last thing on his intoxicated brain. 'Lust is a lozenge I live to savour for days,' drawls Corey lasciviously.

But this time, his philandering philosophy – preaching sinful indulgence at all times – was to land him in some seriously hot water. 'We sequestered ourselves to one of the bedrooms,' Corey continues. 'The lights were soon off and pesky clothes shed in haste. Mouths found skin [. . .] and soon the three of us were a Chinese puzzle with no solution, a delicious triangle of heat and ferocity. As this was taking place, a coup was being plotted downstairs. A bum rush was about to happen . . . Forty people whispered and giggled, determined to inject themselves into our festivities at just the right moment.' As it happens, their timing was perfect. 'Just when it was getting really, really good,' Corey resumes, 'the door burst open; the lights flew on and a multitude of cheers and jeers [. . .] officially put an end to our sweet little tryst.' Lesser men would have dived under the covers along with the girls. But, 'buck naked' Corey was already formulating a plan to 'give these fuckers a taste of their own medicine'. Even back then, it seems class-clown Corey could not resist making a spectacle of himself. 'I'm over the top. I'm loud. I'm boisterous,' he freely admits. 'I want people to have a good time when they're with me.'

'Climbing out of bed, [I] proceeded to throw my soiled yet unfulfilled condom at the closest gawker . . . Watching the crowd, I had a magnificent idea and no one was going to stop me.' Corey's idea was 'simple'. After taking one heroic 'stage dive' out of bed, he'd launch himself into the crowd and effortlessly surf his way down to the kitchen – where he could smoothly fix himself the next drink of the night.

Apparently, lust was not Corey's only deadly sin that night, as there was never any question in the party-god's mind as to how he'd pull it off. 'It bordered on ingenious,' writes Taylor. 'How could it not work? I was *Corey Fucking Taylor*, even then.' But the Holy Bible (and 'that whole religion thing') warns that pride comes before a fall and, in fact, Corey had forgotten one rather significant detail. Whirring above his head were the hefty blades of the 'strongest ceiling fan known to humankind'. Heedlessly, Corey leapt straight into them, sustaining three powerful blows in just two seconds. 'One second I was the coolest dude at the concert, the next I was on my back trying to figure out what the fuck happened,' Taylor laments. He was left with matching black eyes and a particularly nasty gash to the head. 'My friends . . . never told me how fucked up my face was, so I mingled amongst them looking like Rocky Balboa until I caught my own reflection in a bathroom mirror an hour later. I should have just carried around a sign that said, "Take a Picture with the Party Zombie."'

'The thing that really sucked,' Corey recalls, in interview with *Revolver*, 'was I had to play a show the next day and most of the people who were there were at the party. The ongoing joke for years afterwards was, "Oh Corey, be careful, there's a ceiling fan in here!"' In the end however, the last laugh belonged to Slipknot's indestructible number eight. 'I would just go, "Ah if only you knew,"' the Great Big Mouth finally let slip, 'because two days later, I finished that threesome!'

And to Corey's mind, the only true 'sin' would have been to fail to see it through to the end. Beneath the drunken bravado, this tale of his is spiked with a particularly powerful (anti) moral. The sudden loss of Paul Gray (Slipknot's number two) back in May 2004 serves as a tragic reminder that none of us are immortal. Paul was just 38 when he administered a fatal dose of morphine. Months after the lonely death of his friend and bandmate, Corey was subdued but relentlessly upbeat on the subject of Gray's lasting legacy. 'For me,' he explained in interview with *NME*, 'it's important to celebrate life and not revel in death. Paul wouldn't want anyone want to do that, because he absolutely loved doing this . . . if I didn't give it every little bit of gusto I had, he'd be super-disappointed. Vinnie [Abbott, drummer and brother of Dimebag Darrell] looked me right in the eye and he said, "You gotta remember you're living for two now, 'cause that spirit is always with you." And something about that really sticks with me; it helps me remember to embrace life. Don't spend too much time on the darkness; you have to live every single minute with every bit of spirit you have.'

And on the face of it, this is the way Corey has always lived . . . even before Gray's untimely demise. 'For centuries,' he writes in *Seven Deadly Sins*, 'these so-called "weapons of morality" [. . .] have been used as the righteous fist packs by the Right or the Holy Brigade to keep masses of normally free-thinking folks under a multitude of firebrand thumbs.' Conversely, Corey Taylor is one free spirit who refuses to get off what he calls the 'Giddy Wagon' for anything. 'If you are not hurting anyone else, where is the damn sin?' he demands.

Yet something in Taylor's fiery rhetoric rings false. In fact, Corey's career with Slipknot has been anything but a joyous ride on the 'Giddy Wagon', as one member of the Oxford Union appears to have failed to grasp. At the end of Corey's impassioned lecture – urging each of the students in attendance to take some time to discover where their strengths truly lie – the hand of this bespectacled youth shoots up like it's loaded with a spring. 'If it's so important to stay true to yourself,' he demands, 'what do you need the mask for?' There's a tense few moments as the frontman under fire contemplates his answer. The words finally come, but they're from Corey's heart rather than his great big mouth.

'The beautiful thing about Slipknot is I've been able to let go of so much baggage and the mask is a perfect way to visualise that,' explains the slight figure on the podium (clad in a skinny T-shirt emblazoned with Keith Richards's face). 'When you put that mask on you go places you would never imagine. It comes from a spot that's uncomfortable and really dark. The mask was a way to visualise everything I was feeling in my heart and my gut – all that pain I was holding onto. I didn't have the worst childhood but I didn't have the best either, and when you grow up like that you have certain limitations invariably stuck inside you. Slipknot was a way to work it out. I was able to tear those walls down and feel like that.'

Contrary to popular belief, Corey's mask conceals nothing. By the same twisted paradox that's captured onscreen in 'Vermillion, Pt 1' (in which the band cover up their monstrous countenances with sickly skin), the act of donning their masks – physical manifestations of the group's deepest neuroses – leaves them more exposed than ever. And, swear as he might by this unusual form of sonic therapy, the 'Knot's schedule of punishing live shows was clearly doing Taylor few favours in the long-term.

'Slipknot is like a family reunion,' sighed Corey in interview with *Revolver*. 'It's good to see those people, but you can't wait to get away from them. It's the tension between the nine of us that helps make the music. Because we don't get along and I'll be the first to fucking admit it. People keep wanting me to candy-coat it, like we're some fucking fraternity that lives together when we're at home. That's not what happens. We love each other, but we also stay the fuck away from each other, you know?'

But on the road, there was no escape from his antagonists (eight other people who 'don't wash as much as you'd like them too', Corey reveals). And, following Clown's masochistic lead, he was a star performer in the band's twisted displays of self-mutilation. 'It doesn't have to be that boring a party before I'll set myself on fire,' the frontman confessed, live on air with 97X – and he still bears the scars to prove it, including one unsightly patch of hairless, blue-tinged flesh on his leg. 'I'd just be like, "Oooh, let's make some cool patterns,"' he laughs. And though the 'Knot's always been governed by a code of seventeen sacred rules – 'Rule number one,' recites Clown in creepy mindless monotone, 'no. Rule number two: Fuck space. Rule number three: Fuck Egypt . . .' – it's unlikely that any of them pertain to health and safety.

'After a show, you never feel so beaten up in your life,' muses Corey, 'but at the same time, you never feel so good. I float for a couple of hours, just an odd drifting feeling. You've got extreme adrenaline plus exhaustion – it's the weirdest.' A living, breathing oxymoron – as embodied by the most intricate of his tattoos, a two-faced god that's part-sun, part-moon – Corey came closer than ever to articulating the striking duality of his career at the Oxford Union in summer 2011. A secret shared between him and the 200 academics in attendance that day, Corey revealed: 'With Slipknot, it's a whole different beast. When you put that mask on, it's a big responsibility and you can go places that you would never have imagined. Stone Sour is much more laidback. It's a bigger part of my personality – you know, I'd rather make you laugh than make you cry! But Slipknot is probably a more important part of who I am . . . because I let that out and tap that valve [and] I can be myself . . . that part of me that is always going to play the class clown! I'm the guy who will fucking scream in your face and I think that's why a lot of people are drawn to what we do. My job is to give you that voice . . . it's the primal scream; it's more healthy than a lot of people would admit, because I'm free. I'm a better person because I'm in a band like Slipknot.'

Yet, Corey was in need of something more than just catharsis.

Fortunately for the frontman – and legions of maggots everywhere – Scarlett was unwilling to watch her husband ride the same downward spiral as his tragic bandmate Paul. The night of Corey's attempted suicide, she hit him with a powerful ultimatum: either he sober up or she and the children would be out of his life for good. In fact, Corey's crazed behaviour was hurting the people he cared for most in the world – and this was a revelation that stung.

'I would disappear for long periods with no regard for my own safety or anyone else's,' Corey revealed in interview with *MTV News*. 'I wouldn't even know where I was until the next morning. I didn't care about myself, my family, anything. I'd just remember being at a bar and then all of a sudden – nothing. I took a good long look in the mirror and I hated what I saw. I was very bloated, I looked like crap. It wasn't me.' Confronted with the grim reality of what he'd become, Corey made up his mind to put an end to the hedonism once and for all. And though it's a resolution echoed by countless saints before him (many of whom were claimed by the very poison they vowed to forgo), Corey's decision to stay clean was inspired by something more than Scarlett's threats.

'If you can realise you're an addict, you can get through it,' stressed a newly sober Taylor in interview with *Kerrang!* months later. 'It takes a lot of strength and a lot of work, but I think at the end of the day an

> *'If you can realise you're an addict, you can get through it, but I think at the end of the day an addict is only going to get clean if he wants to. Nobody's going to help themselves until they're ready to do it.'*
>
> *– Corey Taylor*

addict is only going to get clean if he wants to. And, nine times out of ten, they don't; they're just kind of going through the motions to appease the people who are around them. Nobody's going to help themselves until they're ready to do it.'

And Corey has recently acquired a whole new set of family members to 'appease' thanks to the efforts of ex-wife Scarlett. Enlisting the services of a private detective, she managed to track down Corey's estranged father – a man who never wanted to be absent from his son's life. 'I never knew who my dad was,' explained Corey in interview with *Contact Music*. 'I didn't even know his name. He knew I had been born but my mum told him to stay out of my life, basically. Anyway, my wife really got in my mum's face about it. She realised I was older now and have kids of my own, so she sent me a letter and gave me his name and all the information she had about him. My wife took that and found him.'

Despite the fact that they'd never met, Corey felt an instant connection with his long-lost father. 'He's one of the coolest dudes on the planet,' he gushed. 'The first time I talked to him [. . .] was really fucking emotional. We must have cried for about twenty minutes, it was really intense [. . .] I can't even express how happy I am at the moment. A whole new chapter in my life has opened.'

Sadly, this new chapter also called for a new leading lady. Ironically, sobriety helped Corey to realise that 'my relationship wasn't right for me. My wife and I had damaged each other too much,' he stated regretfully in interview with *Revolver* in 2007.

However, Corey has since found love with Stephanie Luby. And with a new bride (Corey tied the knot – pun intended – for the second time in November 2009, to the strains of Metallica's 'For Whom the Bell Tolls'), a new book and a string of gigs with Slipknot (most notably as the headliners of the travelling metal circus that is Sonisphere Festival) on the horizon, there's a sense that this thrilling new chapter is still very much a work in progress.

'People = Surprised' was the headline buzzing around the blogosphere when the illustrious Oxford Union opened its doors to 'Corey Fucking Taylor'. Yet, compared to the hysterical reaction of the frontman himself, 'surprise' is a word that barely registers. In contrast to the dulcet tones of the Union's affable young president, the Great Big Mouth seems dangerously close to motoring out of control. 'This is hilarious to me,' he attempts to explain, breaking off as a chortle bubbles up from the same place as his compellingly strangled vocals. 'The fact that we're sitting in the Oxford Union and I'm gonna speak – it's ridiculous! And just the fact that people requested this is baffling. I gotta be honest. I mean this'll probably be the most times that someone has used the f-word on these grounds to these people . . . you need to know what you're in for! This is fucking hilarious.'

But behind the hysteria, Corey is far from immune to the city of dreaming spires. 'I'm blown away,' says the frontman, having accepted his invitation to speak based on the promise of 'two bottles of water and a packet of smokes'. 'I've been a fan of history my whole life . . . so whenever I'm somewhere that you can feel the history, you can feel the legacy in the air, the walls around you, like you're surrounded by it – I get very humbled and I get very ecstatic and excited . . . you know, I want to look at everything, I want to smell everything! You can feel the heritage here and I'm very, very honoured to have been asked to come here. It's just one more thing that I can say I've done and I'm very emotional about it really to be honest. It's one of those things that you never thought you'd be able to do – it was never even on the list!' Given Corey's passionate commitment to 'living for two', who's to say what will happen next?